Participatory Creativity

Participatory Creativity: Introducing Access and Equity to the Creative Classroom presents a systems-based approach to examining creativity in education that aims to make participating in invention and innovation accessible to all students. Moving beyond the gifted-versus-ungifted debate present in many of today's classrooms, the book's inclusive framework situates creativity as a participatory and socially distributed process. The core principle of the book is that *individuals* are not creative, *ideas* are creative, and that there are multiple ways for a variety of individuals to *participate* in the development of creative ideas. This dynamic reframing of invention and innovation provides strategies for teachers, curriculum designers, policymakers, researchers, and others who seek to develop a more equitable approach towards establishing creative learning experiences in various educational settings.

Edward P. Clapp is Senior Research Manager at Project Zero and Lecturer on Education at the Harvard Graduate School of Education, USA.

Participatory Creativity

Introducing Access and Equity
to the Creative Classroom

Edward P. Clapp

Routledge
Taylor & Francis Group

NEW YORK AND LONDON

First published 2017
by Routledge
711 Third Avenue, New York, NY 10017

and by Routledge
2 Park Square, Milton Park, Abingdon, Oxon OX14 4RN

Routledge is an imprint of the Taylor & Francis Group, an informa business

Library of Congress Cataloging in Publication Data
Names: Clapp, Edward P., author.
Title: Participatory creativity : introducing access and equity to the creative
classroom / Edward P. Clapp.
Description: New York, NY : Routledge, 2016. | Includes bibliographical
references and index.
Identifiers: LCCN 2016006521 | ISBN 9781138945241 (hardback) |
ISBN 9781138945265 (pbk.) | ISBN 9781315671512 (ebook)
Subjects: LCSH: Creative ability—Study and teaching | Creative ability in
children. | Classroom environment.
Classification: LCC LB1590.5 .C55 2016 | DDC 370.15/7—dc23
LC record available at https://lccn.loc.gov/2016006521

ISBN: 978-1-138-94524-1 (hbk)
ISBN: 978-1-138-94526-5 (pbk)
ISBN: 978-1-315-67151-2 (ebk)

Typeset in Galliard
by Keystroke, Station Road, Codsall, Wolverhampton

MIX
Paper from
responsible sources
FSC
www.fsc.org   FSC® C013056

Printed and bound in Great Britain by
TJ International Ltd, Padstow, Cornwall

Contents

Figures and Tables

Figures

Tables

Preface

During the early 2000s I worked in New York City trying to make it as a practicing artist, gigging as a teaching artist, and paying the rent with an arts administration position. By night I would either try my luck on the stages of the downtown spoken word scene or work with actors and other artists as part of a small theater company a friend and I ran out of our apartments. By day I would teach creative writing, journalism, and even graphic design for any number of after-school programs—teaching in schools, community colleges, homeless shelters, and juvenile detention centers—while also holding together a full-time job designing and facilitating professional development experiences for artists and educators. Scattered as my life may have been at the time, one might suggest that *creativity* was a throughline that tenuously held all of my experiences together.

As it turned out, part of my professional life at the time involved developing partnerships between New York City public school teachers and a broad range of teaching artists. Working in collaboration with various educational researchers, I remember being compelled by the effectiveness of the protocols we used for looking carefully at student work. These protocols were developed by researchers at Project Zero—a place with a funny name that I began to hear more and more about as my work with educators and teaching artists progressed.[1] While I enjoyed this work and found it deeply rewarding, inside I knew that what I was doing could be done a lot better. The question was, *how?* Noting my interest in Project Zero frameworks and my hankering to do better, one day a colleague of mine said, "You need to go find these Project Zero people, and see what you can learn from them."

Within a year I found myself working as a research assistant at Project Zero, which I now understood was a research center at the Harvard Graduate School of Education in Cambridge, MA. While at Project Zero, I also began my career as a graduate student at the Harvard Graduate School of Education. It was then that my journey down the windy path of creativity research began; more specifically, it was during my enrollment in an interdisciplinary class exploring the intersection of mind, brain, and education research. As I recall, our final assignment for this class invited my classmates and me to conduct a mini-project that further explored an aspect of the course we each wanted to learn more about. It so happened that a number of months back we had been assigned an article about creativity. The article had caught my attention but, given the breadth of content we had to cover, exploring creativity from the perspective of mind, brain, and education was not a focal part of our class discussions for very long. This presented the perfect opportunity for me to dig deeper, and to learn more. And so, with my curiosity piqued, I proposed to further investigate the concept of creativity for my final project.

Having sketched up a brief plan for a pilot study that engaged participants in what I imagined to be creative activities, I met with one of the teaching assistants for the course to see if I was on the right track. After presenting my research question and a brief outline of my proposed inquiry, the teaching assistant gave me a quizzical look and asked me what I now understand to be the most obvious question: "How are you defining creativity?" I looked back, with what must have been a very puzzled expression. How was I defining creativity? I had no idea. No one had ever asked me that before. At that moment, I didn't see the need to define creativity. I probably even thought this question was absurd. "You know, creativity is creativity—everyone knows what it means." Of course, looking back, I now understand the nature of creativity is far more complex than I naively thought at the time.

This first fumbling experience as a graduate student sparked a decade-long odyssey into the exploration of creativity studies, which brought me back to New York, where I had the good fortune to work with creativity researcher Michael Hanchett Hanson, and then back to Cambridge, where my work at Project Zero and the Harvard Graduate School of Education continued. Now on the other side of my graduate studies experience I find that, as much as my perspectives have changed, there is much that has stayed the same. I continue to be deeply interested in the study of creativity and widely influenced by the work of Project Zero—where I have had the unique privilege of being nurtured and supported as an emerging scholar. What's different is that, not only do I find it essential to engage young people in creative learning experiences in ways that help them better understand the world, themselves, and others, I also find it to be of utmost importance to make such experiences as equitable and accessible as possible. As my early work as a teaching artist in New York has taught me, students of all backgrounds and ability levels have the propensity to engage and excel in the creative classroom, if only given the chance.

My goal in writing this book is two-fold: first, I find it essential that we broaden our perspectives of what it means to participate in creativity—especially within schools—so that the widest array of young people may see themselves as creative participants in the world; second, I believe it is essential that we break down the barriers to creative participation so that all students, regardless of race, class, or zip code, may be given the opportunity to live up to their full potential. That being said, I do not expect that this book on its own will eradicate the forces of inequality that make participation in invention and innovation more accessible to some students than to others, but I do hope that it will offer a change in perspective for many educators, administrators, researchers, parents, and policymakers and, as a result, act as an important first step towards introducing a greater sense of access and equity into the creative classroom.

Edward P. Clapp
January 2016
Somerville, MA

Note

1. I later came to understand that one of the primary protocols we used at the time was the Collaborative Assessment Conference for Looking at Student Work designed by Steve Seidel. See www.lasw.org/CAC_steps.html

Acknowledgments

True to the concepts presented throughout this book, the ideas that have been articulated on the pages ahead could not have been developed without the support of others. I wish to express my gratitude to my extended "contributing stakeholder group," especially Shari Tishman and Steve Seidel for their continued mentorship and support, and in particular Michael Hanchett Hanson, whose scholarship helped foster the ideas that are fundamental to this book. I am also greatly indebted to the students, staff, and program mentors at the Boston ArtScience Prize, in particular Andrea Sachdeva, Carrie · Fitzsimmons, Dishon Mills, Kris Price, Tina Lu, Kristen Bonstein, Andrew Churchman, the BiodegradaBall project team—including Ethan Levesque and Jen Roberts, and most especially Shaunalynn Duffy, Rosalie Norris, and all of the members of the Static Fashion and Reverse Outlet project teams. I would further like to thank all of my colleagues at Project Zero, especially the Agency *by* Design research team (Shari Tishman, Jessica Ross, and Jennifer Oxman Ryan), the Creating Communities of Innovation research team (Liz Dawes Duraisingh and Andrea Sachdeva), the Thinking and Learning Today and Tomorrow teaching team (Carrie James, Mara Krechevsky, Jessica Ross, and Carin Aquiline), and also Daniel Wilson, David Perkins, and Howard Gardner for their intellectual leadership as well as Jordy Oakland, Sarah Alvord, Margaret Rundle, Faith Harvey, Flossie Chua, and Dami Seung—and so many others—for their collegiality, good humor, and professional support. I am also greatly indebted to all of the people who have generously provided feedback on previous drafts of this manuscript, including Shari Tishman, Liz Dawes Duraisingh, Karen C. Yeyinmen, and especially Raquel L. Jimenez. In addition, I am greatly appreciative for the artistry of Craig Bostick, whose illustrations helped bring the ideas in this book to life; Jim Reese, Odette Schuler, and everyone at CASIE for helping me share my work with educators around the globe; Tatiana Chemi, for the ongoing intellectual dialogue from across the sea; Mindy Kornhaber, who helped fine tune my understandings of equity in the educational sphere; Janine de Novais, whose friendship and collegial support has continually helped me make sense of issues concerning race and class in the classroom; Laura Clos, for her help in navigating the sometimes uncertain waters of academic publishing; Metta McGarvey, for her friendship and spiritual grounding; Greer Muldowney and Matt Gamber for their camaraderie and cat care; Barry Shauck, whose commitment to the arts and creativity studies has been an inspiration to me; and Chris Clapp, Amanda Clapp, and the Young family for generously allowing me to camp out in their Gilsum, NH cabin, where many of these words were written. I would like to also thank Alex Masulis and Daniel Schwartz at Routledge for their com mitment to this project and their patience and care throughout the editorial process. Lastly, I would like to thank my family for all of their support over the years, especially my wife, Angela Mittiga, for her patience, love, and compassion throughout this process.

Introduction

On a blustery winter afternoon in New England a group of five teens bustles about in an old brick building in the heart of downtown Boston. Diverse in talents, skills, and cultural perspectives, these five teens have come together through an after-school program that challenges public high school students to develop cutting-edge ideas at the intersection of the arts and sciences. In one corner of the space Danny and Reggie use brightly colored balloons and a burnt-out fluorescent bulb to try to register a static electric charge on a multi-meter.[1] The two form a peculiar pair: Danny tirelessly cracks jokes as he makes a performance out of rubbing balloons on himself to generate a static charge. Meanwhile, Reggie meticulously records data gleaned from the multi-meter with each successive attempt. Nearby, Jenny toils over the wordsmithing for an upcoming presentation while her colleague, Maria, surrounded by fabric samples, sits close by her side sketching out designs for an eclectic line of winter apparel. In yet another corner of the space Dana can be found dancing—with arms and legs rhythmically pulsing to a beat—recording a promotional video on an iPad. Though each may appear to be engaged in a separate task, these five young people combine to form Static Fashion—an idea development team committed to inventing clothing capable of powering small electronic devices with everyday static electricity.

Weeks into the program it is hard to know where the idea to develop clothing that harnesses the power of static electricity originated. Danny, Reggie, Jenny, Maria, and Dana have each contributed to the development of this idea in their own unique way. What's more, the winding path of the team's idea development has been deeply influenced by the contributions of adult program mentors, interactions with field professionals, hours of online research, guidance from the program's administrative staff, and innumerable chance encounters with a host of other individuals, tools, and materials.

The work of the Static Fashion team illustrates an important concept that may appear intuitive in the moment, but which also seems to go against the grain of what we know about invention and innovation. Simply put: creativity is not an individual capacity, but rather a socially distributed and participatory process.

Throughout the West—and especially here in the United States—we have developed a fond affection for our heroes, our valedictorians, our Oscar winning actors, and our Olympic medalists. Our achievement-based culture has taught us to praise the accomplishments of individuals. Even when a sports team collectively wins a national title, we are quick to seek out the hero amongst heroes—and award that person the honor of MVP. But if we take the time to parse out the work of the most accomplished amongst us, we'll quickly come to understand that no feat of excellence, and certainly no act of creativity, can take place in isolation.

The same is true with learning and development. Prior research with pre-school teachers in Reggio Emilia, Italy, has taught us that "much, if not most, of the learning that goes on in and out of schools happens through the interactions of groups."[2] Likewise, the work of famed psychologist Lev Vygotsky asserts that all learning and development is social.[3] Consistent with these perspectives, one may further suggest that creativity is not a solitary endeavor, but rather a socially distributed and participatory process.

As the above glimpse into the work of the Static Fashion team illustrates, when we look at creativity in action, we can see that creative ideas emerge socially.[4] Nonetheless, a focus on individual achievement still grips the educational sphere.[5] This focus on individual achievement is particularly distressing when one considers the status of creativity in education. In the creative classroom, the successful student is too often seen as being gifted, as having that certain *spark* about him or her, as being *more* creative than others. Such individual-based orientations towards creativity are not only out of synch with contemporary creativity theory and practice, they also impose unnecessary barriers to creative participation for the majority of students.

But what might it mean to take a new tack towards how we think about creativity in practice and how we foster creativity through education? What new concepts might we have to grasp—and what old ways of thinking might we have to let go of in order to make a shift from understanding creativity as being a cognitive capacity associated with the most gifted amongst us, to a more socially distributed and participatory process that busts open the doors to invention and innovation—and makes creative participation accessible to everyone?

In this book I suggest a new way of thinking about creativity that aims to do just that. Utilizing original case study research and examples from the worlds of science, design, and popular culture, I make the case for a systems-based orientation towards idea development that I call *participatory creativity*. While many theorists have put forth group-based and collaborative models of creativity in the past, my intention is to build on these models by emphasizing the ways in which young people and adults participate in creativity in various ways. While this reorientation towards creativity incorporates the contributions of individuals, it also takes a turn away from a focus on independent individual achievement.

For many of us, an individual orientation towards invention and innovation is deeply rooted in how we understand creativity—and perhaps even how we understand the world. Our social studies textbooks, art history classes, newspaper articles, television shows, and blockbuster movies are filled with stories of unique individuals who have somehow been able to see the world differently and, as a result, have changed the way we understand the sciences, the arts, and the humanities. These domain changers are not hard to recount. The names of such celebrated creators as Albert Einstein, Vincent van Gogh, and Steve Jobs are all but synonymous with creativity. Indeed, for decades creativity researchers have focused on the lives and work of just such individuals.

As a visit to the bookstore or a quick Google search will reveal, countless books and scholarly articles have been written about the creative individual— many in pursuit of the question: *how did they do it?* The "it," in this scenario can be understood as the symphonies, scientific theories, computer plat-forms, and other groundbreaking products purported to be developed by individuals. The "how" may refer to a variety of things. Amongst them are the unique cognitive capacities—or even the unique neurological structures—of individual creators.

In many circles, the emphasis placed on eminence in creative inquiry is colloquially referred to as a "great man" approach to creativity research. From this perspective, those who have achieved greatness are probed for the nature of their greatness. In some cases, the goal of such studies is to understand how the traits of creative individuals can be fostered in others. In other cases, creative individuals are romanticized as extraordinary examples of our species, intellectually gifted, or even genetically endowed in ways that portray them as being superior and beyond the grasp of the rest of us.[6]

Not only does a great man approach to creativity exhibit a bias towards a narrow set of individual abilities, given the list of names above, it also suggests a gender bias towards men and a racial bias towards the achievements of great *white* men. Of course, not all creativity research is centered on the work of white men, but the dominant creativity narrative is arguably skewed in this direction. For many young people, participating in creativity does not seem like an option—simply because the stories of creativity they hear are about people who don't look like them. Even creativity narratives that do celebrate the achievements of women and people of color have the potential to alienate young people due to the greater-than-thou genius status that is granted to creative individuals.

While the chapters ahead do not ignore the racial, cultural, and gender biases inherent in great man orientations towards creativity, a participatory reframing of creativity ultimately problematizes the individualism associated with our traditional understandings of creative achievement. Regardless of their race and gender, we know that the individuals most commonly associated with creativity have not existed in isolation but have rather lived their lives situated within various social, cultural, and political systems.

In our increasingly globalized and interconnected world, our engagement with systems is perhaps richer now than it ever has been before. It makes sense then that a contemporary theory of creativity should look beyond the creative capacities of individuals, and instead consider how individuals participate in socially distributed systems. But the myth of the lone creative genius is strong and our culture of individualism makes it difficult to accept a theory of creativity that does not romanticize the sole efforts of gifted individuals. What is needed is a compelling case that emphasizes the great strides individuals make when they do things together.

Do It Together

> *If you were successful, somebody along the line gave you some help. There was a great teacher somewhere in your life. Somebody helped to create this unbelievable American system that we have that allowed you to thrive. Somebody invested in roads and bridges. If you've got a business—you didn't build that. Somebody else made that happen. . . . The point is, is that when we succeed, we succeed because of our individual initiative, but also because we do things together.*
>
> Barack Obama
> July 13, 2012

During the summer of 2012, President Barack Obama was campaigning for his re-election throughout the United States. While speaking to supporters at a campaign stop in Roanoke, Virginia, the president gave an impassioned speech that sparked a lively political debate. Within his speech Obama argued that successful business people in the United States have not achieved their success on their own, but rather owed their success (and a portion of their earned income) to those who supported them—either directly or indirectly—along the way.[7]

Focusing on the phrase "you didn't build that," the president's opponents accused Obama of dismissing the hard work and ingenuity of American entrepreneurs and small business owners. As a retort to Obama's speech, then presidential candidate Mitt Romney said:

> To say that Steve Jobs didn't build Apple, that Henry Ford didn't build Ford Motors, that Papa John didn't build Papa John's Pizza. . . . To say something like that, it's not just foolishness. It's insulting to every entrepreneur, every innovator in America.[8]

Placed in context, Obama's intention was not to diminish the hard work and ingenuity of American entrepreneurs and innovators. Instead, Obama was trying to make the case that the success of any one American cannot be understood as an individual achievement—but rather as the cumulative work and collective effort of a variety of individuals and agencies. In essence, Obama was situating the success of individual American business owners within greater systems. If we link creativity to innovations that yield successful business enterprises, one can argue that Obama was taking a systems-based approach to understanding creativity. Conversely, when Romney intimated that individuals such as Steve Jobs, Henry Ford, and Papa John (John Schnatter)[9] created their respective companies on their own, he both extended the myth of the lone creative genius and dismissed the networks of support that scaffolded Jobs, Ford, and Schnatter's success. Romney's perspective was focused on the individual. Obama's perspective situated individuals within broader systems.

Of course, Obama's comments were meant to achieve a higher political end (that wealthy business owners should feel obligated to pay higher taxes as a means of paying back the support systems that have contributed to their success), but in the process Obama shed new light on the idea that innovation and entrepreneurial success do not occur solely as a result of the efforts and ingenuity of individuals, but rather "because we do things together." From this systems perspective, we can see that creativity is distributed all around us, and that embracing a culture of collaborative invention is a pathway to "success."

We can also see how difficult it is to embrace a distributed understanding of achievement that recognizes the contributions of multiple people at the expense of romanticizing the work of the lone individual.

Speaking from a much less politically charged perspective, after losing his job as a programmer at a Bay Area start-up, David Lang described his journey into the Maker Movement and his efforts to participate in what is widely known as the new DIY, or "Do-It-Yourself," revolution. However, upon entering this space, what Lang soon came to learn was "how unthinkably hard it is to make anything, let alone [to] do it by yourself."[10] Lang wrote:

> Initially, the concept of DIY created a mental image of a lone inventor toiling away in his basement workshop or a MacGyver-type-know-it-all. It was precisely that stereotype that kept me away from making for so long. I didn't have an engineering degree. I didn't know how to use most of the tools in a workshop, and calling me "uncreative" was an understatement. I figured making was something I just didn't get—it was for *them* and not me. But making, as I discovered early on, was about the art of finding other people—seeking out teachers, creating and joining like minded groups, collaborating with strangers—and co-creating together. As long as you have an initiative to get started, [Do-It-Yourself] quickly evolves to Do-It-Together, or DIT.[11]

In line with Obama's concept of "you didn't build that," Lang first argued that no one does anything by him-/herself. Invention and innovation are always the result of a process of distributed co-creation. Second, Lang made the case that maintaining an understanding of creativity as an independent occurrence carried out by highly skilled and/or gifted individuals poses a barrier to creative participation. And third, Lang argued that, not only can anyone engage in creative work, but also understanding how best to *participate* in the interdependent process of co-creation is elemental to successful innovation:

> Making is about sharing ideas, tools, and processes. The most prolific makers I met weren't the people who did everything themselves. In fact, they were the individuals most skilled at navigating the web of collaboration and adapting it to their will.[12]

Lang made an excellent point—that referring to the Maker Movement (or any systems-based process of making or invention) as the new DIY revolution is a misnomer, and that DIT is a more appropriate acronym. Nonetheless, it is difficult to imagine that the acronym DIT will replace DIY any time soon. (Rebranding an entire movement is no small feat!) While making the shift from Do-It-Yourself to Do-It-Together may involve little more than a simple tweak of language, making the epistemological shift from an individual-focused to a distributed understanding of making and invention will require a much greater effort. But as Lang pointed out, this is a necessary shift to make.

In order to become an effective maker, one has to participate in the broader movement. Being a "maker," as Lang defined it, is not a solitary position one holds, but a participatory experience. Similarly, one can argue that in order to become an effective scientist, artist, or educator, it is necessary to engage with a community of practice in the process of interdependent co-creation. To do so, it is important to both understand the distributed nature of the creative process and to identify how best to participate in that process.

From Individuals to Ideas

As Obama's and Lang's stories illustrate, we are far more successful when we do things together than when we attempt to do things on our own. Beyond simply arguing for power in numbers, what these two anecdotes suggest is that there is no one way to be creative, but rather multiple ways to participate in creativity. Indeed, in a maker context, someone may participate in creativity by contributing code to a project while another person employs his or her skills as a welder. Yet another person may contribute to the same project by developing a marketing campaign or managing social media. If we return to the opening vignette of the Static Fashion team working together to develop an apparel line capable of charging small electronic devices with static electricity, we see that Danny, Reggie, Jenny, Maria, and Dana were each participating in creativity in different ways.

In this sense, creativity can be said to be socially distributed. No one person is *doing* the creativity or *being* creative. Instead, all members of the team are *participating* in creativity—and each member's participation looks different. This is not to say that participation in group creativity is equally distributed. Indeed, on any given project some individuals are likely to participate in creativity more than others. It is also important to note that participation in creativity is not limited to specific groups of people. In the case of Static Fashion, dozens of people contributed to the team's idea development who were not immediate members of the group.

But establishing a participatory orientation towards creativity goes beyond making the simple shift from an understanding of individuals as being creative, to an understanding of groups as being creative. The individuals who compose a group are certainly participating in creativity, but it is not the group that is creative. After all, groups are just collections of individuals and to focus our attention on groups would be to overlook the complexity involved with the greater mechanics of creative systems.[13]

In the chapters ahead I present a systems-based perspective of creativity that aims to embrace the roles that both individuals and groups play in invention and innovation, while also presenting a more participatory and socially distributed understanding of creativity. More specifically, I put forth the following definition: *Creativity is a distributed process of idea development that takes place over time and incorporates the contributions of a diverse network of actors, each of whom uniquely participate in the development of ideas in various ways.*

In this definition, ideas are the center of gravity that hold a participatory understanding of creativity together. The rationale for this reframing of creativity is simple: if we switch the focus of creativity from individuals to ideas, then we set up the opportunity for multiple people to participate in creativity in unique and varied ways. Here, ideas are viewed as social, not psychological, making creative idea development something all students can participate in, not something only a few students *are* or *have*. While the theory of participatory creativity advocates for a distributed approach to invention and innovation, the individual does not become lost in the process. Instead, individuals who participate in creativity develop *profiles of participation* based on the unique talents, skills, and cultural perspectives they bring to the work of creative idea development.

Placing such a strong emphasis on ideas begs an answer to the question: *what is an idea?* My response is that an idea may be understood as an ever-evolving conceptual throughline that is embodied through a succession of innovative products. Products—ranging from concrete objects to utterances and speech acts—serve as the artifacts of evolving ideas.

To understand how creative ideas develop, I introduce a biographical approach to the case study method that focuses on ideas—not individuals—as the primary unit of analysis. Reframing creativity as the *biography of an idea* not only helps make visible the evolution of an idea over time—but also reveals the broadly distributed network of individuals, environments, and technologies that participate in the development of an idea as it wends its way in the world.

Of course, not all ideas are creative. In order to establish a criteria for creativity, it is important to differentiate between a quirky idea (e.g., a group of friends decides to have breakfast for dinner) and a creative idea—arriving at a new concept that provides a significant shift in understanding. While such a criteria may seem straightforward, within creativity research circles the magnitude of a "shift in understanding" can be a point of contention. Whereas some theorists have argued that creativity only occurs when an individual makes a lasting effect on a domain of practice,[14] others have made the case that creativity takes place on a much smaller scale—such as when a minor discovery shifts the perspective of a small group or single individual. The former position is known as *Big C* creativity, whereas the latter is known as *little c* creativity. Rather than enter the Big C/little c debate, a participatory and distributed approach to invention and innovation argues that no creative ideas develop in isolation. Whether in the big leagues of Big C creativity or the little leagues of little c creativity, the creative process is always socially distributed.

Rethinking Creativity in Education

Creativity research has long been a concern of psychologists, educators, parents, and policy makers. However, where socially distributed approaches to creativity are concerned, there is an interesting divide in the literature. Whereas many academic creativity texts do indeed wrestle with systems-based creativity theory and research, few, if any, apply these concepts to education. Conversely, the contemporary texts that promote creativity in education almost exclusively do so from traditional individual-based perspectives that reify the gifted/ungifted dichotomy prevalent in so many schools and after-school settings. In *Participatory Creativity: Introducing Access and Equity to the Creative Classroom* my goal is to offer a counter-narrative to the traditional creativity in education story by presenting an inclusive, systems-based approach to creativity in education that aims to make participating in creativity accessible to all students.

Before engaging with the argument I present in the chapters ahead, I find it useful to define some terminology upfront. To begin, it is important to understand how the words *creativity, invention,* and *innovation* are used throughout this text. Other authors have drawn distinctions between these three terms, and though I am aware of many nuanced definitions for each of these words, here I use them interchangeably. The decision to use creativity, invention, and innovation as synonyms is mostly a practical one—as it has been necessary to have more than one word to describe a single term to avoid repetitive language.

Another use of synonyms that is perhaps more tactical than practical is my association of the word "traditional" with individual-based understandings of creativity. From a historical perspective, individual-based understandings of creativity have certainly preceded the more contemporary systems-based understandings of creativity that theorists consider today. In this way, individual-based understandings of creativity can be thought of as coming from an older "tradition" of creativity theory. However, my use of "traditional" is meant to suggest, in a quite forward way, that individual-based understandings of creativity are literally old fashioned and, in that way, poorly suited for contemporary times. In our increasingly interconnected and globalized world, it is essential that we understand the inherently networked nature of our cultural participation in all aspects of life. To do so, we must cognitively embrace systems-based models of invention and innovation over more traditional models of individual-based creativity—which fail to accept the reality of our times.

Throughout the chapters ahead I use the term *creative classroom* in a very deliberate way. Creative learning experiences happen in a multitude of settings. Some of these settings are formal learning environments, such as within classrooms in K–12 schools. Sometimes these classrooms are studios, dark rooms, computer labs, fablabs, or makerspaces; other times they are spaces that have not been designed for creative learning experiences, such as hallways, cafeterias, or outdoor spaces, but where committed educators find a way to make such experiences happen. As many well know, creative learning experiences do not only take place in schools. Quite often, creative learning experiences happen in informal learning environments such as in museums, libraries, or within after-school settings that may be run by the local Boys and Girls Club, or some other not-for-profit organization. Creative learning experiences may also take place within the home—perhaps on the kitchen table, in the basement, in the garage, or within a home workshop. And lastly, creative learning experiences regularly happen online through various platforms across the Internet. The phrase "creative classroom" is meant to encapsulate all of these settings—and many others that I haven't listed here. In short, the creative classroom can be defined as any setting where creative learning experiences take place.

As with the word creativity, the words *access* and *equity* are often used colloquially in everyday speech, in a casual way, perhaps without much thought as to how these words are used or what they really mean. Of course—as with creativity—the words access and equity may mean many things. So it helps, then, to explicitly define these words when using them in an intentional way.

When I use the word access in the chapters ahead, my goal is to do so in a most straightforward way. Having access to the creative classroom quite literally means having the opportunity to engage with creative learning experiences in an unbounded, uncomplicated, and unencumbered way. Creative classrooms that are easily accessible to young people include those that are universally available in schools or through after-school programming free of charge, regardless of race, class, or address. Young people need to know where the creative classroom is and to feel comfortable walking through the door. Once inside, young people need to understand the language of the creative classroom, and the rules for engaging in that space. Creative classrooms that meet these conditions are most likely to be accessible to all students.

In addition to this quite literal definition of access, in Chapters 3 and 4 I aim to bring nuance to this term by suggesting that the creative classroom is further restricted by the variety of cognitive capacities, personality characteristics, and cultural perspectives it favors. In this way, the creative classroom is more accessible to some students than others.

Equity might be best understood in comparison with a related concept that it is often confused with: *equality*. Conducting a Google image search of the phrase "equity vs. equality" will likely yield a popular Internet meme that illustrates this point. In this two-part image three young men are pictured at the back of a baseball field, each attempting to peer over the fence that separates them from the game taking place in the field in front of them. Each of the boys is a different height. The boy on the left is the tallest, the boy on the right is the shortest, and the boy in the middle is of medium height.[15] The first image shows each boy standing on an equally sized crate, so that they may all have equal opportunity to see over the fence and enjoy watching the game on the other side. However, because the boys are of different heights, only the tallest boy and the medium height boy can see over the fence, the shorter boy, despite standing on the same size crate as his friends, still cannot see over the fence. The caption at the bottom of this image reads "equality." And indeed, each boy has an equal opportunity to stand on a crate of the same size, but because of their varying heights, the supports provided for them have varying effects.

In the second image, the tallest boy is not standing on a crate at all, he can see over the fence all on his own. The medium height boy is standing on the same sized crate as in the previous image. As in that first image, this support is just the right size for him, and he can see over the fence and enjoy watching the game as well. The shortest boy is pictured standing on top of two crates to compensate for his disadvantage. Now he can see over the fence and watch the game, too. The caption beneath this image reads "equity." The comparison between the two images is meant to suggest that a one size fits all approach to supporting young people may appear to provide equal opportunity but, in reality, in order to achieve equity of experience, supports must be structured to meet the specific needs of each student.

In a recent article concerning equity and the Common Core State Standards Initiative, educational researchers Mindy Kornhaber, Kelly Griffith, and Alison Tyler presented three different conceptions of the word equity based on the use of this term in educational research, rhetoric, and policy.[16] Amongst these conceptions of equity, Kornhaber and her colleagues presented an *equalizing conception* of equity. Like the second image described above, the equalizing conception of equity suggests providing proportional resources and supports to students within an educational system, in a manner by which those resources and supports may yield more equalizing results. "To generate more equal outcomes, it is not enough that classrooms and schools have equal resources and are open to all students," they wrote, "instead, policies and practices within the education system need to distribute resources in a compensatory way."[17] The equalizing conception of equity offers what some refer to as a vertical approach to equity, wherein resources and supports are meant to support students in a manner that compensates for their strengths and weaknesses and, in turn, is designed to equalize student outcomes, with the hopes of closing achievement gaps across different populations of students. Where the word equity appears in the chapters ahead, it is meant to be used in this way.

A Roadmap to the Journey Ahead

Participatory Creativity has been structured to take the reader on a journey towards a new way of thinking about the individual and group potential that lies at the heart of the creative classroom. Chapter 1 establishes a systems-based understanding of the concept of creativity by presenting a review of the scholarly literature associated with more socially distributed theories of invention and innovation. In particular, this chapter discusses Howard Gruber's evolving systems approach to understanding the creative individual, Mihaly Csikszentmihalyi's sociocultural theory of creativity, and several theories of group, collaborative, and distributed creativity as presented by R. Keith Sawyer, Vlad Petre Glăveanu, and others.

Chapter 2 formally outlines a participatory and distributed theory of creativity. Beginning with a discussion of Michael Hanchett Hanson's thoughts on *the emergent participatory synthesis*,[18] here participatory creativity is defined as a distributed process of idea development that takes place over time and incorporates the contributions of a diverse network of actors, each of whom uniquely participate in the development of ideas in various ways. This chapter further discusses how ideas are embodied in the artifacts of creative work, and how individuals who participate in creativity develop unique *profiles of participation*. The chapter concludes with examples of the many ways that participatory and distributed instantiations of creativity are all around us.

Chapter 3 argues that our culture of individualism inclines us to seek out heroes and scapegoats for more socially distributed acts by ascribing what Michel Foucault refers to as *author function* to individuals who are not solely responsible for the achievements (or failures) that are most associated with them.[19] In particular, this chapter illustrates how maintaining traditional, individual-based orientations towards creativity within the creative classroom is actually harmful to young people in five distinct ways.

Building on the five crises in creativity presented in Chapter 3, Chapter 4 identifies three additional crises of creativity in education that are based less on our culture of individualism, but more on our cultures of power. Combined together, the five crises of creativity in education derived from a culture of individualism plus the three crises of creativity in education derived from a culture of power amount to what are described at the end of this chapter as the eight barriers to access and equity in the creative classroom.

Chapter 5 suggests that shifting epistemologies requires new methodologies. In order to reframe creativity as a participatory and distributed process, it is therefore necessary to establish a new means of investigating the social origins of ideas. To do this, Chapter 5 argues that instead of telling the biography of purportedly creative individuals, it is more useful to tell the biographies of the ideas those individuals are most known for. This new approach to inquiry is described as the *biography of an idea* methodology. To exercise the biography of an idea approach, the biography of Albert Einstein is briefly retold as the biography of the special theory of relativity; the biography of Kurt Cobain is briefly retold as the biography of Grunge Rock; and a brief biography of Hip Hop is presented as a socially emergent phenomenon.

Having established the biography of an idea methodology as a valid means of investigating the social origins of ideas, this approach is applied to the joint efforts of young people working together at an art- and science-based after-school program on an innovative product design called BiodegradaBall. This chapter quite literally illustrates the biography of the BiodegradaBall idea, while highlighting the ways in which invention and innovation are socially distributed.

Similar to the biography of the BiodegradaBall idea presented in Chapter 6, Chapter 7 illustrates the story of yet another student developed project idea: the biography of Static Fashion. Whereas the goal of Chapter 6 is to make visible the socially distributed nature of invention and innovation, Chapter 7 emphasizes the various ways young people and adults participate in the idea development process. Following the presentation of the biography of the Static Fashion idea, this chapter concludes with an analysis of each participant's unique profile of participation.

Chapter 8 begins by reflecting back on the biography of Static Fashion presented in Chapter 7 to discuss the learning outcomes associated with a participatory reframing of creativity before then establishing a pedagogical framework for the creative classroom based on a *double-loop* model of dial-ectical learning and development. Translating theory into practice, Chapter 8 concludes with a discussion of thirteen implications for education.

Before bringing *Participatory Creativity: Introducing Access and Equity to the Creative Classroom* to a close, I argue that not only do we have a responsi-bility to make creativity in education more equitable and accessible to all young people, we also have a responsibility to consider the ethical dimensions of creativity. Having discussed the importance of addressing issues of ethics in the creative classroom, I ultimately express an overall positive outlook for the collective, creative capacities of human invention—and offer hope for the future of creativity in education.

Ultimately it is my hope that readers will come away from this book with a new sense of urgency to bring opportunities to engage in creative participation to all students. My worry is that in contemporary culture, too many young people are driven away or denied access to the creative classroom and, as a result, we all miss out on the contributions to the sciences, the arts, technology, politics, and so many other aspects of public life which those young people may have enhanced—had they only been given the chance. If we endeavor to live in a world driven by progress and shaped by the richness of our global culture, then it is imperative that all young people have access to creative learning experiences. Policy and educational reform will come, in due time, but a change in mindset, a shift in epistemology must come first. To this end, I believe that adopting a participatory and distributed understanding of the creative process is the necessary first step towards introducing access and equity to the creative classroom. I hope that after reading this book, you believe that, too.

Notes

1. All student names are pseudonyms.
2. See Mara Krechevsky & Ben Mardell, "Four Features of Learning in Groups," in *Making Learning Visible: Children as Individual and Group Learners*, ed. Project Zero and Reggio Children (Reggio Emilia, Italy: Reggio Children, 2001), p. 284. See also Mara Krechevsky, Ben Mardell, Melissa Rivard, & Daniel Wilson, *Visible Learners: Promoting Reggio-Inspired Approaches in All Schools*, (San Francisco, CA: Jossey-Bass, 2013).
3. See Lev Semenovich Vygotsky, *Mind in Society: The Development of Higher Psychological Processes* (Cambridge, MA: Harvard University Press, 1978).
4. See R. Keith Sawyer, *Social Emergence: Societies as Complex Systems* (New York: Cambridge University Press, 2005), and R. Keith Sawyer & Stacey DeZutter, "Distributed Creativity: How Collective Creations Emerge from Collaboration," *Psychology of Aesthetics, Creativity, and the Arts*, 3, no. 2 (2009): 81–92.
5. See Paul Duncum, "Creativity as Conversation in the Interactive Audience Culture of YouTube" *Visual Inquiry*, 2, no. 2 (2013): 115–125.
6. See Vlad Petre Glăveanu, *Distributed Creativity: Thinking Outside the Box of the Creative Individual* (Springer Briefs in Psychology, 2014).
7. See Aaron Blake, "Obama's 'You Didn't Build That' Problem." *Washington Post* (2012, July 18). Retrieved from https://www.washingtonpost.com/blogs/the-fix/post/obamas-you-didnt-build-that-problem/2012/07/18/gJQAJxyotW_blog.html
8. Romney in Blake. See Blake, "Obama's 'You Didn't Build That' Problem," para 20.
9. John Schnatter is the founder and CEO of Papa John's Pizza, the third largest pizza chain in the world. In the spring of 2012 Schnatter and his wife hosted a campaign fundraising event for Mitt Romney at their home in Kentucky. See Joseph Gerth, "Presidential Hopeful Mitt Romney to Visit Louisville for Fundraiser Next Thursday." *Courier-Journal* (2012, April 17).
10. See David Lang, *Zero to Maker: Learn (Just Enough) to Make (Just About) Anything* (Sebastopol, CA: Maker Media, 2013), p. 18.
11. Ibid., p. 19.
12. Ibid., p. 19.
13. See Glăveanu, *Distributed Creativity*.
14. See for example Mihaly Csikszentmihalyi, "Society, Culture, Person: A Systems View of Creativity," in *The Nature of Creativity*, ed. Robert J. Sternberg (New York: Cambridge University Press, 1988); Mihaly Csikszentmihalyi, *Creativity: Flow and the Psychology of Discovery and Invention* (New York: HarperCollins, 1996); Mihaly Csikszentmihalyi, "Implications of a Systems Perspective for the Study of Creativity," in *Handbook of Creativity*, ed. Robert J. Sternberg (New York: Cambridge University Press, 1999). See also See Howard Gardner, *Creating Minds: An Anatomy of Creativity Seen through the Lives of Freud, Einstein, Picasso, Stravinsky, Eliot, Graham, and Gandhi* (New York: Basic Books, 1993).

15. The images suggest nothing about the race or class of the young people depicted in the graphics, which are important factors to consider when addressing issues of equity in the creative classroom, or any classroom.
16. See Mindy L. Kornhaber, Kelly Griffith, & Alison Tyler, "It's Not Education by Zipcode Anymore—But What is It? Conceptions of Equity under the Common Core." *Education Policy Analysis Archives, 22* (4), 2014. Retrieved from http://dx.doi.org/10.14507/epaa.v22n4.2014
17. Ibid., p. 6. See also C. Jencks, "Whom Must We Treat Equally for Educational Opportunity to be Equal?" *Ethics*, 98, no. 3 (1988): 518–533.
18. See Michael Hanchett Hanson, *Worldmaking: Psychology and the Ideology of Creativity*, (New York: Palgrave Macmillan, 2015).
19. See Michel Foucault, "What is an Author?" in *Language, Counter-Memory, Practice: Selected Essays and Interviews* (Ithaca, NY: Cornell Paperbacks, 1980).

Chapter 1

Establishing a Systems-based Understanding of Creativity

Educational researcher David N. Perkins has thought a lot about the future. In particular, he has thought about the future of learning. In a world shaped by shifting economies, social change, climate change, globalization, and digitally mediated life, it is important to consider how best to equip today's students for an unpredictable tomorrow. For these reasons, Perkins has puzzled deeply over how we might best prepare our young people for the lives they are likely to live. But, as he will be first to admit, while we can make educated guesses, we cannot surely know what knowledge, skills, and dispositional ways of thinking will be most useful to the learners we teach today in 15, 20, or 25 years' time.

Though Perkins cannot see into the future any more clearly than the rest of us, in his book *Future Wise*, he offers his best bets on what learning will matter most to today's young people once they arrive in tomorrow's world. Having carefully considered "the expanding universe of what's worth learning,"[1] Perkins has identified six important educational trends as his best bets for what learning really matters. He calls these educational trends the *six beyonds: beyond basic skills, beyond the traditional disciplines, beyond discrete disciplines, beyond regional perspectives, beyond mastering content,* and *beyond prescribed content.*[2] Spend a little time with them, and you will likely find that Perkins's six beyonds do indeed seem like pretty good bets for the future of learning. You might even think, *well if that's what's worth learning tomorrow, then why don't we teach like that today?* But changing the way we teach—and what we teach—is not so easy. And sometimes such change requires hard choices.

When discussing the six beyonds, Perkins has noted that in order to develop a curriculum that makes room to teach what is most worth learning, educators (and administrators) must consider what they might need to let go of in their classrooms. Letting go is never easy—especially when what one needs to let go of is an embedded practice, a familiar habit, or even something as deeply engrained as a core belief. But in order for change to take place, letting go of the old to make room for the new is almost always a necessity.

Like Perkins's six beyonds, participatory creativity is a consideration of what will matter most in the lives young people are likely to live tomorrow. In a world where invention and innovation are increasingly distributed processes, participatory creativity asks that we look beyond individual-based orientations towards invention and innovation, and consider how all people may participate in creativity in different ways.

Developing a new understanding of creativity as a participatory and distributed process requires a not-so-subtle epistemological shift. In order to make this shift, one may have to first make cognitive room for a more systems-based understanding of creativity by letting go of the individual-based orientations towards creativity that he or she may be holding on to. Letting go of the idea that individuals are creative may seem like a radical move. Have no fear. What is being suggested here is not to entirely erase the individual from the creative equation, but rather to open one's mind to the possibility that when creativity takes place, it is less of a psychological event, and more of a social affair.

To ease this transition, the goal of this chapter is to establish a foundational understanding of creativity from a systems-based perspective before then presenting a more participatory model of invention and innovation in Chapter 2. In order to establish this perspective, it is helpful to dip into the history of creativity in education at a pivotal point in time, before then moving quickly into a discussion of creativity as a participatory and distributed process.

From Trait Theory to Distributed Understandings of Invention and Ideation

At the dawn of both the Cold War and the cognitive revolution, a psychometrician by the name of J. P. Guilford was elected president of the American Psychological Association. During his 1950 inaugural address, Guilford directed his fellow psychologists' attention to the field's lack of consideration for creativity in education. In the first minutes of his speech Guilford famously asked: "Why is there so little apparent correlation between education and creative productiveness? Why do we not produce a larger number of creative geniuses than we do, under supposedly enlightened, modern educational practices?"[3]

Though creativity has become a popular and highly prized commodity today, during the first half of the twentieth century the study of invention and innovation received little attention by comparison. Guilford, however, believed that supporting creative young people would be necessary if the West were to stave off the threat of communism that loomed over the United States and Europe after the end of World War II. As creativity researcher Robert W. Weisberg has noted, "Guilford argued that creative children were our most valuable resource and that it was important that they be identified and nurtured as early in life as possible to maximize the likelihood that they would put their potential to use."[4] In order to identify creative young people—or more specifically young people who exhibited creative potential—Guilford suggested a series of measures that could be used to test students for the cognitive skills and personality traits that were presumed to be associated with creative genius.[5]

Interestingly, Guilford made a distinction between genius and intelligence. He understood genius to mean "someone who made unique creative contributions" to the world,[6] not someone who simply had a high IQ. However, just as intelligence could be measured with an IQ test, Guilford and many others set out to develop tests to measure the creative potential of young people.

Following Guilford's lead, throughout the latter half of the twentieth century creativity researchers largely set their sights on exploring the individual as the primary unit of analysis. From this perspective, there was a specific set of traits and cognitive abilities associated with creativity. Depending on how well young people scored on creativity tests, some students were deemed to be more creative—or more potentially creative—than others. In Chapter 3 we will explore the inequality and othering that creativity tests promote, but for now, the key point to be made is that, for decades after Guilford's 1950 address, one of the principal goals of creativity research was to understand, identify, and further develop creative individuals.

After decades of developing frameworks, models, and psychometric tests rooted in Guildford's mid-century trait theory conceptions of creativity, towards the tail end of the twentieth century the field of cognitive psychology took a curious turn. During the 1980s the concept of *distributed cognition*— the idea that cognitive processes were not restricted to individuals but rather distributed across social groups, environments, and technologies—came into play. Distributed cognition researchers "realized the importance of the fact that cognition was socially distributed"[7] and argued that "the content and process of thinking . . . are both distributed as much among individuals as they are packed within them."[8] This new approach to understanding cognition stretched beyond the isolation of the individual mind—suggesting that cognition and human ideation are situated within broader social and environmental systems.

Cognitive scientist Edwin Hutchins is known as one of the primary originators of distributed cognition theory. Hutchins and his colleagues conducted in-depth case study research on U.S. Navy vessels and in airplane cockpit flight simulators to better understand how "cognitive accomplishments can be joint accomplishments, not attributable to any individual."[9] They found that, whether in the air or at sea, navigation was a distributed process that depended on the contributions of a variety of actors, each playing a unique role that interdependently relied on the others. Referring to the performance of a Captain, a First Officer, and Second Officer in a Boeing 727 passenger jet cockpit, Hutchins and Klausen made this case:

> The question of interest to you as a passenger should not be whether or not a particular pilot is performing well, but whether or not the system that is composed of pilots and the technology of the cockpit environment is performing well. It is the performance of that system, not the skills of

any individual pilot, that determines whether you live or die. In order to understand the performance of the cockpit as a system we need, of course, to refer to the cognitive properties of the individual pilots, but we also need a new, larger, unit of cognitive analysis . . . [that] permit[s] us to describe and explain the cognitive properties of the cockpit system that is composed of the pilots and their informational environment. We call this unit of analysis a system of *distributed cognition.*[10]

Hutchins's research on distributed cognition emphasized the importance of interactions amongst individuals, access to information, overlapping expertise, communication, building on prior knowledge, and the role of context. Overall, Hutchins made a systems-based case for cognition by "mov[ing] the boundaries of the cognitive unit of analysis out beyond the skin of the individual person and treat[ing] the navigational team as a cognitive and computational system."[11]

Being that the study of human creativity parallels the investigation of human intelligence,[12] it follows suit that during the rise of distributed cognition, systems-based understandings of creativity began to emerge. Just as many scholars now acknowledge the distributed nature of cognition; today, many creativity researchers recognize that the myth of the lone creative genius no longer applies when creativity is understood as being socially constructed.[13]

Though the scholarly literature on creativity is vast, participatory creativity is situated within research that emphasizes systems-based approaches to invention and innovation rooted in social interactions. To bring this landscape into focus, it is helpful to review three key concepts that support a participatory understanding of creativity—Howard Gruber's *evolving systems* approach to creativity, Mihaly Csikszentmihalyi's *sociocultural* approach to creativity, and various considerations of *group, collaborative,* and *distributed creativity* as proposed by R. Keith Sawyer, Vlad Petre Glăveanu, and others.

Howard Gruber and the "Evolving Systems" Approach

A student of Jean Piaget and a pioneer in the developmental psychology study of creativity, Howard E. Gruber was among the first theorists to shift the focus of creativity research away from the personality traits of the individual, and instead look towards the creative work of that individual.[14] Gruber believed that "the necessary uniqueness of the creative person argues against efforts to reduce psychological description to a fixed set of dimensions."[15] Creativity, Gruber suggested, was unique. And likewise, creative people were "unique in unexpected ways."[16] The premise of Gruber's research was that there was no one way to be creative, but rather that creative work took many different forms. Therefore, no trait theory of creativity could universally describe the psychological (or characterological) profile of the creative individual.

To make his case, Gruber and his colleagues put forth the *evolving systems approach* to studying unique creative people at work.[17] Using the case study method to review the work of Charles Darwin and others,[18] Gruber analyzed creative individuals as evolving systems composed of loosely coupled, developing subsystems of knowledge, purpose, and affect.

Gruber's definition of creativity stated that "a work is creative if it is (a) original, (b) purposeful on the part of the creative person, and (c) in harmony or compatible with other human purposes, needs, or values."[19] In addition to these three tenets, Gruber rejected the popular notion of reducing creativity to the *Eureka!* or *A-ha!* moment. Instead, Gruber highlighted the role of "continuance" in creative work.[20] Making a case for the long sequence of events involved in the creative process, Gruber and Davis playfully challenged the appropriateness of using a single bolt of lightning as a metaphor for creativity:

> A bolt of lightning is by no means a unitary event. It has inner structure and temporal development. There is a period of preparation in which electrical charge is built up; the charge is not a "trait" of the thundercloud, but a relationship between cloud and ground below, or between cloud and cloud (i.e., a difference in electrical potential). The build up of potential difference involves a positive feedback mechanism in which myriad collisions of ice pellets or water drops produce the charge; these earlier events, though of low intensity, prepare the way for intensification later on.[21]

What we recognize in the sky as a dramatic flash of lightning is the result of all that preceded it. Gruber and Davis argued that lightning bolts do not exist in isolation, they are instead part of thunderstorms, which are in turn part of a global system of weather events taking place around the world. Similarly, creative insights are not flashes of brilliance without precedence; instead, "insights, like lightning strokes, represent not a break with the past but the steady functioning of the creative system at work."[22] As Gruber noted, "serious creative work does take a long time. Compared to the few milliseconds of a lightning bolt, with which the creative act is sometimes compared, the actual process is very long indeed, to be reckoned in months, years, and often decades."[23]

Through in-depth case studies, Gruber and his associates found that the creative individuals they studied functioned as unique systems. Their works emerged from the dialectical interaction between concepts and enterprises. The concepts these individuals pursued formed an emergent sense of purpose that drove their creative work forward. In this context, an "enterprise" could be understood as "an enduring group of related activities aimed at producing a series of kindred products"[24] and a network of enterprises was a collection of interrelated enterprises:

> Another way of looking at patterns of interrelationships of this kind is to see them as a web of interruption and resumption, such that a task or

project undertaken in one enterprise becomes an interruption in another. Seen in this way, the interruption itself eventually moves the creator to resume work in the interrupted enterprise . . . [this approach] evokes a picture of the creative mind as a system.[25]

While Gruber's theory of creativity was indeed a systems-based approach, it was nonetheless still a theory of the creative individual. This approach, at least in part, was a great man theory: "we are certainly not criticizing the creative efforts of those below the summit of Mt. Olympus," he argued, "But we insist that the serious study of creative work requires careful and prolonged attention to the individual and must pay special attention to the very great."[26] Even though he contended that the study of creativity must include the luminaries of history, Gruber's emphasis on creativity as *work*, rather than *trait*, also laid the foundation for a more participatory view of creativity. "Even in the loneliest creative effort there is some communication with others," he conceded, "and often creative work is not so lonely."[27] Indeed, Gruber saw the critical role of creativity in the future as broadly participatory work for the survival of humanity: "broad spectrum creative collaboration is needed to guide the course of events in another direction,"[28] he wrote. In this way, Gruber envisioned like-minded individuals working together—first locally, then globally—collectively organized by a common sense of purpose.

Mihaly Csikszentmihalyi and the "Sociocultural" Approach to Creativity

A contemporary of Howard Gruber, Mihaly Csikszentmihalyi is widely known for his theory of *flow*, which describes a state of complete engagement in an activity to the extent that time seems not to exist and one's cognitive energy is entirely focused on the task at hand.[29] In addition to his psychological research on optimal experience and flow, Csikszentmihalyi is also known as a seminal creativity theorist. Like Gruber, Mihaly Csikszentmihalyi also developed a systems-based approach to creativity research.[30] However, in contrast to Gruber, Csikszentmihalyi was one of the first scholars to locate creativity within a system external to the individual self: "what we call creativity is a phenomenon that is constructed through an *interaction between producer and audience*. Creativity is not the product of single individuals, but of social systems making judgments about individuals' products."[31]

Arguing that "the phenomenon of creativity . . . is as much a cultural and social as it is a psychological event,"[32] Csikszentmihalyi's systems model of creativity moved away from a strictly individual-based orientation towards creativity. Instead, Csikszentmihalyi focused on the *environment* within which creative individuals operate. "This environment has two salient aspects: a cultural, or symbolic, aspect which here is called the domain; and a social aspect called the field."[33] According to Csikszentmihalyi, when an individual offers a contribution to a domain (the symbol system of a discipline of practice or area of study) that is approved by the field—the gatekeepers who oversee that domain—creativity takes place. Creativity, then, exists at the intersection of the individual, domain, and field.

This model of creativity adheres to what R. Keith Sawyer has referred to as the *sociocultural* definition of creativity: "*Creativity is the generation of a product that is judged to be novel and also to be appropriate, useful, or valuable by a suitably knowledgeable social group.*"[34] In this way, Csikszentmihalyi's systems model is naturally social, because it takes place within a specific cultural setting.

What we call creativity always involves a change in a symbolic system, a change that in turn will affect the thoughts and feelings of the members of the culture. A change that does not affect the way we think, feel, or act will not be creative. Thus, creativity presupposes a community of people who share ways of thinking and acting, who learn from each other and imitate each other's actions.[35]

Csikszentmihalyi grounded his sociocultural approach to creativity in the work of Richard Dawkins,[36] specifically Dawkins's concept of *memes* as units of cultural meaning. Dawkins proposed that memes function culturally in the same way that genes function biologically. "Memes are similar to genes in that they carry instructions for action. . . . But whereas genetic instructions are transmitted in the chemical codes that we inherit in our chromosomes, the instructions contained in memes are transmitted through learning."[37] Ordinarily, memes are learned by individuals within a culture and then reproduced (imitated) by others without change. However, when an individual introduces a new meme into a culture in a manner that is socially accepted (and therefore alters that culture), then creativity has taken place. In this way, new, combined, or altered memes may have an evolutionary effect on culture in the same way that new, combined, or altered genes may affect biological evolution.

While Csikszentmihalyi's sociocultural perspective did indeed situate creativity within broader systems, it still clung to a great man understanding of creativity, as it focused exclusively on domain changing contributions to culture frequently associated with genius. By equating creativity with long-term cultural change within a domain, the individuals who purportedly generated the ideas in Csikszentmihalyi's model were "often assumed to require some level of eminence, even if in theory 'unsung heroes' could change the domain without seeking or getting credit."[38]

Widely known for his *theory of multiple intelligences*, Howard Gardner employed Csikszentmihalyi's sociocultural model of creativity in his studies of highly successful creative individuals. Gardner's use of Csikszentmihalyi's framework to develop seven case studies of creativity in the Modern era was an eminence-based application of Csikszentmihalyi's sociocultural approach to creativity.[39] Focusing his investigation of creativity on the lives of Sigmund Freud, Albert Einstein, Pablo Picasso, Igor Stravinsky, T.S. Eliot, Martha Graham, and Mahatma Gandhi—and the impact they each had on their respective cultural domains—Gardner placed a clear emphasis on the eminent individual. Gardner's investigation of these seven specific "creating minds" supports a further point made by Csikszentmihalyi and others—namely, that creativity (like intelligence) is domain specific.[40] As Gardner had previously debunked the concept of *g*, or *general intelligence*, with his theory of *multiple intelligences*, so too did he make a pluralistic case for creativity. Scaffolded by Csikszentmihalyi's sociocultural approach to creativity, Gardner argued that "creative breakthroughs in one realm cannot be collapsed uncritically with breakthroughs in other realms. . . . A single variety of creativity is a myth."[41]

Sociocultural theory has changed the terms of the ongoing debate about the definition of creativity and has had its critics. For example, pushing back on the eminence focus of Csikszentmihalyi's sociocultural model, Weisberg has argued that what Csikszentmihalyi refers to as creativity may better be described as *value*. "I would say that [Csikszentmihalyi's model] determines whether an innovation comes to be *valued*, and I would restrict the use of the term *creativity* to the individual's production of the innovation in the first place."[42] Weisberg redefined creativity as "the production of works that were novel for their creator at the time they were produced"[43] regardless of whether they were of interest or in other ways valued by the external gatekeepers of any given cultural domain. Referring to the triple helix model of DNA originally developed by James Watson and Francis Crick (before they developed the domain-changing double helix model of DNA) and the lesser-known painting *Minotauromachy* that was produced by Pablo Picasso as an antecedent to his widely recognized cubist masterpiece *Guernica*, Weisberg included an individual's failed attempts as being equally creative as his/her more successful works. His reason for doing so was that, from his perspective, the cognitive processes involved in producing a failed work were no different from the cognitive processes involved in producing a successful work.

Weisberg rejected this systems-based argument made by Csikszentmihalyi's theory (products developed by an individual may only be considered creative if a set of critical gatekeepers places value upon them), and instead emphasized the internal psychological processes of individuals over the social judgment of their work.

> Why should we assume a priori that different cognitive processes are involved in the production of the valued versus the non-valued innovations? . . . the inventor who produced a machine that failed miserably obviously missed some thing or things, but that does not mean that there was a basic difference in the processes involved in producing the successful versus unsuccessful one.[44]

Despite his interest in cognitive activity, in his case study of Watson and Crick, Weisberg presented what may be considered convincing evidence for a more distributed understanding of the process that led to the young scientists' breakthrough discovery of the double helix model of DNA:

in order to initiate their model-building work, Watson and Crick agreed to begin with the working assumption that DNA might be in the shape of a helix. This helical assumption, of course, was correct in general terms, and it, along with the model-building orientation, put Watson and Crick solidly on the path to success [but] . . . Where did they get those two critical ideas—that they should build models and that DNA may be helical? Did they have some magical intuition, some creative sixth sense, that led them along the correct path, where others did not know to tread? It seems not. Both of those critical assumptions were based relatively directly on the work of Linus Pauling, a world-famous chemist who had . . . proposed that alpha-keratin was helical in shape, and had built a helical model of the structure to show how all the atoms fit together.[45]

In addition to Pauling, other scientists such as Maurice Wilkins and Rosalind Franklin had likewise been developing helical models of DNA at the time. Watson and Crick borrowed liberally from them all as they developed their renowned model of DNA. This suggests that, while Watson and Crick certainly were engaged in psychological work, the cognitive processes of the two scientists were both informed by, and situated within, a greater social system.

Through his case study of Watson and Crick, Weisberg refuted Csikszentmihalyi's emphasis on the value of products as determined by a field of gatekeepers, while also attempting to debunk great man approaches to creativity, suggesting that significant creative contributions like Watson and Crick's double helix model of DNA were achieved through basic problem solving—accessible to anyone. But Weisberg overlooked the social dimensions of this work, focusing instead on individual problem solving applied in extraordinary ways, to make his case.

Upholding a model of creativity deeply rooted in the individual, Weisberg did not align himself with arguments made by Hutchins and other distributed cognition researchers, which suggested that "the emphasis on finding and describing 'knowledge structures' that are somewhere 'inside' the individual encourages us to overlook the fact that human cognition is always situated in a complex sociocultural world and cannot be unaffected by it."[46] As Sawyer has argued, even seemingly single-handed creativity is distributed: "even the insights that emerge when [one is] completely alone can be traced back to previous collaborations."[47] In other words, even behind the closed doors of Watson and Crick's laboratories or within the walls of Picasso's studio, the creative activity that happened in those places was the result of more than individual cognitive processes.

Group, Collaborative, and Distributed Orientations Towards Creativity

Over the past twenty years an array of researchers have proposed group, collaborative, and distributed understandings of creativity that rely less on the eminent individuals that were the focus of previous systems-based creativity studies, and more on the rich webs of interconnectivity that involve a wider array of actors.

A jazz pianist by training—and later a student of Mihalyi Csikszentmihalyi's—R. Keith Sawyer is one of the greatest champions of group, collaborative, and distributed understandings of creativity. Expanding on Csikszentmihalyi's sociocultural approach to the study of creativity and the scholarship on distributed cognition, Sawyer and his colleagues have put forth the idea that "creativity is embedded in social groups . . . and creative products emerge from collaborative networks."[48] Inspired by the work of improvisational theater troupes, mountain bike designers, collaborative working groups, children's fantasy play, and historical innovators such as the Wright Brothers, Sawyer has investigated the creativity that takes place in a variety of group settings. Sawyer's empirical research on improvisational jazz ensembles provides a keen example of group-generated creativity:

> An improvising group of musicians is one of the best examples of group creativity. In jazz, for example, no single musician can determine the flow of the performance: it emerges out of the musical conversation, a give-and-take as performers propose new ideas, respond to other ideas, and elaborate or modify those ideas as the performance moves forward.[49]

Based on their analysis of teenagers participating in a Chicago-based improvisational theater troupe, Sawyer and his colleague Stacy DeZutter have argued that "when cognitive processes are distributed across groups, they become visible, and scientists can observe them by analyzing the verbal and gestural interactions among the participants."[50] In other words, the interactions between individuals make the emergence of creativity visible in a way that individual-based cognitive theories of creative ideation cannot. Thus, a shift towards a more distributed based understanding of invention and innovation demystifies the creativity phenomenon by making it more observable.[51]

Sawyer and DeZutter defined distributed creativity as "situations where collaborating groups of individuals collectively generate a shared creative product."[52] Their research concluded that the outcomes of distributed creativity emerged through a give-and-take process of interaction, wherein members within a group responded to and built upon one another's contributions. The outcomes that resulted from such processes "cannot be reduced to the intentions or actions of any [one] participant."[53] This emergent brand of creativity that involves the collaboration of multiple contributors is a process that Sawyer has labeled *collaborative emergence*.[54]

Reviewing transcripts from improvisational theater performances with a professional theater troupe and brainstorming sessions conducted by artists and writers developing animated episodes for the Cartoon Network, Sawyer provided further examples of collaborative emergence. As a result of these studies, Sawyer identified several "essential characteristics of collaborative emergence"[55]; among them, the concept of *moment to moment contingency*, which suggests that collaborative emergence is unpredictable. The improv scene or the cartoon plot being developed in a brainstorming meeting can take a wild turn at any moment, "and no single actor's action ever fixes the future flow of the performance."[56] Sawyer also identified the concept of *retroactive meaning*, which suggests that an individual's contribution does not take on meaning until someone else in the group responds to that contribution. In this way, "the meaning of each line is retroactively determined by the collective flow of the dialogue."[57] For instance, if an actor were to say, "Well, well, well . . . what have we here?" during an improvisational theater performance, the question "What have we here?" means little until there is a response. If another actor were to respond by saying "It appears to be a rack of lamb," then the question "What have we here?" takes on a different meaning from if the responding actor were to say, "Allow me to introduce you to my sister." In this simple example, the word "what" literally changes meaning from something to eat to someone to meet based on the response that proceeds it.

Overall, Sawyer found that within instances of collaborative emergence, the study of creativity could not be reduced to the cognitive activity of any given individual member, because each individual contribution was in turn "transformed and reinterpreted by the ensuing thought processes of the group."[58]

Combining the domains of cultural psychology with creativity studies, Vlad Petre Glăveanu has put forth a theory of creativity as distributed action.[59] Simply put, Glăveanu has made the case that to create is to act on the world. But creative action does not happen in isolation. Instead, creativity is always situated within society and culture. Consistent with John Dewey's conception of *art as experience*,[60] creativity "emerges as an encounter between person and world."[61] To develop a visual image of his thinking, Glăveanu reinterpreted Mel Rhodes's popular four Ps of creativity (person, product, process, and press),[62] as five interrelated As: actors, audiences, artifacts, actions, and affordances. As he has explained:

> Creativity can no longer be said to reside "within" the person, the product, etc. It emerges as a form of action engaged in by various actors (individual or groups), in relation to multiple audiences (again individuals or groups), exploiting the affordances of the cultural (symbolic or material) world and leading to the generation of artefacts (appreciated as new and useful by self and/or others).[63]

But Glăveanu's five As model of creativity is not a simple rebranding of Rhodes's four Ps,[64] instead, what Glăveanu has aimed to do is to *integrate* Rhodes's Ps, which are too often (and mistakenly) considered separate from one another. "In distributed creative acts we cannot easily disentangle the psychological from the physical, the social from the individual, nor should we be concerned with such segmentations."[65] Actors, audiences, artifacts, actions, and affordances exist in relationship to one another: "actors are defined by their interaction with audiences, action engages existing affordances and generates new ones, artefacts can become agents within creative work, etc."[66]

To further illustrate his point, Glăveanu presented an interesting case study: the art of Romanian Easter egg decoration. As Glăveanu has explained, the traditional folk art of decorating Easter eggs in Romania is not based on the work of any one individual, but instead involves many actors, and takes place over time. Glăveanu's case study emphasized the importance of audiences in his model. The egg decorators in his study were responsive to the needs and interests of the people who bought their eggs at fairs (who may be local experts, or visiting tourists) and other events, just as they were to the scrutiny of those who judged their designs at Easter egg festivals. Within the domain of Romanian Easter egg decoration "the views of others and dialogue with them (at the church, at the fair, at the local museum) are crucial for creative action."[67] Innovations in Romanian Easter egg decoration, therefore, cannot be solely attributed to individual artists, but instead are the result of a broader system.

The group, collaborative, and distributed theories discussed above all serve as systems-based conceptions of creativity that stand in opposition to the idea of the lone creative genius. However convincing these arguments may be, systems-based understandings of invention and innovation have a scant representation throughout popular culture. It is therefore understandable that socially distributed theories of creativity may be disorienting to the man-on-the-street (or educator in the classroom) who maintains a traditional understanding of invention and innovation steeped in the foundations of our individualistic culture. "How can you tell me that Albert Einstein, or Frida Kahlo, or Duke Ellington are not creative," one might ask. Indeed, as the current chapter has discussed, the tractor beams of our individualistic culture are strong—and even renowned scholars deeply embedded in the study of creativity have likewise struggled to fully grasp socially emergent explanations of creativity that look beyond the cognitive processes of individuals.

Many theorists have suggested that we are inclined to recognize the Einsteins, Kahlos, and Ellingtons of the world as creative people—if not creative geniuses—for two reasons. First, our individualistic Western culture naturally favors orientations towards individual achievement (and the hero worship that accompanies it) and second, the study of creativity is deeply rooted in psychology, which is largely biased towards studies of the cognitive processes of the individual self.[68]

At the beginning of this chapter, I suggested that in order to develop a systems-based understanding of creativity, it may be necessary to let go of traditional, individual-based understandings of invention and innovation that placed the locus of creativity within the gray matter of solitary actors. But I also urged readers not to erase the individual from the creative process entirely. In order to adopt a participatory approach to understanding creativity, it is necessary for individuals to *participate* in distributed creative processes—just as Sawyer and Glăveanu have suggested. Therefore, we must resist the bifurcation of creativity theories into individual vs. social constructs, and instead develop an orientation towards invention and innovation that both embraces individual agency while also emphasizing the socially distributed nature of discovery.[69] Chapter 2 presents a participatory and distributed theory of creativity that intends to do just that.

Notes

1. See David N. Perkins, *Future Wise: Educating Our Children for a Changing World* (San Francisco, CA: Jossey-Bass, 2014), pp. 225–226.
2. Ibid., p. 226.
3. See J. P. Guilford, *Creativity*. Address of the President of the American Psychological Association. September 5, 1950. Pennsylvania State College, University Park, PA, 1950.
4. See Robert W. Weisberg, *Creativity: Understanding Innovation in Problem Solving, Science, Invention, and the Arts* (Hoboken, NJ: John Wiley & Sons, 2006), p. 450.
5. Ibid.
6. Ibid., p. 449.
7. See Edwin Hutchins, *Cognition in the Wild* (Cambridge, MA: MIT Press, 1995), p xii. See also Gavriel Salomon (ed.), *Distributed Cognitions: Psychological and Educational Considerations* (New York: Cambridge University Press, 1993).
8. See Michael Cole & Yrjo Engeström, "A Cultural Historical Approach to Distributed Cognition," in *Distributed Cognitions: Psychological and Educational Considerations*, ed. Gavriel Salomon (New York: Cambridge University Press, 1993), p. 1.
9. See Edwin Hutchins, "Learning to Navigate," in *Understanding Practice: Perspectives on Activity in Context*, eds. Seth Chaiklin & Jean Lave (Cambridge, UK: Cambridge University Press, 1996), p. 35; see also Hutchins, *Cognition in the Wild*, and Edwin Hutchins & Tove Klausen, "Distributed Cognition in an Airplane Cockpit," in *Cognition and Communication at Work*, eds. Yrjo Engeström & David Middleton (New York: Cambridge University Press, 1996).
10. See Hutchins & Klausen, "Distributed Cognition," p. 17.
11. See Hutchins, *Cognition in the Wild*, p. xiv.
12. See Howard Gardner, *Creating Minds: An Anatomy of Creativity Seen through the Lives of Freud, Einstein, Picasso, Stravinsky, Eliot, Graham, and Gandhi* (New York: Basic Books, 1993).
13. See, for example, Vlad Petre Glăveanu, *Distributed Creativity: Thinking Outside the Box of the Creative Individual* (Springer Briefs in Psychology, 2014), Lone Hersted, "Creativity in a Relational Perspective," in *Behind the scenes of Artistic Creativity*, pp. 229–245, eds. Tatiana Chemi, Julie Borup Jensen, & Lone Hersted (Frankfurt am Main, Germany: Peter Lang, 2015), and R. Keith Sawyer & Stacey DeZutter, "Distributed Creativity: How Collective Creations Emerge from Collaboration," *Psychology of Aesthetics, Creativity, and the Arts*, 3, no. 2 (2009): 81–92.
14. See Reijo Miettinen, "The Sources of Novelty: A Cultural and Systemic View of Distributed Creativity" *Creativity and Innovation Management*, 15, no. 2 (2006): 173–181.
15. See Howard E. Gruber & Doris B. Wallace, "The Case Study Method and Evolving Systems Approach for Understanding Unique Creative People at

Work," in *Handbook of Creativity*, ed. Robert J. Sternberg (New York: Cambridge University Press, 1999), p. 93.

16. Ibid., p. 93.
17. See Howard E. Gruber, "The Evolving Systems Approach to Creative Work," in *Creative People at Work: Twelve Cognitive Case Studies*, eds. Doris B. Wallace and Howard E. Gruber (New York: Oxford University Press, 1989); Howard E. Gruber & Sara N. Davis, "Inching our Way up Mount Olympus: The Evolving Systems Approach to Creative Thinking," in *The Nature of Creativity*, ed. Robert J. Sternberg (New York: Cambridge University Press, 1988); Gruber & Wallace, "The Case Study Method" in *Handbook of Creativity*, ed. Robert J. Sternberg (New York: Cambridge University Press, 1999) and Doris B. Wallace, "Studying the Individual: The Case Study Method and Other Genres," in *Creative People at Work: Twelve Cognitive Case Studies*, ed. Doris B. Wallace & Howard. E. Gruber, (New York: Oxford University Press, 1989).
18. See Howard E. Gruber, *Darwin on Man: A Psychological Case Study of Scientific Creativity*, second edition (Chicago: University of Chicago Press, 1981), and: Gruber & Wallace, "The Case Study Method."
19. See Gruber, "The Evolving Systems Approach," p. 4.
20. See Wallace, "Studying the Individual," p. 29.
21. See Gruber & Davis, "Inching Our Way Up Mt. Olympus," p. 243.
22. Ibid., p. 244.
23. See Gruber, "The Evolving Systems Approach," p. 14.
24. See Gruber & Wallace, "The Case Study Method," p. 105.
25. Ibid., p. 107.
26. See Gruber, "The Evolving Systems Approach," p. 6.
27. Ibid., p. 7.
28. See Howard E. Gruber, "Creativity and Human Survival," in *Creative People at Work: Twelve Cognitive Case Studies*, eds. Doris B. Wallace and Howard E. Gruber (New York: Oxford University Press, 1989), p. 282.
29. See Mihaly Csikszentmihalyi, *Flow: The Psychology of Optimal Experience* (New York: HarperCollins, 1990).
30. See Mihaly Csikszentmihalyi, "Society, Culture, Person: A Systems View of Creativity" in *The Nature of Creativity*, ed. Robert J. Sternberg (New York: Cambridge University Press, 1988); Mihaly Csikszentmihalyi, *Creativity: Flow and the Psychology of Discovery and Invention* (New York: HarperCollins, 1996); Mihaly Csikszentmihalyi, "Implications of a Systems Perspective for the Study of Creativity," in *Handbook of Creativity*, ed. Robert J. Sternberg (New York: Cambridge University Press, 1999).
31. See Csikszentmihalyi, "Implications of a Systems Perspective," p. 314.
32. Ibid., p. 313.
33. Ibid., p. 314.
35. See R. Keith Sawyer, *Explaining Creativity: The Science of Human Invention* (New York: Oxford University Press, 2006/2012), p. 8.
35. See Csikszentmihalyi, "Implications of a Systems Perspective," p. 316.
36. See Richard Dawkins, *The Selfish Gene* (Oxford: Oxford University Press, 1976).
37. See Csikszentmihalyi, "Implications of a Systems Perspective," p. 316.
38. Personal communication with Michael Hanchett Hanson, January 8, 2014.
39. See Gardner, *Creating Minds*.
40. See John Baer, "The Case for Domain Specific Creativity," *Creativity Research Journal*, 11, no. 2 (1998): 173–177, and John Baer, "Is Creativity Domain Specific?" in *The Cambridge Handbook of Creativity*, eds. James C. Kaufman & Robert J. Sternberg (New York: Cambridge University Press, 2010).

41. See Gardner, *Creating Minds*, p. 7.
42. See Weisberg, *Creativity: Understanding Innovation in Problem Solving*, p. 64.
43. Ibid., p. 65
44. Ibid., p. 68.
45. Ibid., pp. 17–18.
46. See Hutchins, *Cognition in the Wild*, p. xiii. See also, Hutchins, "Learning to Navigate"; Hutchins & Klausen, "Distributed Cognition"; Cole & Engerström, "A Cultural and Historical Approach to Distributed Cognition"; and David Perkins, "Person-Plus: A Distributed View of Thinking and Learning," in *Distributed Cognitions: Psychological and Educational Considerations*, ed. Gavriel Salomon (New York: Press Syndicate/University of Cambridge, 1993).
47. R. Keith Sawyer, *Group Genius: The Creative Power of Collaboration* (New York: Basic Books, 2007).
48. See R. Keith Sawyer & Stacey DeZutter, "Distributed Creativity," p. 81. See also R. Keith Sawyer, *Explaining Creativity*; R. Keith Sawyer, "Improvisational Theater: An Ethnography of Conversational Practice," in R. Keith Sawyer, *Creativity in Performance* (Greenwich, CT: Ablex, 1997); R. Keith Sawyer, *Group Creativity: Music, Theater, Collaboration*, (Mahwah, NJ: Lawrence Erlbaum Associates, 2003); R. Keith Sawyer, *Group Genius*; R. Keith Sawyer, "Individual and Group Creativity," in *The Cambridge Handbook of Creativity*, eds. James C. Kaufman & Robert J. Sternberg (New York: Cambridge University Press, 2010).
49. See Sawyer, *Group Creativity*, p. 4.
50. See Sawyer & DeZutter, "Distributed Creativity," p. 81.
51. Yrjö Engeström, known for his work on activity theory, likewise asserted that "collaborative thinking opens up access to direct data on thought processes." See Yrjö Engeström, "Teachers as Collaborative Thinkers: An Activity-Theoretical Study of an Innovative Teacher Team," in *Teachers' Minds and Actions: Research on Teachers' Thinking and Practice*, eds. I. Calgren, G. Handal, & S. Vaage (Bristol, PA: Falmer, 1994), p. 45. This assertion is consistent with investigations conducted by Project Zero researchers in collaboration with educators in Reggio Emilia, Italy who have argued that observing collaborative working groups is a means of *making learning visible*, see Mara Krechevsky & Ben Mardell, "Four Features of Learning in Groups," in *Making Learning Visible: Children as Individual and Group Learners*, eds. Project Zero and Reggio Children (Reggio Emilia, Italy: Reggio Children, 2001).
52. See Sawyer & DeZutter, "Distributed Creativity," p. 82.
53. Ibid., p. 90.
54. See Sawyer, "Individual and Group Creativity." See also, Sawyer & DeZutter, "Distributed Creativity."
55. See Sawyer, "Individual and Group Creativity," p. 369.
56. Ibid., p. 369.
57. Ibid., p. 370.
58. Ibid., p. 371.
59. See Vlad Petre Glăveanu, *Distributed Creativity*, and Vlad Petre Glăveanu, *Thinking through Creativity and Culture: Toward an Integrated Model* (New Brunswick, NJ: Transaction Publishers, 2014). See also, Vlad Petre Glăveanu, Alex Gillespie, & Jaan Valsiner, eds. *Rethinking Creativity: Contributions from Social and Cultural Psychology* (cultural dynamics of social representation), (New York: Routledge, 2015).
60. See John Dewey, *Art as Experience*, (New York: Perigee Books, 1934).

61. See Glăveanu, *Distributed Creativity*, p. 27.
62. See Mel Rhodes, "An Analysis of Creativity." *Phi Delta Kappan*, 42 (1961): 305–310.
63. See Glăveanu, *Distributed Creativity*, p. 27.
64. In a chapter entitled "Theories of Creativity," Kozbelt, Beghetto, & Runco suggest *place, persuasion*, and *potential* as further Ps of creativity to consider. See A. Kozbelt, Ronald A. Beghetto, & Mark A. Runco, "Theories of Creativity," in *Cambridge Handbook of Creativity*, eds. James. C. Kaufman & Robert. J. Sternberg (New York: Cambridge University Press, 2010).
65. See Glăveanu, *Distributed Creativity*, p. 26.
66. Ibid., p. 27.
67. Ibid., p. 35.
68. See Lone Hersted, "Creativity in a Relational Perspective."
69. See Albert Bandura, "Exercise of Human Agency through Collective Efficacy," *Current Directions in Psychological Science*, 9, no. 3 (2000): 75–78, and Michael Hanchett Hanson, *Worldmaking: Psychology and the Ideology of Creativity* (New York: Palgrave Macmillan, 2015).

Chapter 2

Reframing Creativity as a Participatory and a Distributed Process

Imagine coming across a 35-foot tall structure composed of steel and nylon sculpted umbrellas, the lowest of which emit a delicate mist, the highest of which burst with flames while the structure itself radiates from within, illuminating a complex pattern of light. Each element of the structure is interactive—mist, flame, and light are controlled by the observer, who is not an observer at all, but rather an active participant in the aesthetic of the piece.

Imagine coming across an equally gigantic form situated far out in the desert—nearly three stories tall—built of translucent materials, suggestive of seedpods and fertility. Twisting upwards from the sand, the structure is sinuous, meandering, and organic in its original state—and then it changes form. Dramatically burning away its outer shell, a new structure is revealed—pulsing with flame, light, and fountain effects. Like the last, this structure, too, invites interaction. Each flame- and light-emitting effect triggered by movement and sound.

The above sculptural descriptions are neither hallucinations nor alien forms from a sci-fi fantasy. Instead, they are large-scale, interactive public art works developed by the Flux Foundation, an Oakland, California-based consortium of artists, engineers, metal workers, programmers, pyro technicians, fund raisers, crowdsourcers, contractors, and dozens of others. Respectively referred to as BrollyFlock (2011/2012) and Zoa (2012), both of these large-scale works of public art necessitated the coordinated efforts of a wide range of individuals, each bringing his or her personal talents and experiences to bear on the collective outcome of the group's work.[1,2]

Born of the Burning Man tradition, the Flux Foundation deeply believes that large-scale public art projects are ripe with learning opportunities, collaboration, and empowerment. The fire-breathing, shape shifting, luminous, interactive sculptures that the organization envisions, fabricates, and installs can only be achieved through the hands-on effort of a committed group of stakeholders, where each person's individual contribution is integral to the success of the whole. This is a process that the organization refers to as *radical collaboration*, which not only demands coordinated collaboration in the making process, but also emphasizes the importance of establishing a relationship between the artwork and the audience members who interact with it to bring about a socially formed aesthetic experience.[3]

By nature, the Flux Foundation does not separate the creative process from the learning process. Both art and making become educational events—where the diversity of the group engaged in the work serves as the muscle to make things happen, but also as the knowledge bank that propels a creative idea—and an artistic vision—forward. Without the concerted efforts of each member of its community, the work of the Flux Foundation—and all of the learning that takes place along the way—may never come to be. Both the group, and the individuals who make up that group, are what make the work of the Flux Foundation possible.

The Participatory Synthesis

The radically participatory and distributed approach to creativity practiced by the Flux Foundation is akin to what Michael Hanchett Hanson has referred to as the *emergent participatory synthesis* of creativity theory.[4] Hanchett Hanson has wisely called this new approach to creativity a *synthesis* because it is based on the convergence of several elements. Most importantly, participatory creativity combines individual agency with sociocultural models of creativity, emphasizing the roles that people play in change. By suggesting that creativity is a process one may participate in in many different ways, a participatory reframing of creativity opens up engagement in invention and innovation to everyday practice, as opposed to the extraordinary feats of ideation favored by more eminence based models of creativity.[5]

As has been suggested by Hanchett Hanson's idea of the emergent participatory synthesis, a participatory approach to creativity incorporates the contributions of multiple actors exerting their individual agency in various ways, within a broader system driven by a sense of collective purpose. In this way, participatory creativity can be understood as a form of *collective agency*.

Originated by the psychologist Albert Bandura,[6] collective agency is a form of human agency that derives from social cognitive theory. Different from the more popular brand of *personal agency* that is widely discussed in the psychology literature, collective agency involves the coming together of many individuals to bring about an intended social effect. As Bandura has argued, people do not live their lives separate from others, but are instead socially situated. As a result, the pursuit of particular goals involves the interdependent action of various individuals. In order to exercise collective agency, "groups," as Bandura referred to them, have to act with synergistic purpose. "A group's attainments are the product not only of shared knowledge and skills of its different members," he has written, "but also of the interactive, coordinative, and synergistic dynamics of their transactions."[7]

But Bandura's theory of collective agency (which is also referred to as collective efficacy) is not merely a variant of group creativity; instead, collective agency acknowledges the personal agency of individuals within the efforts of the greater collective. As he has argued, social cognitive theory rejects the bifurcation of individual and group theories of efficacy that "pits psychological theories and sociostructural theories as rival concepts of human behavior"[8]; instead, "personal agency and social structure operate interdependently. Social structures are created by human activity, and sociostructural practices, in turn, impose constraints and provide resources and opportunities for personal development and functioning."[9]

Much in the same way that Hanchett Hanson has framed the emergent participatory synthesis as embracing both individual development and sociocultural theories of creativity, so too does Bandura's notion of collective agency incorporate individual action within collective efforts. Though I have made a strong case against the hero worship and individualism associated with many traditional theories of creativity, I too believe that a participatory reframing of creativity must not abandon individual agency. Quite the contrary—reframing creativity as a participatory and distributed process would not be possible without individual action.

Establishing a Framework for Participatory Creativity

If one is to merge individual agency with collective participation, it makes sense to investigate creativity from multiple angles. To do this, the sections below consider the *what*, *where*, and *when*, as well as the *who* and the *how*, of creativity. By doing so, socially emergent invention and innovation reveals itself to be an evolutionary, distributed, and participatory process rooted in ideas that are expressed through artifacts developed by stakeholder groups through purposeful work.

The What, Where, and When of Creativity: Ideas and their Artifacts

While group, collaborative, and distributed orientations towards creativity stretch beyond the idea of solitary geniuses, when considering these socially emergent understandings of creativity, it is frequently unclear as to who or what is creative instead. Some theories suggest co-created *products* are what is creative, others suggest that group *processes* are what is creative, and still others suggest that the collaborative *groups* themselves—composed of many *people*—are what is creative. In developing a framework for participatory creativity for education, it is helpful to look for *what* is creative by first asking *where* creativity takes place. To do this, it is useful to return to Csikszentmihalyi's sociocultural model of creativity, which flipped the question, 'What is creativity?' on its head by asking 'Where is creativity?'

Within Csikszentmihalyi's sociocultural model, *products* developed by individuals appear to be the unit of creative analysis. As Gardner wrote:

> According to Csikszentmihalyi, creativity occurs when—and only when— an individual or group *product* generated in a particular domain is recognized by the relevant field as innovative and, in turn, sooner or later, exerts a genuine, detectable influence on subsequent work in that domain.[10]

Here, Gardner clearly identified products as the primary unit of creative analysis that the gatekeepers of a field make judgments upon. And he was right to do so, for as Csikszentmihalyi has written himself, "Creativity is not the product of single individuals, but of social systems making judgments about individuals' *products*."[11] Even though the products themselves are not necessarily creative until the system casts judgment on them, there is still an emphasis on products. From an educational perspective, focusing on a product—presumably a final product—tells one very little about the learning that may have taken place during the development of that product. Instead, focusing on the arc of experience throughout the creative process—and the learning that accrues to young people along the way—is what brings value to a participatory reframing of creativity. Within this reframing, *ideas* are positioned as both the focal point of creative work, as well the primary unit of analysis. From this perspective, an idea is not an internal thought or thought process maintained by a single individual, but rather a social phenomenon that may be engaged with and re/articulated by any number of individuals via a multitude of modalities. In other words, ideas are social, not psychological.

This idea-centric orientation towards creativity further suggests that creative ideas exist in a dialectical relationship with the products that represent them. In this sense, an idea can be understood not as a final product, but as a throughline that is enacted through a series of iterations of a concept within a certain area of practice that is ever evolving, and that may be articulated in any manner of mediums. A succession of products makes creative ideas visible at each stage of their evolution. In other words, products serve as the artifacts of ideas throughout their development.

In order to fully understand creativity, one must look beyond the single creative product and rather consider the multiple forms a creative idea has taken throughout its evolution, as well as the steps, missteps, and interactions that took place along the way. As Hanchett Hanson has noted, "we tend to forget the process that produced the artifacts and the chain of references that construct creative ideas."[12]

Focusing on the succession of products that contribute to the development of a creative idea further allows us to understand the creative process as a *learning* process. At its heart, Csikszentmihalyi's sociocultural theory is a learning model of creativity. Within this model individuals acting within a culture learn and replicate memes. When new memes are created, they are socially adjudicated. New memes that are deemed novel and useful are added to the culture, and therefore change the practice of the domain. In the process of adopting a new meme the culture—and all of its constituents—learn something new. In Csikszentmihalyi's definition, the application of the word "culture" is meant to describe a system of domains and their relationships to one another. But a "culture" can be as small as a classroom or even as intimate as a small working group within a classroom. Regardless of the breadth of culture, ideas may still be developed and socially assessed for their novelty and utility.

Returning once again to Weisberg's case of Watson and Crick, the *idea* of the double helix model of DNA was developed over an extended period of time, included successive models, and was informed by a variety of actors who participated in the development of what later came to be known as one of history's most significant contributions to our understanding of genetics. Each next model in this process in some way referenced the last. As the group of scientists developing the DNA models acquired new knowledge, skills, and understanding, their ideas—embodied in their models—became more sophisticated. And as their ideas/models became more sophisticated, the broader group of scientists in turn gained further knowledge, skills, and understandings from the products of their creative work—and from one another.

Within the educational sphere, there have been several attempts to make the learning associated with the creative idea development process visible. Whereas traditional portfolios have highlighted the end products of student work, early Project Zero research on *processfolios* emphasized the iterative nature of idea development by including the multitude of drafts students make in pursuit of developing and refining an idea.[13] Processfolios, therefore, tell the story of idea development over time. A more contemporary interpretation of the processfolio concept is the notion of an idea translation map, as developed by the Boston ArtScience Prize.[14] Like processfolios, idea translation maps tell the story of students' idea development throughout the design process, placing an even greater emphasis on the "translations" that take place from one iteration of an idea to the next. Both processfolios and idea translation maps illustrate the idea development process, while also making visible the learning that takes place along the way.

As stated above, participatory creativity suggests that ideas are both the *what* and the *where* of creativity. But the *when* of creativity still needs to be sorted out. It can be argued that the idea of the double helix model of DNA became creative when it was approved by the field. This is an important moment in the *when* of creativity, as per Csikszentmihalyi's sociocultural theory. But it also raises a point of contention from the perspective of teaching and learning.

Csikszentmihalyi's sociocultural approach has frequently received pushback from educators because, with its emphasis on longstanding domain changing contributions to culture, it suggests that children cannot be creative. Csikszentmihalyi has explicitly stated that "because creativity does not exist until it produces a change in the culture, it cannot be observed or measured in children."[15] In a creative learning environment, it is less important that an idea achieves field approval and changes a domain in some way, but more important that the young people participating in the development of an idea learn something as a result of their creative participation.[16] Throughout the idea development process, young people (and supportive adults) make judgments on their work, which inform their decisions to make new products that advance their ideas—leading to the development of a "change in the culture" within the creative classroom. Once again, each of these moments of reflection, assessment, and further iteration marks important moments in both the idea development and learning process. It is more helpful, then, to suggest that the *when* of creativity is not a single moment in the idea development process, but rather the longer arc of time associated with the evolution of an ever-changing creative idea.

In review, ideas are what comprise both the *what* and the *where* of creativity and a succession of artifacts give shape to the evolution of an idea over time. The *when* of creativity is neither a single flash of insight nor the moment a field ordains a single artifact of an idea worthy of the domain, but rather the arc of an idea's development over time.

The Who and the How of Creativity: Stakeholder Groups and Purposeful Work

In addition to addressing the *what, where,* and *when* of creativity, a participatory reframing of invention and innovation must also consider the *who* and the *how* of the creative process. One way to identify the who and the how of participatory creativity is to replace the *individual* in Csikszentmihalyi's model with a *contributing stakeholder group.* A contributing stakeholder group can be understood as the broad set of actors that have a vested interest in developing a creative outcome. A contributing stakeholder group plays a similar role as Csikszentmihalyi's individual; the primary difference is that a contributing stakeholder group acknowledges the distributed nature of creativity in the more dispersed manner that Glăveanu, Sawyer, and others have suggested.

Making the shift from individuals in Csikszentmihalyi's model, to a contributing stakeholder group begs the question, "What is a group?" This is a dilemma that French philosopher, anthropologist, and sociologist Bruno Latour has wrestled with through his presentation of Actor-Network Theory.[17] Latour's Actor-Network Theory suggests that "action is distributed amongst agents,"[18] and while phenomena may arise as a result of the work of groups, if we trace the associations between actors in groups, what is a group becomes difficult to define. According to Latour, there are no groups, only group formation.[19] In other words, the boundary of a group is always expanding and contracting to include more or less players as the work of the group moves forward.

Consider a standard rock band (rhythm and lead guitar, bass guitar, drums, and vocals). When a drummer leaves the band, and a new drummer joins is one way to think of a group as a dynamic entity that changes membership over time, but Latour's ideas on group formation are more complex than that. Sometimes the band is in the recording studio—and then the sound technicians, mixers, and studio personnel become a part of the group. Sometimes the group is on tour, and then a host of others are part of the group. Of course, sometimes the members of the band are at home with their families and friends—are those individuals also part of the group?

In addition to the people mentioned above, the band also uses instruments to make their music, technology to record their music, and the Internet to market their music and connect with their fans. Could it be that these non-human actors are part of the group, too?

Imagine that in addition to the standard instruments the band uses, one day someone gives the band a Moog synthesizer or a sitar. As the band begins to play with these new instruments, their ideas about music begin to change—and their sound as a band begins to change. Even though these instruments are inanimate "actors," they become part of the group as well. What's more, the band works within a culturally situated tradition of music that has an influence on the band's work—as does the popular culture, popular media, and literature of the day. All of these inanimate actors have an effect on the work of the band. We only have to look so far as the Beatles for an example. When Beatles' guitarist George Harrison traveled to India to study sitar with Ravi Shankar, not only did the Beatles' sound change, but the idea of raga rock—popular Western music incorporating traditional Indian instruments and tonal aesthetics—began to emerge.

Some argue that groups need to be bounded systems, and that their membership needs to be clearly defined and consistent. But what the group is at any given point in time depends upon what associations one makes with the group at that time. As suggested above, as the work of the group changes, so too does the very nature of the group: *there is no group, only group formation.* Of course if there is no group, then one cannot say it is the group that is creative. The what and the where of creativity are rooted in socially situated ideas. The actors within a contributing stakeholder group at any given time *participate* in the development of those ideas. A contributing stakeholder group is therefore dynamic because who or what *contributes* to creativity changes as the work of the group takes different tacks.

From this perspective, it is important to note that a participatory reframing of creativity does not suggest a shift towards "group work" in the traditional classroom sense. Indeed, many times young people will work together in physical groups to pursue the development of creative ideas, but due to the expansive and always changing nature of "groups," it is also possible that young people can work on their own, at a distance, and still be participating in more broadly distributed contributing stakeholder groups.

To recap, the *who* of participatory creativity are the various individuals that make up an ever-changing *contributing stakeholder group*. A contributing stakeholder group is organized by a sense of common purpose and collectively engaged in dedicated work that takes place over time. In keeping with Gruber's vision of an evolving systems approach,[20] the *how* of participatory creativity can be simply understood as *purposeful work over time*. As with any effective learning experience, the work of creativity is meaningful and relevant to the individuals who comprise an idea's contributing stakeholder group, while also being potentially meaningful and relevant to the broader community outside of the creative classroom. The individuals who help shape a creative idea see value in that idea, and therefore pursue its development with great intention.[21] This pursuit is not only purposeful, it is work and therefore requires time and effort. As the phrase "purposeful work" suggests, the development of a particular creative idea must be perceived by the individuals shaping that idea as work worth doing. But this emphasis on purposeful work may raise concerns about degrees of participation.

When one considers that group membership evolves based on time and context, then surely some members of the group may be more purposeful than others. A contributing stakeholder group is therefore composed of two different types of group members: primary and secondary contributing stakeholders. As Figure 2.1 suggests,[22] revolving around any one creative idea there is a relatively stable *primary contributing stakeholder group* whose members are in close proximity to the idea development process, and therefore form and shape an idea in a direct and purposeful way. Ideas are also shaped by a more distant *secondary stakeholder group* whose membership is less stable and consistent, and whose contributions to the development of the idea may be direct, or indirect. In other words, sometimes members of the secondary contributing stakeholder group influence the development of an idea in an immediate way, and sometimes members of the secondary contributing stakeholder group influence an idea by association—for example, by influencing members of the primary contributing stakeholder group.

When we think of group or collaborative orientations towards creativity, we often think in terms of a primary contributing stakeholder group, whose membership is relatively easy to understand and define. However, limiting a socially distributed view of creativity to such a confined group fails to consider the broader system within which that group acts. A participatory and distributed approach to understanding creativity demands a more expansive view of group membership and participation. Whether a primary or secondary group member, all participants in a contributing stakeholder group have agency.

While members of the secondary contributing stakeholder group may come and go, the way that various actors in the primary contributing stakeholder group enact their agency and participate in creativity can be further discussed by addressing both the roles young people play when they work together to develop creative ideas, as well as the profiles of participation they develop along the way.

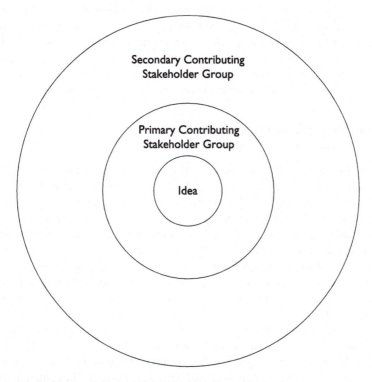

Figure 2.1 Defining a Contributing Stakeholder Group.

Note: A contributing stakeholder group is composed of primary and secondary stakeholder group members. Though all membership in groups fluctuates over time and in response to context, a primary contributing stakeholder group based on relatively consistent membership is responsible for directly shaping a particular idea over time in a purposeful way. A secondary stakeholder group, based on less consistent membership, may also directly shape the development of an idea in a purposeful way, or indirectly shape the development of an idea (e.g., by influencing members of the primary contributing stakeholder group) in a less purposeful way.

Developing Roles and Dynamic Profiles of Participation

As Hanchett Hanson has argued, within the emergent participatory synthesis identifying the roles that people play through the process of creative idea development may be the link between individual development and the sociocultural models of creativity presented by Csikszentmihalyi and others:

> Introducing roles into the analysis preserves the value of individual initiative and the particularity of individual interpretation of the roles. At the same time, it makes that value context dependent and emphasizes the development and expression of individual initiative through culturally meaningful interactions with other actors.[23]

When considering a participatory reframing of creativity, there are many ways to discuss the various roles individuals play when they enact their agency through their contribution to the development of creative ideas. As will be discussed below, when considering the various roles one may play throughout the creative idea development process, it is important to keep in mind the dynamic nature of cultural participation.

Field Roles, Collaborative Roles, and the Role of the Material World

In his discussion of the emergent participatory synthesis, Hanchett Hanson has noted that there are a variety of roles suggested by systems-based theories of creativity. These include field roles, collaborative roles, and material roles. Field roles entail those who offer social judgment on creative products, as per Csikszentmihayli's sociocultural theory, but they also include those who act as audience members, as per Glăveanu's theory of creativity as distributed action. Lone Hersted has even suggested that there may be *imaginary audiences* that influence the development of creative ideas. In other words, during the process of making, a particular artist may imagine how a given audience might respond to her creative work as she is in the process of developing that work. Hersted has described these imaginary, perhaps fictitious players as *inner social audiences*, "that can both motivate and inhibit creativity."[24]

Collaborative roles suggest the broad range of actors who are engaged in the construction of products that embody creative ideas. These include producers who, as Glăveanu has noted, play a central role in the development of creative products. In describing his theory of Collaborative Innovation Networks (COINs), Peter Gloor has identified three key producer roles: *visionaries* who develop big ideas, *collaborators* who form networks to bring big ideas to life, and *communicators* with a strong business sense, who bring the products associated with big ideas (and the big ideas themselves) to the world.[25] Within Gloor's three categories of collaborative innovation, any number of other, more specific roles may be identified as well—and group membership changes over time and in relationship to the task at hand.

While there are a broad range of collaborative roles that one may play in real time, it is also important to recall Sawyer's suggestion that, even when an individual appears to be working in isolation, he or she is always drawing upon his or her past collaborations. Hersted has expanded upon this point through her research on the creative processes of artists. "The ideas that emerge when we are alone can be traced back to previous relationships, traditions, other arts works and collaborations,"[26] she wrote. Citing the connections Vygotsky made between interpsychological and intrapsychological development of higher order mental functions,[27] Hersted has added "that all private thought is a derivative of social experience, or in other words: people learn to think about the world through interactions with others."[28] Referencing Karl Tomm and his colleagues,[29] Hersted has referred to these internal collaborators as *internalized others.* She has further argued that the individuals who participate in creativity today, are simultaneously in dialogue with longstanding traditions—a point that Sawyer and Glăveanu have made as well. In this sense, entire domains—with all of their historical knowledge, practices, traditions, and past actors—participate as collaborators in the creative enterprise.

The final variety of role that Hanchett Hanson presents is the role of the material world. This refers to the notion that even inanimate objects—tools, technologies, materials, and environments—may participate in the development of creative ideas. In some instances, these inanimate objects and environments are used instrumentally but, in other instances, a particular tool, technology, material, or environment may play a greater role in informing the development of a particular idea. This is a concept that Hutchins, Glăveanu, and Latour have all emphasized through their work. Glăveanu has even suggested that, by engaging with a particular tool, one is in conversation with the long history of individuals who have participated in the development of that tool. When working on a canvas, the painter in her studio is in dialogue with all of the individuals who have participated in the development of the tools and materials of her trade (e.g., brushes, paints, mediums, pallet knives, etc.). In the same way, the gamer in his basement is in dialogue with all of the programmers who have designed the massively multi-player online role playing games (MMORPGs) he participates in—not to mention the developers of all of the hardware he uses to access and engage with these online worlds.

When considering the role played by the material world in the process of invention and innovation, an interesting question to ask is: "To what degree do objects and environments have agency in the development of creative ideas?" When addressing this question, one must keep in mind that the degree to which objects and environments have influence over the development of a creative idea is always mediated by human agency—the way individuals employ and/or negotiate objects and environments throughout the creative process.

Considering the field roles, collaborative roles, and material roles involved in the development of creative ideas sheds light on both the distributed and the participatory nature of invention and innovation. However, it is important to note that the nature of these roles are not as fixed as, say, Csikszentmihalyi's sociocultural model suggests. Especially where field roles and collaborative roles are concerned, one may bounce back and forth between these two different roles. Kurt Luther and Nicholas Diakopoulos have used examples from online video remixing to emphasize how "people take on roles which correspond to different facets of the creative process at different times as they see fit."[30] In other words, at one instant in the online video remixing process an individual may be taking on a collaborative, or producer role, but in the next minute, that same individual may be taking on a field role, assessing value and making judgments on the work of others. As will be discussed further below, a participatory approach to creative idea development embraces the notion that roles are dynamic and flexible, rather than rigid and fixed.

Beyond Roles: Establishing Profiles of Participation

A participatory reframing of creativity allows space for young people to contribute to the development of creative ideas in ways that best suit their talents, skills, background experiences, and cultural perspectives. As a result, there is no one way to be creative, but rather multiple ways to participate in creativity. But here it is necessary to underscore an important point: *young people play various roles when they participate in creativity, but those roles are neither fixed nor unidimensional.* In other words, when young people participate in creativity they do not merely play narrowly defined parts; instead, they develop dynamic, unique, and multi-faceted *profiles of participation.* To better understand what is meant by a profile of participation, it is helpful to briefly visit an earlier pluralistic approach to understanding cognition and human engagement: Howard Gardner's theory of multiple intelligences.[31]

In 1983 developmental psychologist Howard Gardner released the ground-breaking text *Frames of Mind: The Theory of Multiple Intelligences.*[32] Here, the young psychologist argued against traditional schools of psychology that suggested that intelligence was a singular entity, known as g (for general intelligence), that could be assessed through psychometric tests that produced intelligence quotients. One's intelligence quotient—or IQ score—was there-fore thought to represent one's general intelligence. But Gardner had a much different understanding of intelligence. Through his research with children who expressed talents in the arts and adults who had experienced strokes—and as a result, exhibited isolated cognitive impairments—Gardner found that the participants in his studies exhibited unique profiles of ability and disability.[33] Building on further research, Gardner translated these patterns of ability and disability into what he first identified as eight, and then extended to nine, different *intelligences.* Gardner's original suite of intel-ligences included the following: *linguistic, logical-mathematical, musical, spatial, bodily-kinesthetic, interpersonal, intrapersonal, naturalistic,* and *existential* intelligence.

Though, as Gardner has noted himself, many psychologists before him had been building towards a more pluralistic approach to understanding intelligence,[34] Gardner's theory of multiple intelligences (also known as *MI theory*) was a radical departure from the popular—and relatively narrow—understandings of g in the early 1980s. Despite the disagreement many psychologists expressed for Gardner's pluralistic approach to understanding the intelligences, upon learning about MI theory, educators, who had long known that young people were smart in many different ways, sighed a breath of relief. As Gardner has noted:

> If some psychologists expressed skepticism about the theory of multiple intelligences, educators around the world have embraced it. MI theory not only comports with their intuitions that children are smart in different

ways; it also holds out hope that more students can be reached more effectively if their favored ways of knowing are taken into account in curriculum, instruction and assessment.[35]

Here, Gardner justified how his pluralistic approach to intelligence opens doors to a new world of intellectual possibilities for a wide range of young people. In essence, Gardner's theory of multiple intelligences makes access to intellectual achievement a possibility for an extended breadth of young people, if not, presumably, all young people. Similarly, the goal of presenting a distributed and participatory approach to invention and innovation is to introduce greater access and intellectual equity to the creative classroom.

Just as Gardner argued that there is no one type of intelligence, but rather multiple intelligences, so too does a distributed and participatory reframing of creativity suggest that there is no one way to be creative, but rather multiple ways to participate in creativity. In much the same way that Gardner suggested that curriculum, instruction, and assessment should be designed to capitalize on the many ways that young people are intelligent, so too does a distributed and participatory approach to creativity suggest that curriculum, instruction, and assessment should be designed to be more accessible to young people who certainly possess different types of intelligences, but also enter the creative classroom equipped with different skills and abilities, driven by different interests, formed by different cultural perspectives, embracing different background experiences, and overall—possessing different worldviews. From a social, cognitive, cultural, and individualized perspective, an argument for a participatory approach to creativity is therefore an argument for greater access to and equity within the creative classroom.

The Schism of Cognitive and Creative Pluralism

While there are many parallels between Gardner's theory of multiple intelligences and a distributed and participatory theory of creativity, my goal in making this connection is to address a major pitfall that both MI theory and a participatory approach to creativity are subject to. As Gardner and others have noted, there have been many ways in which educators have misinterpreted and misapplied his theory of multiple intelligences.[36]

In her essay "Expanding Our 'Frames' of Mind for Education and the Arts," Jennifer Groff outlined how Gardner's theory of multiple intelligences has been interpreted and applied in ways that belie the psychologist's original intentions. In particular, she highlights two primary "foible-ings" of MI theory. The first is a conflation of the intelligences with disciplines and domains, and the second, as she puts it, is "*Labeling kids and putting them in buckets.*"[37] While the first of Groff's concerns about the misinterpretation and misapplication of MI theory is certainly valid, it is the second of her concerns that applies to associating roles to young people, based on their participation in the development of creative ideas. As Groff has written:

Not long after MI theory began gaining traction in schools, a commonly heard phrase was "Johnny is a visual learner" or "Sarah is a very active and bodily-kinesthetic learner." The intelligences were conflated with learning styles, both of which were, and still are, confused and misapplied. Gardner . . . too, has acknowledged this frequent misuse. In reality, such a misapplication of MI theory has often led to putting kids into "buckets" and labeling them as being a certain way, which not only falsely categorizes young people but also prevents their full development and expression across the variety of their true intelligences.[38]

As has been noted above, Gardner himself has been very well aware of the pitfalls of his theory if misapplied in ways which suggest that each student falls into one of eight (or nine) intelligence buckets, as opposed to his true intention which suggests that individual students are intelligent in unique and varied ways. All students have access to all of the intelligences—and all students express their abilities (and disabilities) in each of these intelligences in unique ways. As Gardner has argued:

> The theory of multiple intelligences . . . makes two strong claims. The first is that all humans possess all these intelligences: Indeed they can collectively be considered a definition of *Homo sapiens*, cognitively speaking. The second claim is that just as we all look different and have unique personalities and temperaments, we also have different profiles of intelligences. No two individuals, not even identical twins or clones, have exactly the same amalgam of profiles, with the same strengths and weaknesses.[39]

Gardner has argued that individuals do not possess a single type of intelligence, but instead possess all of the intelligences, and that it is the unique combination of an individual's strengths in certain of those intelligences that comprise one's profile of intelligences. A participatory approach to creative idea development does not suggest the same suite of capacities from which to mix and match, but the notion that individuals do not participate in creativity in just one way, but rather in many ways, yields what can be understood as one's *profile of participation*.

It is my hope that a distributed and participatory understanding of creativity may indeed be of interest to educators—who have long known that there are many ways in which young people participate in creativity. At the same time, I urge educators to remember not to pigeonhole young people by labeling them as participating in creativity in one way, without recognizing the many other ways they may participate in creativity as well. While it is important to understand the roles young people play when they participate in creativity, it is also important to understand that just as young people possess different profiles of intelligence, so too do they possess different profiles of participation in the creative classroom. By doing so, educators may provide young people with the opportunity to engage in creativity in the many ways that maximize their full potential—while also challenging them, from time to time, to push beyond the comfort zones of their established talents, skills, background experiences, and cultural perspectives.

Participatory Creativity is All Around Us

Participatory creativity can be described as a process of invention and innovation centered around the development of ideas that are generated by a diverse network of actors each of whom contributes to the idea development process in unique and varied ways. In summary, zeroing in on the *what, where, when, who,* and *how* of creativity brings to the surface six core principles:

1. Individuals are not creative, ideas are creative;
2. Ideas function as conceptual throughlines that are embodied in a succession of artifacts that evolve over time;
3. Creative idea development is distributed amongst a diverse and dynamic set of actors known as a contributing stakeholder group;
4. The development of creative ideas is purposeful work;
5. There is no one way to be creative, but rather multiple ways for a variety of individuals to participate in the development of creative ideas, and;
6. Individuals play various roles when they participate in creativity, but those roles are neither fixed nor unidimensional.

Beyond the radically collaborative sculptures of the Flux Foundation, the tradition of Romanian Easter egg decoration, and the discovery of the double helix model of DNA, examples of distributed and participatory approaches to creativity are all around us. Creativity researchers have looked to the technological structures that shape our contemporary culture—such as information systems, online platforms, and social media—as examples of socially distributed creativity.[40] Like Glăveanu, Sawyer, and Cskiszentmihalyi, these researchers have argued that "the transition from an individualistic into a systemic, contextual or sociocultural view of creativity" is in order,[41] and that "social creativity involves the emergence of meaning involving synergistic interaction among creative individuals—not just the sum of individual contributions."[42] Reijo Miettinen has made the case that users who contribute code to open-source software initiatives help the producers who originate such software innovate or co-evolve their ideas to build better products. Similarly, in an investigation of YouTube videos produced by young people, Paul Duncum has asserted that "videos are conceived as creative conversations, their productions being the consequence of social networks and self-organizing systems rather than individual psychology."[43] Utilizing hashtags on social media platforms as virtual social organizers, Alexis Ditkowsky has argued that *crowdsourced creativity* occurs when "participants are encouraged to channel an idea into something else (e.g., photos, videos, writings, performances, code) and then share it in a way that can be aggregated, reformatted, and reshared as a multi-faceted body of work."[44] In Ditkowsky's brand of crowdsourced creativity, hashtags function as vehicles of creative action and creativity exists in the aggregate of individual contributions—which are always emerging. Taking a similar experiential approach to creativity, Peter Gloor has invoked the concept of *swarm creativity* to describe flash mobs, online cyber composition collaborations, opensource software development, and even the collaboratively edited online encyclopedia Wikipedia as embodiments of his concept of *collaborative innovation networks* (COINs), which rely on the participation of multiple individuals driven by a common purpose and organized around a core idea.[45]

Participatory creativity is perhaps most prevalent in the physical and online spaces where young people participate in the development of socially emergent ideas. These environments include:

- *Makerspaces, hackerspaces, and fablabs*, where an opensource ethos and a culture of information sourcing and sharing knowledge and expertise drive invention, innovation, and learning;
- *Open world video games*, such as Minecraft, where young people use digital tools to construct new worlds, engage in online forums, and build on the knowledge and expertise of others;
- *Massively multiplayer online roleplaying games (MMORGs)*, such as World of Warcraft, where young people develop new narratives, characters, and plotlines with others;
- *Web-based visual programming platforms*, such as Scratch, where young people have the opportunity to design games, videos, and other digital content, upload their work to a community of users, and remix the work of their peers, and;
- *Social media platforms*, such as Instagram, Snapchat, and Twitter, where young people have the opportunity to share media, establish and remix memes, and use hashtags to aggregate information.

Whether in the face-to-face or digital world, contemporary creativity necessitates access and engagement with others. Even within the realm of the traditional arts disciplines (e.g., visual art, music, theater, dance, creative writing, etc.), the creative experiences of young people are socially distributed. As Mimi Ito and her colleagues at the Digital Media and Learning Research Hub have argued, adopting a connected learning approach to supporting young people relies on the collective capacities of a community of people—and yields collective outcomes.[46]

Despite the ubiquity of participatory creativity in contemporary culture, many teachers, administrators, and policy makers within the educational sphere still cling to individual-based understandings of creativity. In a world where invention and innovation are increasingly socially distributed endeavors, maintaining such traditional orientations towards creativity within schools has the potential to massively limit access to creative learning experiences for the majority of young people. As Chapters 3 and 4 discuss, adopting a more participatory stance towards invention and innovation is an imperative for the creative classroom.

Notes

1. To learn more about Brollyflock, see: www.fluxfoundation.org/brollyflock/
2. To learn more about Zoa, see www.fluxfoundation.org/zoa/
3. To learn more about the Flux Foundation's approach to radical collaboration see http://library.fora.tv/2012/05/20/Flux_Foundation_The_Radical_Art_of_Collaboration; see also the Stanford d. school's approach to radical collaboration http://dschool.stanford.edu/our-point-of-view/, and James W. Tamm & Ronald J. Luyet, *Radical Collaboration: Five Essential Skills to Overcome Defensiveness and Build Successful Relationships* (New York: Harper Collins, 2005).
4. See Michael Hanchett Hanson, *Worldmaking: Psychology and the Ideology of Creativity* (New York: Palgrave Macmillan, 2015).
5. Here, it is helpful to look back at Weisberg's efforts to refute great man theories of invention and innovation (see Chapter 1) by suggesting that creativity was based on everyday cognitive capacities.
6. See Albert Bandura, "Exercise of human agency through collective efficacy," *Current Directions in Psychological Science*, 9, no. 3 (2000): 75–78.
7. Ibid., pp. 75–76.
8. Ibid., p. 77.
9. Ibid., p. 77.
10. See Gardner, *Five Minds for the Future*, (Boston, MA: Harvard Business School Press, 2006), p. 81, emphasis added.
11. See Csikszentmihalyi, "Implications of a Systems Perspective," p. 316.
12. Personal communication with Michael Hanchett Hanson, January 22, 2014.
13. See Howard Gardner, "The Assessment of Student Learning in the Arts," in *Evaluating and Assessing the Visual Arts in Education: International Perspectives*, pp. 131–155, eds. Doug Boughton, Elliot W. Eisner, & Johan Ligtvoet (New York: Teachers College Press, 1996). See also www.pz.harvard.edu/projects/arts-propel
14. See www.artscienceprize.org/asp/
15. See Mihaly Csikszentmihalyi and colleagues, "Key Issues in Creativity and Development," in *Creativity and Development*, ed. R. Keith. Sawyer (New York: Oxford University Press, 2003), p. 220.
16. As Hanchett Hanson has argued, "even though Csikszentmihalyi's cultural systems theory is not supposed to apply to children, the kinds of dynamics for integrating new ideas that he has analyzed occur in classrooms" (personal communication, January 22, 2014). Hanchett Hanson has gone on to make the case that the underlying principles of Csikszentmihalyi's sociocultural model—understanding how one participates in culture, how domains are socially mediated by gatekeepers, how new ideas are socially adopted and spread throughout culture—are in themselves important learning objectives and examples of good education.
17. See Bruno Latour, *Reassembling the Social: An Introduction to Actor-Network Theory* (New York: Oxford University Press, 2005).
18. Ibid., p. 50
19. Ibid.
20. See Gruber, "Creativity and Human Survival."

21. See Mara Krechevsky, Ben Mardell, Melissa Rivard, & Daniel Wilson, *Visible Learners: Promoting Reggio-Inspired Approaches in All Schools* (San Francisco, CA: Jossey-Bass, 2013).

22. This concentric circles model of a contributing stakeholder group is based on the "Groups of Decision Makers" model for quality in arts education originally developed by the Qualities of Quality research team at Project Zero. See Steve Seidel, Shari Tishman, Ellen Winner, Lois Hetland, & Patricia Palmer, *The Qualities of Quality: Understanding Excellence in Arts Education* (Cambridge, MA: Project Zero, 2009).

23. See Hanchett Hanson, *Worldmaking*, p. 184.

24. See Lone Hersted, "Creativity in a Relational Perspective," in *Behind the Scenes of Artistic Creativity*, pp. 229–245, eds. Tatiana Chemi, Julie. B. Jensen, & Lone Hersted (Frankfurt am Main, Germany: Peter Lang, 2015), p. 238.

25. See Intelligent Collaborative Knowledge Network http://www.ickn.org/collaboration.html

26. See Hersted, "Creativity in a Relational Perspective," p. 237.

27. See Lev Vygotsky, *The Psychology of Art* (Cambridge, MA: MIT Press, 1971).

28. See Hersted, "Creativity in a Relational Perspective," p. 237.

29. See Karl Tomm, Michael F. Hoyt, & Stephen B. Madigan, "Honoring Our Internalized Others and the Ethics of Caring: A Conversation with Karl Tomm," in *Handbook of Constructive Therapies: Innovative Approaches from Leading Practitioners*, ed. M. F. Hoyt (San Francisco, CA: Jossey-Bass, 1998).

30. See Kurt Luther & Nicholas Diakopoulos, "Distributed Creativity" (paper presented at Creativity & Cognition: Supporting Creative Acts Beyond Dissemination, Washington, D.C., June 13, 2007), p. 3.

31. Though Howard Gardner (and others) has written many books on his theory of multiple intelligences, *Frames of Mind: The Theory of Multiple Intelligences* (New York, Basic Books, 1983) is widely known as the seminal text in which Gardner first revealed his pluralistic theory of the intelligences. In addition to *Frames of Mind*, here I also reference a more concise and more recent work by the psychologist: Howard Gardner, "A Multiplicity of Intelligences," *Scientific American Presents, Exploring Intelligence*, 9, no. 4 (1993): 19–23. Readers may also find interesting Howard Gardner, *Multiple Intelligences: The Theory in Practice*, (New York: Basic Books, 1993).

32. See Gardner, *Frames of Mind*.

33. See Gardner, "A Multiplicity of Intelligences."

34. Ibid.

35. Ibid., p. 21.

36. See Gardner, *Multiple Intelligences: The Theory in Practice*; Howard Gardner, *Intelligence Reframed* (New York: Basic Books, 1993), and Howard Gardner, "The Happy Meeting of Multiple Intelligences and the Arts," *Harvard Education Letter*, 15, no. 6 (1999): 1–6. See also Jennifer Groff, "Expanding Our 'Frames' of Mind for Education and the Arts," *Harvard Educational Review*, 83, no. 1 (2013): 15–39.

37. See Groff, "Expanding Our 'Frames' of Mind," p. 18 (emphasis in original).

38. Ibid., p. 18.

39. See Gardner, "A Multiplicity of Intelligences," p. 21.

40. See Cecilia R. Aragon & Alison Williams, "Collaborative Creativity: A Complex Systems Model with Distributed Affect" (paper presented at CHI 2011, Vancouver, BC, May 7–11, 2011); Alexis Ditkowsky, (Unpublished student paper, Harvard Graduate School of Education, Cambridge, MA, 2013); Paul Duncum, "Creativity as Conversation in the Interactive Audience Culture of YouTube" *Visual Inquiry*, 2, no. 2 (2013): 115–125; Kurt Luther & Nicholas Diakopoulos, "Distributed Creativity"; Reijo Miettinen, "The

Sources of Novelty: A Cultural and Systemic View of Distributed Creativity" *Creativity and Innovation Management,* 15, no. 2 (2006): 173–181.

41. See Miettinen, "The Sources of Novelty," p. 174.
42. See Luther & Diakopoulos, "Distributed Creativity," p. 2.
43. See Duncum, "Creativity as Conversation," p. 115.
44. See Ditkowsky, p. 1.
45. See Peter A. Gloor, *Swarm Creativity: Competitive Advantage through Collaborative Innovation Networks* (New York: Oxford University Press, 2006).
46. See Mizuko Ito and colleagues, *Connected Learning: An Agenda for Research and Design,* (Irvine, CA: Digital Media and Learning Research Hub, 2013). Retrieved from http://dmlhub.net/wp-content/uploads/files/Connected_Learning_report.pdf

Chapter 3

A Culture of Individualism and the Five Crises of Creativity in Education

On Thursday, October 22, 2015, New York Mets relief pitcher Jeurys Familia struck out Dexter Fowler, the center fielder of the Chicago Cubs, sweeping the Cubs four games to none in a seven game series and earning the Mets the title of National League champions for the fifth time in the team's history. As exciting as this moment may have been, earlier during the game an even more historic event took place. During the eighth inning, Mets second baseman Daniel Murphy hit a two-run homerun off of Cubs relief pitcher Fernando Rodney—making him the only player in the history of Major League Baseball to hit a homerun in six consecutive post-season games. Sure enough, as soon as the final strike was called, Murphy was named the National League Championship Series Most Valuable Player—and the Mets were soon on their way to face the Kansas City Royals in the 2015 World Series.

This shouldn't surprise anyone. Here in the United States—and in many other countries throughout the East and West—naming MVPs and celebrating feats of high achievement is what we do. We love our heroes, our valedictorians, our Oscar winning actors, and our Olympic medalists. Even when a sports team collectively wins a national title, the first thing we do is to seek out the hero amongst heroes, and award that person the title of MVP.

Whether in baseball, the arts, or the sciences, feats of greatness, like Murphy's post-season performance, inspire us, they fill us with awe, and urge us to celebrate the outer reaches of human achievement. But when we take a closer look at these moments of greatness, we come to understand that no feat of excellence, and certainly no act of creativity, takes place in isolation. Greatness—and creativity—are always socially and culturally situated. Indeed, Murphy's contributions to the Mets' 2015 victory were significant, but few people—if any—would argue that Murphy won the team's National League pennant all by himself. To begin, one would first consider the rest of the Mets' team roster: all of the various players who worked hard, not just in the post-season, but throughout the year to lead up to the team's National League Championship victory. Less visible to the average fan, one may also point to all of the coaches and trainers who supported the team throughout the year—and over the years. Of course, a variety of other individuals also supported the team in ways that are even less visible—groundskeepers, equipment suppliers, nutritionists, physical therapists, agents, and security guards. This is all not to mention the affective support that many of the players (and all of the above mentioned contributors) received—or had received—from their parents, spouses, siblings, children, friends, and communities.

The truth of the matter is that there were many unseen individuals who contributed to the Mets' 2015 post-season victory. For this reason, when the Mets were crowned National League Champions, there was just as much cause to celebrate in the Mets' locker room as there was to celebrate in living rooms throughout the United States—and beyond. And why celebrate? Because thousands of people who were not on the field for the closing pitch of the 2015 National League Championship Series were not only connected to the Mets' victory, they had contributed to it, too.

In the Introduction to this book I referenced former presidential candidate Mitt Romney's push back on Barack Obama's 2012 "you didn't build that" campaign comments. Here, I stated that Obama took a system's view of achievement, whereas Romney took a more traditional individual-based approach to the conversation. And indeed, within that exchange, this appears to be the case. But beyond the 2012 Obama/Romney tit-for-tat, looking back on some of Romney's earlier comments concerning the distributed nature of human achievement is illuminating, especially within the context of feats of athletic excellence. During the opening ceremonies of the 2002 Winter Olympics—of which Mitt Romney was the Chief Executive Officer—Romney praised the Olympians in a manner that acknowledged the broader systems that support such feats of human achievement:

> You Olympians, however, know you didn't get here solely on your own power. . . . For most of you, loving parents, sisters or brothers, encouraged your hopes, coaches guided, communities built venues in order to organize competitions. All Olympians stand on the shoulders of those who lifted them. We've already cheered the Olympians, let's also cheer the parents, coaches, and communities.[1]

Within his remarks, Romney recognized that even in the Olympics, where (for many events) sole athletes are placed on tiered pedestals and awarded medals, feats of greatness are not attained by the sheer talent of individuals, but rather by the support of greater systems. In his 2002 opening ceremony speech, Romney recognized that, even when the individual figure skater takes to the ice, when the sole snowboarder drops into the half pipe, or when the lone luger propels herself down the track—these individual athletes are never really out there on their own. Make no mistake, they are *by themselves*, meaning there are no hidden other people out there joining them, but they are not alone, meaning their performance has been made possible by an extensive network of support—and those support structures are with them throughout their performances.

Throughout his case studies of seven "creators" of the Modern era, Howard Gardner was keen to understand the relationship between such support structures and the pursuit of a creative enterprise. It is important to remember that, though Gardner applied a systems-based approach to understanding creativity, his unit of analysis was the creative individual, and his area of focus was largely (though not exclusively) on moments of creative breakthrough, and the events leading up to them. Prevalent as they were, the importance of support structures in the creative process was not something that Gardner was expecting to find: "as a psychologist interested in the individual creator, I was surprised by this discovery of the intensive social and affective forces that surround creative breakthroughs."[2] Gardner identified two key types of supports that scaffolded the creators he was studying: "the creator required both affective support from someone with whom he or she felt comfortable and cognitive support from someone who could understand the nature of the breakthrough."[3] Gardner's distinction between these two types of supports is helpful, but a less individual-based take on creativity may suggest that, in addition to affective and cognitive supports, a broad spectrum of other supports also contributes to creative achievement—developing a complex network of support. A further step away from an individual-based approach to creativity may suggest that such a complex network of support is not only present during the time of creative achievement, but throughout the longer arc of creative development. This extension of the idea of support structures as being networks contributing to the development of creativity over time further sets us up to suggest that individuals who contribute to such a network of support may not be considered "supports" at all—but rather actual participants in the process of creativity.

Taking a networked or systems-based approach to creative achievement does not suggest that each actor in this network participates in equal measure, nor in similar fashion, but rather suggests that there are multiple ways for various individuals to engage in creativity aside from the star role that our individualistic culture emphasizes. To draw an example from the story of Daniel Murphy's performance in the 2015 National League Championship Series—the people who designed and crafted Murphy's bats may not have been swinging them at the plate during those late October games, but from a systems perspective, they still participated—in their own way and at a considerable distance—in driving those balls out of the park. Sure, we may not think about innovative baseball bat designers and the skilled technicians who operate and maintain custom bat making lathes, sanders, and chisels when we think of major league MVPs, but those individuals, along with many others, are certainly part of the complex network of actors that helped make Daniel Murphy's home runs happen.

Achievement and Folly, Heroes and Scapegoats

Not only can a systems-based approach be applied towards our understandings of high achievement, it can also be applied towards our understandings of great folly. This is helpful to keep in mind as we address the idea that, just as much as an individualistic culture likes to celebrate heroes, so, too, does it like to point fingers at scapegoats. And, as Mets fans well know, Halloween can do tricky things to a pennant winning baseball team . . . and its MVP. In fact, it was on October 31, 2015 that the unfortunate Daniel Murphy—who was so recently lauded as a hero—was quickly deemed a scapegoat in the span of less than ten days.

After Murphy's remarkable performance in the first two rounds of the 2015 post-season, as soon as the Mets arrived to play game one of the World Series in Kansas City, the crack of Murphy's bat went quiet at the plate. Not only had Murphy delivered a flat offensive performance against the Kansas City Royals, during game four of the World Series on Halloween, a trick was about to transpire to tarnish Murphy's treats. While the Mets were trailing the Royals two games to one, but leading the Royals in the eighth inning and about to tie the series at two games apiece, a routine ground ball hit by Royals' first baseman Eric Hosmer snuck beneath Daniel Murphy's glove and rolled its way into right field. The Royals tied the game on the play—which should have ended the game and tied the series. The Royals then went on to score two additional runs in the inning, winning the game—and the next night—the World Series.

Sportscasters were quick to point fingers at Murphy for blowing it all. The man heralded as the MVP of the National League Championship Series was now the scapegoat for the Mets' failed attempt at the 2015 World Series title. The sports network ESPN even referred to Murphy's error as being the sixth costliest in World Series history.[4] "I just misplayed it," Murphy said, taking responsibility for the error, "It went under my glove and they made us pay for it."[5]

Though Murphy was hard on himself, and perhaps even blamed himself for the team's loss, teammates, such as team captain and third baseman David Wright, looked back on game four and stated that "This is not Daniel Murphy's fault. It's the New York Mets' fault, we lost the game."[6] Nonetheless, many distraught fans, armchair analysts, and professional sports reporters alike, continued to direct their moaning at Murphy.

And indeed, Wright was, well, right. The Mets' loss of the World Series, or even any one game in the series, was not any one player's fault, but a larger systems failure. Pointing to the eighth inning alone, Mets' pitcher Tyler Clippard walked two batters just before Murphy's fielding error, putting the tying and winning runs on base. And, as some have speculated, Mets' manager Terry Collins may have made a poor decision to put Clippard on the mound in the first place.[7] Of course, one cannot dismiss the roles that the Royals played—on the field, in the dugout, and elsewhere—to bring about the chain of events that led to their team's ultimate victory.[8]

But it is not only within the realm of sports that our culture of individualism drives us to point our fingers at scapegoats. Throughout our media-saturated world, there is a constant emphasis placed on "who done it?" Following the

November 13, 2015 terrorist attacks in Paris, France, that left 129 people dead and hundreds of others wounded, the media coverage of the unfolding investigation sought to identify the "ringleader" responsible for the coordination of the attacks. Even though the authorities had confirmed that there were eight assailants associated with these horrific events, our culture of individualism drove the media to develop a narrative that suggested that the French authorities were in the process of identifying the villain amongst villains, the "mastermind" responsible for the attacks on Paris. This man was soon identified as Abdelhamid Abaaoud—and later killed in a raid on an apartment building in the Parisian suburb of Saint-Denis.

Later that week the National Public Radio program *On the Media* discussed the nature of individualizing culprits of such attacks, and overascribing a sense of genius to such individuals. During a segment called the "Breaking News Consumer's Handbook: Terrorism Edition," host Brooke Gladstone dug into the issue: "In the days following an attack like this, there is an urgent need to find the culprit, not just the group behind it, but the actual individual," she said, "we seem to crave a specific human target for our anger and fear. But we don't want it to be just anybody . . . we want it to be a *mastermind*."[9]

To unpack this idea, Gladstone interviewed journalist Jack Shafer to discuss his recent article "The Myth of the Terrorist Mastermind: Why Do We Need to Keep Telling Ourselves that the Plotters are Special?"[10] Here, Shafer argued that there is nothing particularly genius about the plots that terrorists carry out, and that the coordination of such atrocities require little more intelligence than it takes to order a pizza. In Shafer's article, he suggested that hyperbolizing the genius involved in planning terrorist attacks may be due to a need to bottle up all of the evil of such an event into one individual, and then to distance that person from the rest of us. "What makes us so susceptible to the idea that the author of the Paris killings is a 'mastermind'? Why can't he be called something more mundane, like an organizer or a commander?" Shafer wrote, "I think we ascribe evil brilliance to terrorists because we can't accept that a normal working Joe of standard intelligence could kill so freely as this."[11]

The discussion between Gladstone and Shafer continued to compare the ways in which terrorists are portrayed as masterminds in the media to the ways in which villains are portrayed in popular culture—as cunning geniuses capable of elaborate plans. In many ways, the over-inflation of intelligence and ability associated with the terrorist mastermind narrative is related to the hyped-up hero narrative discussed above, with the obvious difference being that the moral compass is flipped. As Shafer noted, equating real world terrorists with made-for-TV villains not only exaggerates the capacities of these individuals, it also provides a false sense of comfort while overlooking the complexity that is involved, not within a particular terrorist plot, but within the broader system within which that plot had been enacted. "When we turn the bad guy into a mastermind," Shafer wrote, "we're offering ourselves an oddly false comfort—a way to make sense of a world that is neither as full of evil geniuses as the TV version would have us believe, nor as comforting."[12]

Indeed, real world terrorism is not like television. The killing of Abaaoud in the early morning hours of November 18, 2015 did not end an episode of any sort. No closing credits began to roll afterwards, and the French sense of *joie de vivre* did not return to the Parisian streets after the final commercial break. Instead, the terror persisted, and will persist for some time—because, mastermind or not, Abaaoud was only ever one actor within a broader system. And it is that system that persists.

The point to be made here is that our individualistic culture concerns itself less with how systems operate to bring about particular effects, and more with identifying standout individuals and highlighting their seemingly singular contributions made towards achieving those effects. While our attention may be drawn to individual acts of heroism or folly or terrorism, great achievements, failures, and atrocities are always socially distributed. Where the 2015 World Series is concerned, all the players noted above, and many others, participated in the events that transpired, each contributing in their own ways. Where the Paris terrorist attacks are concerned, Abdelhamid Abaaoud may have played a lead role in orchestrating these events, but the authorship ascribed to him not only overlooked the other actors involved, but also gave him far more credit than he deserved.

Moving Beyond the *Who* and the *How* of Individualism

Whether in the case of heroes or scapegoats, as soon as significant moments in culture take place, an individualistic orientation towards culture inclines us to seek out the *who* and the *how* of that event. In other words, a culture of individualism is inclined towards determining *who* did it, which is immediately followed by a cultural curiosity that drives us to figure out *how* they did it.

When asked the question, "How did the Mets come to be in the 2015 World Series?", from an individualistic perspective, one might respond, *Daniel Murphy hit homeruns in six consecutive post-season games, he's the MVP! They couldn't have done it without him.* Similarly, when asked, "How did the Mets lose the 2015 World Series?", from an individualistic perspective one might respond, *Daniel Murphy let a ground ball roll between his legs on a clutch play—he blew it for everyone.* But from a systems perspective, both of these outcomes require much more intricate explanations. Without a doubt, Daniel Murphy did the things that Daniel Murphy did, but the fate of the Mets, for better or for worse, did not rely on his actions alone.

Moving beyond the drama of post-season Major League Baseball, the *who* and the *how* of achievement resonates with our understandings of creativity just as much as it does with our understandings of sport. In both arenas, we seek out heroes and scapegoats and try to figure out *who* did what and *how* did they do it? We grant, what one may call, *author function* to individuals who are actually better understood as primary contributors within much broader systems. The term "author function" comes from Michel Foucault's popular

1969 lecture "What is an Author?"[13] Here, Foucault questioned the very relationship between the author, the reader, and the "work" and suggested that the idea of an author not only pertains to a particular text or work, but rather functions at the level of discourse.

> The author's name manifests the appearance of a certain discursive set and indicates the status of this discourse within a society and a culture. . . . The author function is therefore characteristic of the mode of existence, circulation, and functioning of certain discourses within a society.[14]

Foucault's concept of author function has many facets, and may be understood from multiple angles. One interpretation suggests that when the name of an author has significance that stretches beyond merely ascribing the origination of a work to a particular individual, then that author's name is functioning in a way that suggests a greater cultural meaning. To say that a comment, idea, or individual is "Marxist" is to say that Karl Marx's name has meaning within our culture beyond simply identifying Karl Marx as being the author of a particular work. Without a doubt, towards the end of his life in the late 1800s, Karl Marx authored *Das Kapital*, but Karl Marx cannot be said to have physically authored a "Marxist" text written today, during the second decade of the twenty-first century. Nonetheless, within a society that recognizes Marx's ideas as having a certain signature and cultural significance, Marx may frequently be granted author function for any number of texts, artifacts, or speech acts that will have been originated long after Karl Marx, the man himself, has been dead and buried. In other words, the concept of author function explains how certain individuals may be given credit for things they have not done.

In the spirit of Foucault, I use the term "author function" to indicate the sociocultural process of naming an individual as the sole actor responsible for a particular outcome or occurrence, whereas in actuality, that outcome or occurrence was the result of a greater social process. In many ways, ascribing Daniel Murphy as the MVP of the 2015 National League Championship Series—or as the scapegoat for the Mets' prompt loss of the 2015 World Series—is to assign him author function for these more socially distributed occurrences. The same can be said of Abdelhamid Abaaoud, and the author function he was granted for the November 2015 Parisian terrorist attacks.[15] It is more accurate to say that these individuals *participated* in these cultural occurrences, perhaps in significant ways, but neither Murphy nor Abaaoud "authored" these events all by themselves.

Returning to the *who* and the *how* of an individualistic culture's orientation towards high achievement, when author function is granted to a particular *who*, the next step is to understand *how* the *who* did it. The pursuit of *how* is complicated, however, when we understand that feats of high achievement are distributed amongst a complex network of actors. In the case of Daniel Murphy and the 2015 New York Mets, this may soon become all too apparent.

However, when author function is granted to an individual for feats of invention and innovation that are socially distributed, seeing the complex network of actors behind creative achievement may not be so easy. In these cases, a stubborn attachment to an individualistic perspective overlooks the multiple actors connected to events of cultural significance. With tunnel vision focused on a seemingly sole author, the blinders of our individualistic culture may prevent us from seeing anyone else around, and therefore drive us to explore the biography of the *who* we have identified as the author, in search of the *how* that may be hidden in his or her personal history. The who and the how of a traditional orientation towards creativity, is quite different from the who and the how of creativity discussed from a participatory perspective in Chapter 2. Here, the who is quite literally seen as an individual, and the how is commonly understood as that individual's solitary work.

The process of assigning individuals author function is, in itself, a function of individualistic culture. As we will see from the discussion below, this inclination to call out individuals for social occurrences not only plays itself out on the ball field, but also affects how we understand, nurture, and support invention and innovation in the creative classroom.

Who's On First—But More Importantly— How Did He/She Get There?

Understandably, the above section of this chapter, with its back and forths between the *whos* and the *hows* of individualistic culture, may have felt like an excerpt from the Abbott and Costello "Who's on first?" comedy sketch. But the point to be made is an important one. That is, that looking for the *how* of creativity within the *who*, not only inclines us to overlook the networks of actors that contribute to creativity, but also sets us up to develop false, individual-based explanations for how feats of high achievement come to be. More specifically, the personality traits, past experiences, work ethic, formal schooling, family histories, and even the neurological structures of individuals are mined for evidence that may shed light on how feats of creativity have come about. Once the contributing elements associated with creativity (the *hows*) are surfaced, an individualistic culture then endeavors to understand how these *hows* can be used to make more—and better—*whos*. It makes sense, then, that a culture of individualism that grants author function to individuals will then affect how educators and administrators narrowly, and perhaps misguidedly, structure learning experiences to foster creativity.

Individualism, Achievement, and Assessment

It would not be surprising if some parents and educators reading this chapter may have winced at my consistent use of phrases such as "greatness," "high achievement," and "feats of excellence" throughout the sections above. These words and phrases make me wince as well, but I've been using them quite deliberately, along with their antonyms, such as "failure" and "folly." My intentional use of these words and phrases has been to illustrate how we view educational success and failure through the lens of individualism.

Here in the United States, and in many other countries, our culture of individualism is compounded within the educational sphere by high-stakes testing environments that likewise value individual achievement while stigmatizing, if not outright punishing, failure and folly. The result is that having an individual approach to understanding creativity is inherently tied to assessment.

Whether it's the weekly vocabulary quiz or the Scholastic Aptitude Test, young people in schools are consistently being evaluated on their individual performance on standardized tests. While some tests are standardized far more than others, very few tests are designed to assess understanding from the perspective of multiple learning profiles. Though the concept of differentiated instruction—developing learning environments that benefit students of various abilities—may be on the rise, developing differentiated assessments of student learning are far less common.[16]

The core of the problem here is that, within an environment that applies a one-size-fits-all approach to assessment, educators are forced to develop a narrow conception of what achievement looks like, and then to gauge young people's performance based on that narrow conception of understanding. The more narrow the assessment measure, the more students are squeezed to perform their understandings in narrowly focused (and undifferentiated) ways. Working within such environments, it may not be surprising that many educators maintain traditional orientations towards creativity that are likewise narrowly focused, and therefore individually based.

Though creativity advocates throughout the educational sphere have voiced their frustration with high-stakes tests that favor certain performances of understanding over others, it is ironic to note that many of these individuals have resorted to none other than creativity *tests* to gauge student achievement. The most popular of these tests is the Torrance Tests of Creative Thinking (TTCT),[17] which many contest measures divergent thinking, not creativity, and therefore lacks validity.[18] Whereas some creativity theorists have argued that tightly coupling creativity with divergent thinking overlooks the wider breadth of capacities associated with creativity, others have rejected the validity of such tests entirely, arguing that divergent thinking, though useful in some contexts, may not even be a necessary part of the creative process.[19] Of course, not all creativity tests are designed equally, and while some creativity tests, such as Teresa Amabile's Consensual Assessment of Creativity approach, look beyond divergent thinking and even take social factors into consideration,[20] many practitioners and researchers alike continue to approach creativity tests of all stripes with a sense of great skepticism.

Rather than parse out the differences between this or that approach to measuring creativity, here I find it more interesting—and more important—to ask the core question: "Why would one want to test creativity in the first place?"

Well-meaning educators and administrators may be quick to answer that they need to test creativity to support students throughout their creative development and, on a different level, to show student improvement and thereby make the case that work done in the creative classroom is a valid form of learning. Indeed, these are perfectly good reasons as to why one may establish tests of creativity, invention, and innovation. In fact, these justifications of creativity tests echo the rationales stated for tests of any number of subjects—as well as tests of intelligence and other forms of cognitive competence. On the surface, there appear to be two purposes behind such tests: first, to support student learning; and, second, to make the case that learning is indeed taking place in a particular educational context. But as many students, parents, teachers, and administrators well know, tests also have other, sometimes less obvious, purposes that may lead to more dire educational effects.

Within the creative classroom, I identify the negative effects of individual-based orientations towards creativity in education—as well as the tests that are associated with such a perspective—as *the five crises of creativity*. Discussed below, these five crises of creativity in education derive from my consistent problematizing of an individualistic approach towards creativity and its application within the creative classroom, but also from asking the question: "What are the consequences of an individual-based orientation towards creativity, and the tests used to measure it?"

The Five Crises of Creativity in Education

It is my opinion that traditional, individual-based understandings of creativity in education in general, and the psychometric tests that purport to measure individual student creativity specifically, are not only behind the times from practical and theoretical perspectives, but also detrimental to young people in five specific ways. In the following sections of this chapter I describe what I call the five crises of creativity in education.

- Crisis one: *The "some kids are more creative than others" misconception*
- Crisis two: *The "I'm just not a creative person" syndrome*
- Crisis three: *Narrowly defining creativity privileges some students and alienates others*
- Crisis four: *Denying young people the opportunity to create and invent with others*
- Crisis five: *Ill-equipping young people for success in contemporary life and work*

Not only do these crises in creativity present challenges for educators and administrators hoping to foster creativity and innovation through education but, as we will see in Chapter 4, they also present social and cultural barriers to access and equity in the creative classroom.

Crisis One: The "Some Kids Are More Creative than Others" Misconception

Asking the question "What's the point of testing?" has prompted psychologist Scott Barry Kaufman to argue that, aside from acting as interventions designed to support student learning, most tests—and perhaps especially creativity and intelligence tests—are used in schools to sort gifted students from ungifted students.[21] This is not a new phenomenon. Here in the United States, sorting the gifted from the ungifted has a long history, particularly where intelligence and creativity are concerned.

In Chapter 2 I noted that, during the second half of the twentieth century, creativity tests began to emerge in response to Guilford's 1950 American Psychological Association address. Regardless of the psychometric measures they used, the purpose behind many of these tests was to identify the creative potential of young people and to then channel students who scored highly on such tests into educational tracks that would further develop their creativity. These tests were developed at a precarious time: in the United States, the Cold War was just kicking in. With a growing concern for national safety, J. P. Guilford's question "Why do we not produce more creative geniuses than we do under supposedly enlightened modern educational practices?"[22] was largely prompted by an urgency to develop the next generation of scientists and engineers capable of designing the defense equipment and technology necessary to protect the United States and oppose its aggressors.[23] Though the threat of the Cold War may be far behind us, even today, creativity tests, such as the Torrance Tests of Creative Thinking, continue to be used "for identification of the creatively gifted and as a part of gifted matrices in states and districts in the USA."[24]

The first crisis of creativity in education therefore suggests that a focus on the creative individual sets up the potential for educators and administrators to determine that some students are more creatively gifted than others, or worse—that some students are creative, and others are not. Such an approach to creative development poses the risk of establishing a system of *creativity tracking*. Creativity tracking may best be understood as the process of using some form of individually based determinant to direct students into educational and career tracks that prepare some students to be socially and cognitively equipped for life and work in the creative professions, while doing quite the opposite for other students—preparing them for life and work in less creatively oriented (and likely less lucrative) professions. An individual student's performance on a creativity test, then, may greatly influence the arc of his or her educational experience—which in turn may radically affect his or her higher education and career options. This may work out well for students who are identified as being creatively gifted, but it has the potential to be disastrous for those who are not. In such a scenario, the opportunity for the creative classroom to be an equalizing place where the potential of all students is recognized becomes lost.

The correlation between creativity and giftedness is highly problematic in regards to issues of access and equity in the creative classroom. The nature of this problem can be found directly in the word "gifted." The gifted metaphor that is used in education functions well within our culture of individualism, as it is based on properties that appear to be possessed by the individual. If we were to tease apart the gifted metaphor, we would find that to be gifted suggests that certain individuals are endowed with a set of cognitive capacities in ways that others are not. Though some may suggest these "gifts" were granted from a higher power, others would argue that they are biological or genetic in nature, and still others would suggest that the origin of these gifts is unknowable. Regardless of where these gifts came from, from this perspective, gifted students literally possess something that ungifted students lack. Ungifted students, then, can never excel in the ways that their gifted peers can, because they are perceived as not having or possessing the same "gifts." This sets up a haves/have-nots scenario that in almost every circumstance will favor the haves, or gifted students, over the have-nots, or ungifted students. But compassionate educators know that the gifted vs. ungifted narrative presents a false dichotomy. On the one hand, it is not the case that gifted students have capacities that ungifted students do not have. All students have access to the same cognitive capacities, but some students perform better on certain cognitive tasks than others. On the other hand, if we were to maintain the gifted metaphor, we could argue that all students possess talents and skills unique to their background experiences and cultural perspectives. In other words, all students are gifted in their own unique ways. The problem here is that, within the educational sphere, some "gifts" are valued—and therefore privileged—more than others.

When we use any sort of metric, whether it be a formal creativity test or our own intuition, to determine an individual student's creative capacity—or giftedness—we immediately set up the potential to compare that one particular student with others. Though educators and administrators may have the best intentions in mind, sorting students by presumed creative ability, and then channeling some students towards creative experiences based on their perceived creative potential, sets up a scenario wherein participating in creativity is far more accessible for some students than for others. The challenge for educators in the creative classroom is to see beyond traditional individual-based orientations towards creativity, and to recognize that all students have the potential to participate in invention and innovation in their own unique ways.

Crisis Two: The "I'm Just Not a Creative Person" Syndrome

The second crisis of creativity in education further emphasizes the negative effects of individual-based perspectives on creativity, while underscoring the harm that can be done by creativity tests. Not only do such tests have the potential to separate the creatively gifted from the presumably ungifted, but they can also instill within young people a lasting "I'm just not a creative person" identity.

Imagine this scenario: a group of young people are asked to take what has been presented to them as a creativity test. After engaging with the test—whatever form it may take—their responses to the prompts they have been given are scored by outside experts and, soon after, they each receive an individual *creativity quotient.*

It was J. P. Guilford's original intention to develop psychometric tests that could establish creativity quotients for young people, much like intelligence tests had been designed to establish intelligence quotients for their test takers. Since Guilford's contributions to the field of creativity research, many creativity tests have been established with the aim of developing accurate metrics that might yield reliable creativity quotients. Some of these tests are still being designed today.[25]

Though such tests are used in many high stakes settings—in some instances to determine giftedness and creative potential of young people, in other instances to identify talent and make employment or college admissions decisions—the scoring of creativity tests can be highly subjective, if not arbitrary.[26, 27] While establishing the reliability of a creativity test is arguably a tricky business, educators in the creative classroom have more cause for alarm over the negative psychological effects that may result when young people are given numerical scores to mark their creative ability.

Naturally, after taking a creativity test some students will receive higher creativity scores—or quotients—than others, which, as discussed above, may signal to educators where to channel certain students and where to channel others. This is problematic. But just as worrisome is the idea that when individual students are labeled with creativity quotients, other harmful signals are being transmitted as well.

As with IQ tests—individual-based creativity tests may signal to young people that creativity is a fixed capacity. As a result, students may develop what psychologist Carol Dweck refers to as an *anti-growth mindset* that psychologically discourages them from participating in creative learning experiences.[28] If a young person's creative capacity is fixed, and if certain students perform better on creativity tests than others, then why should young people who are told they have performed poorly on creativity tests have any interest in pursuing future creative experiences? No one likes to engage in activities they are not any good at. So from a student's perspective, opting out of creative experiences after scoring poorly on a creativity test or being told you have a low creativity quotient makes logical sense.

From a growth mindset, one might have a different perspective. Understanding the importance of formative assessment, some educators may argue that a low score on a creativity test is not the end of the world—it indicates room for improvement—and that with hard work, students can score better next time. But creativity tests, as with many psychometric tests, are not necessarily designed in a manner that provides opportunity for growth. Instead, they are deterministic. They offer scores, not grades. And too often, those scores are seen as unmovable markers of creative potential.[29]

Even if it were possible to score better on a creativity test the next time, even if we could "teach for the test," I would argue that the question remains to be asked: "Who says that we should value what creativity tests measure, anyway?"

Crisis Three: Narrowly Defining Creativity Privileges some Students and Alienates Others

More often than not, the instruments that are used to estimate an individual student's creative capacity—or giftedness—are likely to be narrow ones that fail to capture the full breadth of one's creative potential. The third crisis of creativity in education concerns itself with what it is that creativity tests measure, and ultimately suggests that narrowly focusing on a limited set of cognitive capacities—as all psychometric tests must—privileges some students' capabilities and cultural perspectives over others.

All creativity tests need to test something. Whether it be divergent thinking, personality characteristics, or one's ability to solve a Rubik's Cube as quickly as possible, creativity tests, like all social science-based psychometric tests, by their very nature, must be designed to measure a particular capacity, or suite of capacities, according to a set of rules that determine the presence or exhibition of that/those capacity(ies).[30]

As we have learned from Howard Gardner's theory of multiple intelligences, not all people are intelligent, or smart, in the same way. Instead, each individual possesses a unique profile of intelligences that takes into account the full range of their cognitive strengths and weaknesses.[31] If we accept Gardner's theory, then no one psychometric test can accurately measure the full range of the intelligences—and especially not the diverse profiles of intelligences that are unique to each individual. If creativity mirrors the intelligences, as Gardner and others have suggested,[32] then it should be the case as well that not all people are creative (or have the potential to participate in creativity) in the same way. And, therefore, no one test can accurately measure the multiplicity of ways that various people may participate in creativity, including the diverse *profiles of participation* that are unique to each individual.

What is problematic about this third crisis of creativity in education is that the psychometricians who design creativity tests ultimately make choices concerning what creative capacities their tests will and will not measure. The choices these individuals make naturally privilege certain cognitive capacities over others. The privileging that takes place during this decision-making process is vexed in many ways. From an MI theory perspective, one may argue that it is not fair for psychometricians to prioritize certain capacities over others. Rather, to be fair, any sort of instrument designed to gauge creativity must take into account the full range of ways in which young people participate in creativity. As will be discussed further in Chapter 4, one may also argue that from a social-cultural perspective, creativity tests further express the social and cultural biases of their test makers. Whatever perspective one takes, narrowly focusing on a restricted set of cognitive capacities and/or character traits as being the markers for what it means to be creative—and then designing tests to measure those narrow sets of capacities and characteristics—has the detrimental effect of privileging some students, while grossly alienating others.

Crisis Four: Denying Young People the Opportunity to Create and Invent with Others

So far in this chapter I have discussed the creative classroom in the abstract, without specifying many particular learning environments. Perhaps now is a good time to hone in on one. To do so, I'd like you as a reader to imagine a materials rich environment full of arts and crafts supplies, digital cameras, and computers, a place where young people—pre-school-aged students—come together to work on a variety of projects. Picture a group of students working together to draw a map of their city, a schematic that describes how a fax machine works, or a 3-D representation of how to play *Ring Around the Rosie* using their own bodies. All the while, as the young people work together on these projects, adults are documenting their work and scaffolding their learning experiences. It's a group effort, where everyone learns from everyone else.

While the above scenarios may have been drawn from any number of pre-school learning environments, the specific projects noted above come from the pre-schools of Reggio Emilia in northern Italy. Established by Loris Malaguzzi, the *Reggio Emilia approach* is widely known for student-centered learning, documentation, and its emphasis on allowing children to express themselves and explore ideas in as many ways as possible or, as Malaguzzi referred to it, the *hundred languages of children*. The pre-schools of Reggio Emilia are also known for the group- and community-based learning that takes place when young people pursue projects together. To best illustrate what group- and community-based learning looks like in a Reggio Emilia pre-school, the quote below from Malaguzzi describes the process of young people working on a project together, an amusement park for birds:

> Suggestions were made [in class assembly] for houses and nests in the trees, swings for chicks to play on, elevators for the elderly birds. Ferris-wheels and rides with music. And then—everyone laughs—water skiing for the birds, providing them with tiny slats of wood for skis. Then came the fountains which had to be big and real, and spray the water up really high. . . . As part of the project Andrea has drawn an elevator for tired birds. After doing this he goes to the computer corner to build an animation version. . . . Andrea is unable to complete the animation by himself; he takes his project home where his elder sister helps him finish it. The next day Andrea goes to the school workshop area and adds to the animation a picture of a real bird taken with a digital camera, and records

birds singing. Once Andrea has completed his work on the computer he shows it to the class. . . . Now there is a new project. The children go out to observe actual elevators and take pictures of them. Then they discuss and draw how they think an elevator works. With the help of Giovanni, Andrea and Alice made an elevator using Lego motors and a sensor attached to a "programmable brick". The elevator is to be placed in the amusement park for birds.[33]

While this excerpt (which originally appeared in a book chapter focused on creativity, community, and technology) highlights the work of one student, Andrea, what we see is that the learning that takes place is distributed amongst many young people. And, indeed, emphasizing the distributed, or community-based, aspect of learning is a key element of the Reggio Emilia approach. Had Andrea been left to work on the amusement park for birds project by himself, he may have run into several road blocks along the way and the end product of his work would most likely be focused on a much more narrow set of ideas. But with the help of others, Andrea's learning—and the ways in which he participated in the project—was brought to a new level. Not only did Andrea benefit from his participation in this project, but the end product and his peers benefitted as well (and ultimately, one hopes that the birds of Reggio Emilia benefitted, too).

Consistently, as with the amusement park for birds project, documentation drawn from Reggio Emilia pre-schools underscores the many ways in which student learning takes place when young people work together. As many readers will know, the Reggio Emilia approach has been a longstanding interest of researchers at Project Zero. With an emphasis placed on the interplay between individual and group learning, what these researchers have found is that "much, if not most, of the learning that goes on in and out of schools happens through the interactions of groups."[34] If this is indeed the case, then the fourth crisis of creativity in education contests that an individual-based focus on creativity development denies young people access to the important peer-to-peer learning that takes place when students invent, solve problems, and build knowledge together.

Long before Project Zero researchers engaged in their inquiry of individual and group learning with pre-school students in Reggio Emilia, the Soviet psychologist Lev Vygotsky had made a similar assertion about the distributed nature of learning.[35] From Vygotsky's perspective, all learning is social. Perhaps Vygotsky's most well-known work in this regard is a concept he referred to as the *zone of proximal development*. What this theory suggests is that learning and development are interrelated processes, both of which are socially situated. Throughout our lives we are consistently learning from others; in other words, as we engage with others, we learn from them and, as we learn, we develop in a way that makes us more mentally complex. In Vygotsky's own words:

the zone of proximal development . . . is the distance between the actual development level as determined by independent problem solving and the level of potential development as determined through problem solving under adult guidance or in collaboration with more capable peers.[36]

Similarly, social anthropologist Jean Lave has argued that young people learn when they participate as peripheral players in communities of practice. Using Lave's language, *newcomers* learn from *oldtimers* as they become increa singly sophisticated within a particular domain. "Learning is recognized as a social phenomenon constituted in the experienced, lived-in world, through legitimate peripheral participation in ongoing social practice," she wrote, and then further made the connection to self-development via engagement in a community of practice: "the process of changing knowledgeable skill is subsumed in processes of changing identities in and through membership in a community of practitioners."[37] Using an apprenticeship metaphor, Lave further discussed how young people organically learn from adults and more accomplished peers through authentic participation, which becomes more complex over time. Through interaction with more skilled peers and experts, novices themselves become more skilled and demonstrate their evolving mastery through participation in the domain. Access to people, resources, and experiences are key supports in this process.

In the story of Andrea and the amusement park for birds told by Malaguzzi, above, there are several instances where Andrea is scaffolded by his "colla-boration with more capable peers," most notably when his older sister helps him with his computer animation, and when Giovanni helps him and Alice to build an operational elevator using mechanized LEGOs. "What a child can do with assistance today," Vygotsky wrote, "she will be able to do by herself tomorrow."[38] In Andrea's case, what he learned with support from his sister and from Giovanni, he will likely be able to do without assistance in the near future.

Though the work of Vygotsky helped influence the pedagogical approach of the Reggio Emilia pre-schools, it is not only within northern Italy that students learn from one another in such a way. Rather, it is the nature of our human development. If we accept this as being true, then why would we want to maintain an individual-based orientation towards invention and innovation that discourages development through learning with and from others?

Not only do individual-based understandings of creativity have the potential to deny young people the opportunity to learn and invent with one another, but one of the consequences of applying an individual-based orientation towards invention and innovation in the creative classroom is that young people may mistake social learning opportunities for *stealing* from one another. Sharing knowledge, skills, and expertise is an important part of both the learning and the creative processes. But if young people become overly proprietary about their work, there is a risk that they may either guard their ideas from others and/or restrain themselves from engaging with and borrow-ing from the work of their peers. The opposite should be the case—where the ideas and work of students is freely shared so that all students may learn from one another. In order to preempt the development of proprietary thinking in the creative classroom, educators would be advised to emphasize the distributed nature of both learning and innovation, framing all idea development as a participatory process, wherein each student contributes to the collective work of their classmates.

If we are to believe that, as Vygotsky suggested, all learning and development is social, then we must also be open to changing our mindsets towards invention and innovation and likewise embrace the idea that all creativity is social, too. A social approach to creative development must then be at the core of how educators design learning experiences in the creative classroom.

Crisis Five: Ill-Equipping Young People for Success in Contemporary Life and Work

Within the innovation economy, the concept of *design thinking* has been popularized by design firms like IDEO and higher education programs such as the Stanford d. school (Hasso Plattner Institute of Design). Design thinking is a process of inspiration, ideation, and implementation that, according to Tim Brown, the CEO and president of IDEO, "uses the designer's sensibility and methods to match people's needs with what is technologically feasible and what a viable business strategy can convert into customer value and market opportunity."[39]

In the past ten years, design thinking has become increasingly popular throughout both the corporate and social services sectors, and a *Design Thinking for Educators Toolkit* has even been developed for teachers to bring the principles of design thinking to young people in various educational settings.[40] Whether being applied in schools, NGOs, or Fortune 500 companies, one of the core principles of design thinking is that "all design activity is ultimately social in nature."[41] What this first suggests is that the very nature of design is human-centric or, in other words, based on satisfying human needs. Frequently this is discussed in terms of the designer developing empathy and a deeper human awareness of his/her client or "end user." There is an emphasis here on the end product of design being in alignment with the user's needs. But aside from design being socially situated in such a way, it has also been stressed that the *process* of design is social as well. What this means is that more successful innovations and better solutions to the world's most "wicked problems" are likely to come about when diverse groups of individuals with different skills and expertise work together, as opposed to when a homogenous group of designers collaborate on similar projects.

Whether employing the processes of design thinking or some other approach to innovation, the contemporary creative economy puts much less of an emphasis on creative individuals than it does on establishing interdisciplinary teams capable of approaching the process of innovation or creative problem solving from multiple angles.

The fifth crisis of creativity in education therefore makes the case that an educational focus on individual creativity is incongruous with the needs of higher education settings and innovative workplace environments that no longer seek lone innovators, but rather employ collaborative work-groups that incorporate the expertise of diverse individuals. In this regard, teaching and learning environments focused on individual creativity ill-equip young people for success in twenty-first-century life and work.

According to a recent study by David J. Deming, despite the prevalence of increased technology in the workplace, social skills—especially the ability to interact with others and adapt to the changing demands of a team or collaborative work group—are becoming even more valuable throughout the labor market.[42] As a related *Harvard Business Review* article indicated, "nearly all job growth since 1980 has been in occupations that are relatively social skill intensive . . . high-skilled, hard-to-automate jobs will increasingly demand social adeptness."[43] Not only are jobs requiring social skills in higher demand, the same *Harvard Business Review* article further reported that employees with strong social skills earn more money than their less socially adept peers, regardless of education, cognitive ability, and other factors. In other words, knowing how to participate in distributed invention and innovation processes pays off.

While person-to-person social skills are certainly important in the contemporary creative economy, Peter Gloor's research on Collaborative Innovation Networks (COINS) at the Massachusetts Institute of Technology's Center for Collective Intelligence describes how the three-step process of innovation, collaboration, and communication conducted by networks of innovators with a variety of skills may happen deliberately in face-to-face environments, or more organically through virtually connected networks of innovation.[44]

Suffice it to say, the process of collaboration and building upon the talents and expertise of diverse individuals has become an essential part of life and work in the contemporary creative economy. As Keith Sawyer reminds us, "When we collaborate, creativity unfolds across people; the sparks fly faster, and the whole is greater than the sum of its parts."[45] The corporate sector has come to understand this, but many in the education sector still cling to traditional, individual-based understandings of creativity. If we are to truly prepare our young people for success in life and work in the decades ahead, then the challenge for educators in the creative classroom is to look beyond outmoded, individual orientations towards creativity, and to adapt structures for teaching and learning that permit young people to participate in distributed approaches to invention and innovation.

Reframing Creativity as a Participatory Process: What's an Educator to Do?

Despite the five crises of creativity in education discussed above, the heroic narratives presented by our culture of individualism are strong. When great victories take place—or when exciting new innovations are introduced, we experience a cultural inclination to identify a hero, and to grant that person author function for what may initially be perceived as an individual feat of achievement. As we have seen from the story of Daniel Murphy, the same is true when great failures and follies take place. However, if we shift our perspective and take a more distributed stance towards achievement, especially as it concerns creativity and innovation, we will find that there is far more to learn (and perhaps more to celebrate) when we recognize that all acts of invention are socially and culturally situated.

One of the greatest implications for education concerns itself with changing mindsets—of both students and educators. This change in mindset may be brought on by educating our young people, not to believe that one day they will be the best, that they will do great things of their own volition, that they will outperform their peers and be crowned the MVP of their game or domain, but rather to educate our young people to understand that yes, they have the potential to do and achieve great things in their lives, but their achievements will always be socially and culturally situated, and that the greatness they may one day experience will be a result of their own efforts combined with—and amplified by—the distributed efforts of others.

Before moving forward towards developing a distributed and participatory orientation towards invention and innovation, there are still other crises of creativity in education that must be addressed in order for us to fully understand the obstacles to access and equity in the creative classroom. Whereas this chapter addressed the crises of creativity in education that result from our culture of individualism, in Chapter 4 I further present a suite of three additional crises of creativity that emanate from our prevailing cultures of power.

Notes

1. See Romney in Domenico Montanaro, "Romney to Olympians: 'You Didn't get here Solely on Your Own.'" *First Read on NBC News.com* (2012, July 23). Retrieved from http://firstread.nbcnews.com/_news/2012/07/23/12904508-romney-to-olympians-you-didnt-get-here-solely-on-your-own?lite, para 3.
2. See Howard Gardner, *Creating Minds: An anatomy of creativity seen through the lives of Freud, Einstein, Picasso, Stravinsky, Eliot, Graham, and Gandhi* (New York: Basic Books, 1993), p. 44.
3. Ibid., pp. 43–44.
4. See David Schoenfield, "Daniel Murphy's error was sixth costliest in World Series history." *ESPN SweetSpot* (n.d.). Retrieved from http://espn.go.com/blog/sweetspot/post/_/id/65873/daniel-murphys-was-sixth-costliest-in-world-series-history
5. See Daniel Murphy in Bob Nightengale, "Mets' David Wright on World Series game four loss: 'This isn't Daniel Murphy's fault.'" *USA Today Sports* (2015, November 1). Retrieved from http://www.usatoday.com/story/sports/mlb/2015/10/31/world-series-new-york-mets-kansas-city-royals-jeurys-familia-michael-conforto-daniel-murphy-wade-davis/74981610/
6. Ibid.

7. Ibid.
8. It should be acknowledged that a complete counter-narrative could be developed describing what I've been referring to as the Mets' loss of the 2015 World Series as the Royals' win of that same set of games. Some of the characters might be the same, but such a story would likely draw on additional actors and events to describe the team's victory.
9. See *Breaking News Consumer's Handbook: Terrorism Edition, On the Media* (November 20, 2015). Retrieved from http://www.onthemedia.org/story/breaking-news-consumers-handbook-terrorism-edition/
10. See Jack Shafer, "The Myth of the Terrorist Mastermind: Why Do We Need to Keep Telling Ourselves that the Plotters are Special?" *Politico Magazine* (November 16, 2015). Retrieved from http://www.politico.com/magazine/story/2015/11/the-myth-of-the-terrorist-mastermind-213367
11. Ibid., para 4.
12. Ibid., para 9.
13. See Michel Foucault, "What is an Author?" in *Language, Counter-Memory, Practice: Selected Essays and Interviews*, pp. 113–138 (Ithaca, NY: Cornell Paperbacks, 1980).
14. Ibid., p. 211.
15. I should be clear that I am in no way comparing the character of Daniel Murphy to the wickedness of Abdelhamid Abaaoud.
16. It is important, however, to remember that suggesting certain students have certain learning styles runs the risk of placing students into "buckets" that may narrowly define them as learners. For a critique of learning styles see Valerie Strauss, "Howard Gardner: 'Multiple Intelligences' are not 'learning styles'" (*Washington Post*, October 16, 2013). Retrieved from https://www.washingtonpost.com/news/answer-sheet/wp/2013/10/16/howard-gardner-multiple-intelligences-are-not-learning-styles/; Jennifer Groff, "Expanding our 'frames' of mind for education and the arts." *Harvard Educational Review* 83, no. 1 (2013): 15–39.
17. See E. Paul Torrance, *Torrance Tests of Creative Thinking: Norms Technical Manual.* (Princeton, NJ: Personnel Press, 1974). See also Scholastic Testing Services, Inc., Torrance Tests of Creative Thinking, (Bensenville, IL/Earth City, MO, n.d.). Retrieved from http://www.ststesting.com/ngifted.html
18. See Baer, "Why You Should Trust Creativity Tests," *Educational Leadership*, 51, no. 4 (1994): 81–83; Susan B. Crockenberg, "Creativity Tests: A Boon or Boondoggle for Education?" *Review of Educational Research*, 42, no. 1 (1972): 27–45; Arthur J. Cropley, "Defining and Measuring Creativity: Are Creativity Tests Worth Using?" *Roeper Review*, 23, no. 2 (2000): 72–79; Gardner, *Creating Minds*; Michael Hanchett Hanson, "Creativity Theory and Educational Practice: Why all the Fuss?" in *The Creative Imperative: School Librarians and Teachers Cultivating Curiosity Together*, pp. 19–37, eds. Jami Biles Jones & Lori J. Flint (Santa Barbara, CA: ABC-CLIO, LLC, 2013); Keith Sawyer, *Group Genius: The Creative Power of Collaboration* (New York: Basic Books, 2007); and James Haywood Rolling, Jr., *Swarm Intelligence: What Nature Teaches Us About Shaping Creative Leadership*, (New York: Palgrave Macmillan, 2013).
19. See Robert W. Weisberg & Michael Hanchett Hanson, "Inside-the-Box: An Expertise-Based Approach to Creativity in Education," in *The Creative Imperative: School Librarians and Teachers Cultivating Curiosity Together*, pp. 71–84, eds. Jami Biles Jones & Lori J. Flint (Santa Barbara, CA: ABC-CLIO, LLC, 2013), and Hanchett Hanson, "Creativity Theory and Educational Practice."

20. See Teresa M. Amabile, *Creativity in Context* (Boulder, CO: Westview Press, 1996); see also Teresa M. Amabile, "The Social Psychology of Creativity: A Componential Conceptualization," *Journal of Personality and Social Psychology*, 45, no. 2 (1983): 357–376.

21. See Scott Barry Kaufman, *Ungifted: Intelligence Redefined* (New York: Basic Books, 2013), and Crockenberg, "Creativity Tests."

22. See J. P. Guilford, *Creativity.* Address of the President of the American Psychological Association. September 5, 1950. Pennsylvania State College, University Park, PA, 1950.

23. Interestingly, this early impetus to foster creativity through education to develop new defense equipment and technologies mirrors the recent support by the Defense Advanced Research Projects Agency (DARPA) to develop makerspaces in schools to bolster young people's proficiencies and interest in the STEM subjects and professions. See Dale Dougherty, DARPA Mentor Award to Bring Making to Education, *Make* (July 19, 2012). Retrieved from http://makezine.com/2012/01/19/darpa-mentor-award-to-bring-making-to-education/; see also Kevin Driscoll, "The Dark Side of DIY: Makerspaces and the Long, Weird History of DIY Hobbyists and Military Funding," *Civic Paths* (n.d.). Retrieved from http://civicpaths.uscannenberg.org/the-dark-side-of-diy-makerspaces-and-the-long-weird-history-of-diy-hobbyists-military-funding/

24. See Scholastic Testing Services, Inc., *Torrance Tests of Creative Thinking*, para 1.

25. See, for example, Allan Snyder, John Mitchell, Terry Bossomaier, & Gerry Pallier, "The Creativity Quotient: An Objective Scoring of Ideational Fluency," *Creativity Research Journal* (2004), 16, no. 4 (2004): 415–420. Note that, even as recently as 2004, psychometric tests designed to produce creativity quotients still rely on aspects of divergent thinking as determinants of creativity.

26. See, for example, SPARCIT (www.sparcit.com/), an online creativity testing company that offers their clients (e.g., businesses, universities, etc.) products designed to determine an individual's or group's creativity quotient. From the company's website: "Employers can now measure and help enhance employees and teams' creative power through an easy to use online platform. They gain access to an accurate and versatile creativity quotient (CQ) to recruit and train employees, to form teams with appropriate, balanced skill sets." See also Crockenberg, "Creativity Tests."

27. Despite manuals and careful rubrics designed to help analysts score creativity tests, individual interpretations of the responses on such tests are always subjective. Nonetheless, many creativity researchers and psychometricians have claimed that certain creativity metrics have a high degree of reliability. Some creativity tests have even been digitally automated to be scored electronically, presumably removing the potential for variability caused by interpretation, subjectivity, or human error. I would be just as suspicious, however, of a creativity test that had claimed to have developed clear cut measures of what is or is not creative, as I would be of a creativity test that suggested its participants' responses were subject to interpretation.

28. See Carol Dweck, *Mindset: The New Psychology of Success* (New York: Random House, 2006).

29. Though some researchers have argued that cognitive abilities are dynamic, which defies the fixed capacity association with creativity quotients, limiting creativity to a set of cognitive capacities, whether fixed or flexible, upholds an individual-based perspective on creativity.

30. See Stanley Smith Stevens, "On the Theory of Scales of Measurement," *Science* (1946) 7, no. 2684 (1946): 677–680.
31. See Howard Gardner, *Frames of Mind: The Theory of Multiple Intelligences* (New York: Basic Books, 1983), and Howard Gardner, "A Multiplicity of Intelligences," *Scientific American Presents, Exploring Intelligence,* 9, no. 4 (1993): 19–23.
32. See Gardner, *Creating Minds.*
33. This quote from Loris Malaguzzi is excerpted from a chapter by Jenny Leach. Though Leach's intention in using this quote was to highlight "the role that technology can play ... within a community of young learners" (p. 182), I find it to be an excellent exhibition of distributed learning. See Jenny Leach, "A Hundred Possibilities: Creativity, Community, and ICT," in *Creativity in Education*, Anna Craft, Bob Jeffrey, & Mike Leibling, eds. pp. 175–194 (New York: Continuum, 2001). The Malaguzzi quote appears on page 183.
34. See Mara Krechevsky and Ben Mardell, "Four Features of Learning in Groups," in Project Zero and Reggio Children, *Making Learning Visible: Children as Individual and Group Learners*, pp. 284–295 (Reggio Emilia, Italy: Reggio Children, 2001) p. 284.
35. See Lev Semyonovich Vygotsky, *Mind in Society: The Development of Higher Psychological Processes* (Cambridge, MA: Harvard University Press, 1978).
36. Ibid., p. 86.
37. See Jean Lave, "Situating Learning in Communities of Practice," in *Perspectives on Socially Shared Cognition*, L. B. Resnick, J. B. Levine, & S. D. Teasley, eds. pp. 63–82 (Washington, DC: American Psychological Association, 1991).
38. See Vygotsky, *Mind in Society*, p. 87.
39. See Tim Brown, "Design Thinking." *Harvard Business Review* (June 2008), 84–92, p. 86.
40. See IDEO, *Design Thinking for Educators Toolkit* (2011). Retrieved from https://www.ideo.com/work/toolkit-for-educators
41. See Christopher Meinel & Larry Leifer, "Design Thinking Research," in *Design thinking: Understand—improve—apply*, pp. xiii–xxi, H. Plattner, C. Meinel, & L. Leifer, eds. (New York: Springer, 2011), p. xv.
42. See David J. Deming, "The Growing Importance of Social Skills in the Labor Market," Working paper 21473 (Cambridge, MA: National Bureau of Economic Research, 2015). Retrieved from www.nber.org/papers/w21473
43. See Nicole Torres, "Technology is Only Making Social Skills More Important," *Harvard Business Review* (2015, August 26). Retrieved from https://hbr.org/2015/08/research-technology-is-only-making-social-skills-more-important, para 2.
44. See Peter Gloor, *Swarm Creativity: Competitive Advantage through Collaborative Innovation Networks* (New York: Oxford University Press, 2006); see also "Intelligent Collaborative Knowledge Networks," Collaboration in Creative Learning Networks (2013). Retrieved from www.ickn.org/collaboration.html
45. See Sawyer, *Group Genius.*

Chapter 4

5 + 3 = 8: The Eight Barriers to Access and Equity in the Creative Classroom

In Chapter 3 we explored the five crises of creativity that have come about as a result of our traditional, individual-based orientation towards creativity that permeates throughout the educational sphere. This individual-based orientation towards creativity emanates from an individualistic culture that grants author function to sole actors for cultural occurrences that are socially situated. These five crises in creativity present challenges to educators in the creative classroom, not only because they are misaligned with theory and practice and distort the realities of the creative process, but also because they impede access and equity in the creative classroom. Beyond these five crises of creativity that derive from an individual-based orientation towards invention and innovation, in this chapter I identify three additional crises of creativity in education that are based less on our culture of individualism, but more on our *cultures of power*. As will be discussed below, these two cultural forces are not mutually exclusive, and indeed many intersections between the two forces exist. Combined together, the five crises of creativity in education derived from a culture of individualism plus the three crises of creativity in education derived from a culture of power amount to what I describe at the end of this chapter as the eight barriers to access and equity in the creative classroom.

Cultures of Power, Progressive Education, and the Creative Classroom

For the past two years I have co-taught a course at the Harvard Graduate School of Education entitled "Thinking and Learning, Today and Tomorrow: Project Zero Perspectives." Throughout the course my colleagues and I draw on Project Zero frameworks to explore a set of throughlines that consider the nature of understanding, making learning visible, how and where do thinking and learning thrive, and what is worth learning today and tomorrow. In addition to exploring research related to these topics, our students are also engaged in workshop experiences that expose them to a range of strategies for promoting thinking and learning in various settings. As with many models for progressive education, the pedagogical frameworks explored throughout our course are often presented as being socially and culturally neutral. But as our students have been keen to point out, learning is contextualized and not all learners are the same. It is therefore important to always ask the question "Whose thinking and learning are we talking about?" Where the creative classroom is concerned, one may likewise ask, "Whose creativity are we talking about?"

Though many psychometricians might like to believe that the creativity tests they design are both color blind and socially and culturally neutral, the opposite can be said as well: that creativity tests are socially and culturally charged, and therefore favor some populations over others. In the same way, just as much as educators in the creative classroom might like to think that the learning experiences they provide for their students are color blind and socially and culturally neutral, one might equally argue that these experiences are likewise socially and culturally charged.

In a recent *Education Week* blog post entitled "Deeper Learning Has a Race Problem,"[1] educational researcher Jal Mehta enumerated the many ways in which deeper learning experiences are racially biased, and despite well-meaning intentions to support all students, deeper learning is largely geared towards privileged populations. "Deeper learning in the U.S.," Mehta wrote, "is much more white than the nation as a whole."[2] Reading Mehta's blog post struck a chord for me, and made me ask the question: "To the degree that creativity is a form of deeper learning, does creativity in education also have a race problem?" I have concluded that, for many of the same reasons that Mehta articulated in his blog post, one can also make the case that creativity in education likewise has a race problem—and a class problem, too. To be clear, this is not to suggest that the dominant creativity narrative (including research and practice) is racist or classist, but rather to suggest that social and cultural issues, such as race and class, are at play within the creative classroom, just as they are at play within any classroom. What is problematic is that issues of race and class are too often overlooked or dismissed as being inapplicable to the broader creativity narrative, and our failure to explicitly address these issues—whether we be researchers, educators, administrators, or policymakers—when we talk about creativity, inherently biases our discussions.

As Michael Hanchett Hanson has pointed out, because dominant creativity narratives have focused on persistence, overcoming adversity, and self-actualization, "creativity research has largely avoided addressing sociocultural power dynamics directly."[3] Hanchett Hanson has argued that there exist many romanticized examples of individuals who have overcome adversity—poverty, anti-Semitism, ableism, homophobia, racism, sexism, etc.—to achieve creative eminence. As a result, character traits associated with overcoming adversity (what some may call "grit") have over-shadowed the socioculturally related power dynamics that affect creative potential.[4] "Power dynamics have yet to be recognized as centrally important to creativity," Hanchett Hanson has observed. And why?

One reason has been the reliance on historical eminence as a validation criterion. When the starting point is the pronouncement of the most empowered, many questions of power dynamics are taken off the board. This is a costly approach for a construct used to participate in, manage, evaluate and promote change.[5]

The argument made by Hanchett Hanson (who boldly supports participatory models of creativity) illustrates how our culture of individualism with its associated hero worship over-emphasizes (and over-romanticizes) the ability for some individuals to "pull themselves up by their boot straps" while ignoring larger systemic issues related to power. Drawing on social constructivist theory, particularly from the perspective of Michel Foucault,[6] Hanchett Hanson suggests to us that retaining an eminence approach to understanding creativity as being a function of the grittiest amongst us allows imbalanced power dynamics to persist.

Hanchett Hanson raises important points, but his discussion is at the level of broader creativity theory. Issues pertaining to the creative classroom certainly fall within the realm of Hanchett Hanson's argument, but it is also helpful to zero in a bit to engage with arguments that directly address the role of power in education. When addressing the social and cultural implications of progressive education, one text that has been identified as being helpful for developing an understanding of the role that power may play in the classroom is Lisa Delpit's popular essay, "The Silenced Dialogue: Power and Pedagogy in Educating Other People's Children."[7] Within this essay Delpit presented the concept of *cultures of power* and elaborated upon the ways in which those most attuned to the culture of power in the classroom have an advantage over those who are less attuned to that culture of power. Considering the culture-neutral and color-blind manner by which creativity in education is often presented, I find it both useful and important to devote time to explore Delpit's conceptualization of power in education and, in particular, the role that power plays in the creative classroom. To do so, it is necessary to first orient ourselves towards Delpit's five aspects of power:

1. Issues of power are enacted in classrooms.
2. There are codes or rules for participating in power; that is, there is a "culture of power."
3. The rules of the culture of power are a reflection of the rules of those who have power.
4. If you are not already a participant in the culture of power, being told explicitly the rules of that culture makes acquiring power easier.
5. Those with power are frequently least aware of—or least willing to acknowledge—its existence. Those with less power are often most aware of its existence.[8]

Mapping Delpit's five aspects of power over a traditional individual-based conception of creativity suggests that power is indeed at play in the creative classroom and that there are codes and rules for participating in power—just as there are codes and rules for participating in creativity. Here, it can be argued that the rules for participating in creativity—especially traditional, individual-based conceptions of creativity—are derived from those who come from the culture of power. In Delpit's argument, she asserted that "children from middle class homes tend to do better in school than those from non-middle class homes because the culture of the school is based on the culture of the upper and middle classes—of those in power."[9] Whereas this quote from Delpit focuses on social class, she has also extended her argument to race. In this way, Delpit has suggested that white students of privilege have an advantage over students of color, because schooling has been designed to perpetuate white cultures of power. From this perspective the argument can be made that cultural biases in education are exacerbated, not ameliorated, by progressive and process-based approaches to education, because these liberal, alternative approaches to teaching and learning further favor the rules and codes that have been established by white cultures of power.

Though Delpit makes a strong argument for the power structures enforced by progressive and process-based education, earlier arguments made by sociologists Pierre Bourdieu and Jean-Claude Passeron would suggest that progressive and process-based education are but two forms of *pedagogical actions* within a broader system of diverse pedagogies. From their perspective, all forms of education enforce extant power structures, though some of these approaches to pedagogy are more dominant than others.

Cultural and Social Reproduction, Pedagogical Action, and Power

Resonant with Delpit's position on cultures of power are the concepts of cultural and social reproduction introduced by Bourdieu and Passeron. As they discussed in their book *Reproduction in Education, Society, and Culture*, the rules and codes of a culture are passed down from one generation to the next as a means to ensure the continuity of a particular culture.[10] This process, referred to as *cultural reproduction*, leads to what Bourdieu and Passeron have further called *social reproduction*. Different from, though closely related to, cultural reproduction, social reproduction describes the process by which social groups pass along their social structures from one generation to the next in order to maintain the group's social status over time or, as Bourdieu and Passeron defined it, "the reproduction of the structure of the relations of force between classes."[11] The process of social reproduction perpetuates class structures in a way that those in higher social classes retain their social advantages. Educational systems have traditionally been one of the primary mechanisms that drive cultural and social reproduction.

Bourdieu and Passeron referred to all forms of education—whether in formal school settings, within informal settings, or at home—as *pedagogical action* (abbreviated as PA). It is pedagogical action that serves as the vehicle driving cultural and social reproduction. Of course, there is not one, but instead many pedagogical actions within a broader educational ecosystem. As they wrote,

> *In any given social formation the different PAs, which can never be defined independently of their membership in a system of PAs subject to the effect of domination by the dominant PA, tend to reproduce the system of cultural arbitraries characteristic of that social formation, thereby contributing to the reproduction of the power relations which put that cultural arbitrary into the dominant position.*[12]

From this perspective, pedagogical actions contribute to cultural and social reproduction, and therefore reinforce the process of social domination by the dominant social class over the dominated social class. All forms of education perpetuate a cycle of what Bourdieu and Passeron referred to as *symbolic violence*. "*All pedagogic action . . . is, objectively, symbolic violence insofar as it is the imposition of a cultural arbitrary by an arbitrary power.*"[13] Different from physical violence, symbolic violence brings harm to a community by imposing power over that community in a way that retains the power of dominant culture, while further suppressing the dominated culture. Bourdieu and Passeron placed an emphasis on class, but as sociologists—or anyone for that matter—well know, issues related to class reflect issues related to race.[14] Therefore, in order to disrupt the processes of cultural and social reproduction throughout the educational sphere—and the broader social sphere—issues of both race and class need to be addressed.

Reconsidering Critiques of Progressive Education, Process-based Learning, and the Creative Classroom

Critiques of progressive education, process-based learning, and the practices of the creative classroom are important to take seriously, especially where issues of race and class are concerned. However, just as I have found it necessary to address these issues, I also find it necessary to pause here to recognize that the arguments associated with the cultures of power narrative are not without flaw. One may first note that, though many of the power imbalances that the cultures of power narrative presents still persist, the educational landscape has changed—for better and for worse—and much has been done to advance this conversation in the years since Delpit and Bourdieu and Passeron, for example, first presented their ideas.[15] Though a complete review of the evolution of the power in the classroom dialogue is warranted, such a review (more appropriately conducted by a scholar who is more knowledgeable and steeped in the literature than myself) is beyond the scope of this text. Here, however, I would like to address the primary aspect of popular cultures of power arguments that I find problematic, and that is the issue of *essentializing*, *othering*, and *stereotyping*.

When talking about issues of race and class, we must always be vigorous and caution against essentializing broad populations of individuals. No one racial, social, religious, or cultural group uniformly adheres to a given set of cultural norms, just as no one racial, social, religious, or cultural group responds to particular pedagogical practices in a consistent way. There is variability, differentiation, and uniqueness within groups, and therefore sweeping general-izations cannot be made concerning power, potential, or pedagogy. This acknowledgment of differentiation within groups, however, sets up a challenge for those of us who address issues of race and class within the educational and social spheres. The challenge is this: how do we foreground the variability within groups and resist the urge to stereotype, other, and essentialize while also recognizing that it is undeniably the case that our contemporary social structures favor middle and upper class individuals over others, just as they favor white individuals over people of color?

As Delpit has wisely noted, social and cultural groups are not monolithically consistent. There are instead very obvious exceptions to almost every social and cultural rule. Delpit, in her essay, noted that there exist poorer white people who may be outsiders to the culture of power, just as there are affluent people of color who may be insiders to the culture of power—if not members of the social elite.[16] I would add that there are multiple variations and configurations of social and cultural experiences between these two examples. In other words, there are many people—of all racial backgrounds—who comfortably exist within the middle class. And yet, we know that racism and classism persists at all levels of social experience.

I find it important to make these points, but I also find it inappropriate to dismiss the dialogue associated with race and class in education for the pur-pose of acknowledging differentiation within groups. And so, in the sections ahead—and throughout this book—I have applied the terminology of this dialogue when discussing the social and cultural implications of teaching and learning in the creative classroom. When encountering this terminology I encourage readers to keep in mind that there is no one white experience, nor one black experience, nor one brown, red, or yellow experience. Neither is there one lower, middle, or upper class experience. Rather, there is variability within the labels and language we use to discuss issues of race and class, particularly within the educational sphere.

I bring these points up because I feel that recognizing the concept of differentiation within groups is pertinent to the critiques of progressive education and process-based learning—and by association the practices and principles of the creative classroom—from the perspective of the cultures of power narrative. Viewing this argument from 30,000 feet, what I see as being in question here are the core tenets of constructionism. I do not believe, however, that the core tenets of constructivism are woefully flawed. Rather, I believe the locus of the tension between constructivist approaches to educational practice and the cultures of power narrative lies within a greater inability to recognize the importance of understanding the variability of experience both within and across social and cultural groups.

Throwing out the core tenets of constructionism, progressive education, process-based learning, and the pedagogical structures that shape the brand of thinking and learning that happen in the creative classroom, is unwarranted. What is needed instead is the development of a heightened sensitivity to the individual social and cultural perspectives of each student in the creative classroom. Equipped with a focused sense of perspective taking, educators may better exercise social and cultural agility when implementing the pedagogical practices associated with constructivist education, not only within the creative classroom, but within all classrooms.

I have often told my students, when one's pedagogical practice is questioned, it is important to be open to criticism, but also important to take a stance. And this is my stance: though I acknowledge, deeply understand, and in many ways agree with the criticisms that have been voiced against progressive education, process-based learning, and (by implication) constructivism, I do not think that these approaches to pedagogical practice are in any way invalid. Quite the contrary. Instead, I believe that even more work needs to be done to develop practices that *expand* the application of progressive and process-based education in a manner that is equitable and universally accessible. This includes—if not foregrounds—addressing issues of race and class in the creative classroom.

Does the creativity in education conversation need to address issues of race and class? Absolutely. Are all creative classrooms ignorant of these issues? Certainly not. I imagine that many creative classrooms are designed specifically with issues of race and class in mind. If we were to look more closely at these learning environments, we might find that the creativity narrative is quite different from that which we are accustomed to in dominant culture. That being said, there is no one way, and certainly no right way, to facilitate teaching and learning in the creative classroom. There are, however, pitfalls that we can look to avoid, especially where power, cultural reproduction, social reproduction, and symbolic violence play a role. Considering the crises of creativity in education associated with our culture of individualism, as mentioned in Chapter 3, in concert with the crises of creativity in education associated with our cultures of power that will shortly be presented below, may help us better understand, address, and overcome the barriers to access and equity in the creative classroom.

The Crises of Creativity in Education Associated with Cultures of Power

As discussed in Chapter 3, our culture of individualism presents discrete challenges that serve to limit access and equity in the creative classroom. But a prevailing sense of individualism is not the only factor that shapes one's sociocultural experiences. As has been discussed above, all people live within a culture of power that favors the members of certain social classes over others. Below, I add to the five crises of creativity associated with our culture of individualism by presenting three additional crises of creativity associated with our cultures of power:

- Crisis six: *Assuming creativity in education is socially and culturally neutral*
- Crisis seven: *A misalignment of identity in the representation of creative icons*
- Crisis eight: *An imbalance of opportunity*

It is my hope that, naming the crises of creativity in education associated with power—and being cognizant of their effects—will serve as an important step towards understanding how teaching and learning in the creative classroom can be a profoundly enriching experience for all students.

Crisis Six: Assuming Creativity in Education is Socially and Culturally Neutral

Within the field of creativity research, there is a subset of inquiry that explores the relationships between personality traits and creativity. The personality psychologist Gregory J. Feist is well known within this area of study for his research describing the personality traits associated with creative artists, as compared with the personality traits associated with creative scientists. Based on a synthesis of creativity research studies spanning over four decades,[17] Feist concluded that creative artists are inclined to be open to experiences, fantasy-oriented, imaginative, impulsive, emotionally sensitive, driven, ambitious, nonconformist, aloof, and introverted—amongst other traits. Creative scientists are inclined to likewise be open to experiences, driven, ambitious, and introverted, but also flexible with their thinking, achievement-oriented, dominant, self-confident, autonomous, and independent—amongst other traits. Backing up these assertions Feist has argued, that "the creative personality does exist and personality dispositions regularly and predictably relate to creative achievement in art and science."[18]

An implication of this individual-based perspective on creativity might be for institutions in the business of invention and innovation (including schools) to seek out and recruit individuals who possess these personality traits. However, astute educators and business professionals alike will recognize that, though interesting, this list of traits does not fully capture the range of personality characteristics they have seen in the many people they have collaborated with on creative enterprises. To this end, a narrow list of personality traits associated with the creative individual privileges some personality traits, while disadvantaging others. This concept was explored in Chapter 3 when the third crisis of creativity was addressed. But here there is a new twist. And that is to ask "What is the relationship between the perceived cognitive and person-ality traits associated with creativity and those associated with our cultures of power?"

Without attention to the many ways that young people may participate in creativity, narrowly focused, individual-based orientations towards creativity not only privilege certain cognitive profiles over others, they also privilege certain social and cultural profiles over others. Here, there is an intersection between our cultures of individualism and power—and their effects on what teaching and learning (and testing) may look like in the creative classroom. From the cultures of power perspective that Delpit presented as well as the cultural and social reproduction perspective presented by Bourdieu and Passeron, one may question the degree to which the capacities and character traits associated with creativity from a traditional, individual-based perspective (such as those identified by Feist and others) and the skills generally thought to be associated with creative engagement (e.g., comfort with ambiguity, brainstorming and "outside-the-box" thinking, learning from failure, chal-lenging authority, etc.) are not only associated with the aspirations of progres-sive and process-based education, but also coupled with the capacities, character traits, and skills associated with the dominant culture of power.

I want to be clear that I would never suggest that poorer students and students of color are incapable of these presumably "higher order" thinking skills. Indeed they are capable. What is at issue here is that, in the creative classroom, poor students and students of color may be at a disadvantage compared with their more privileged middle and upper class white peers who have been raised within a culture of power, and who have therefore been equipped with the knowledge and skills that are necessary to excel within classrooms that support the cultural structures and rules of engagement that have shaped their upbringing. Mehta expanded on this point when he wrote,

> the kind of open-ended exploration and play that is prized in inquiry-oriented instruction is fine for students who come with a significant background in "basic" or "core" knowledge and skills, but to pursue that approach with students who lack this background is likely to be ineffective.[19]

While not over-emphasizing skills-based instruction, Delpit made much of the same argument when she wrote,

> I do not advocate a simplistic "basic skills" approach for children outside of the culture of power. It would be (and has been) tragic to operate as if these children were incapable of critical and higher-order thinking and reasoning. Rather, I suggest that schools must provide these children the content that other families from a different cultural orientation provide at home.[20]

The bottom line here is that, as creativity in education has been traditionally understood, some students may be more equipped to engage in the creative classroom than others, and these students are most likely to come from the dominant culture of power. We should not separate these students from their peers, but instead wrestle with ways in which we can design learning environments that promote equity in the creative classroom, in much the way that this concept was discussed in the Introduction to this book: to raise up all young people in a manner that meets their needs as learners. In order to do this, we must acknowledge that not all students arrive in the creative classroom from a place of equal footing.

The sixth crisis of creativity in education is the assumption that what is taught in the creative classroom is socially and culturally neutral. What's needed here is for educators in the creative classroom to both disrupt the trend towards favoring certain cognitive capacities, character traits, and skills over others, while at the same time disrupting the cultures of power that are perpetuated by traditional, individual-based orientations towards creativity, and the tests designed to measure it.

Writing from my perspective as a white man who has long been engrained in the culture of power, it is hardly my place to offer solutions to educators in the creative classroom where such issues are concerned. However, I do feel a sense of responsibility to surface what I see as the socially and culturally based challenges that ought to be faced by those who facilitate and administer creative teaching and learning experiences for young people.

The first challenge to educators has to do with awareness. How does one acknowledge not only how what is taught (and how it is taught) in the creative classroom may privilege some students' skills and capacities more than others, but also how what is taught (and again, how it is taught) in the creative classroom may privilege certain social and cultural perspectives more than others? For many educators—especially for those who are products of the culture of power—it may be difficult to see how one's teaching practices are socially and culturally biased. Indeed, this is one of Delpit's five aspects of power: that those with power are frequently least aware of it. But in order for what's learned in the creative classroom to be as accessible and as equitable as possible, acknowledging the role of power in the creative classroom is necessary work to be done.

Having identified the role that power plays in one's work with young people, the second challenge to educators is to disrupt the cultures of power that are prevalent in the creative classroom without diluting or "dumbing down" the creative learning experience. In this regard, differentiation, not dilution, may be of great importance. As Delpit has noted, "I believe that the actual practice of teachers of all colors typically incorporates a range of pedagogical orientations."[21]

Lastly, throughout the process of differentiating instruction and diversifying creative learning experiences to appreciate the wide range of students' background experiences and cultural perspectives, another challenge faced by educators in the creative classroom is to find explicit ways to inform students of the rules and the codes of the creative classroom, so that all students may approach their work in the creative classroom from a place of equal understanding—and equal opportunity. One should never assume that young people will implicitly develop an awareness of the rules associated with the culture of power in the creative classroom. Being explicit about what these rules are makes understanding them most accessible for young people.

Crisis Seven: A Misalignment of Identity in the Representation of Creative Icons

As discussed in Chapter 3, our individualistic culture propels us to grant certain individuals author function for socially distributed achievements. Sometimes these individuals are even heralded as creative geniuses for their work. Either implicitly or explicitly, creative icons are frequently referenced in the creative classroom as exemplars of a particular domain, or perhaps as exemplars for a particular way of thinking. Sometimes the likenesses of these individuals are portrayed on posters that hang on the walls of the creative classroom, with a pithy inspirational quote beneath. Other times, the likenesses of these individuals are less visible, but they are still with us in the creative classroom, their names being bandied about throughout the day.

Historic innovators such as Albert Einstein, Vincent van Gogh, and Charles Darwin are frequently heralded as just such creative idols. And sometimes, it almost appears as though these individuals have been raised to the status of gods sitting on a hill, high above us. Perhaps this summit of the gods of creativity is a precipice that's just the next peak over from Mt. Olympus.[22] If we were to go there we might find Einstein in front of a chalkboard, working through equations. Darwin might be around the way, categorizing insects. Not far from him we might find van Gogh, painting a sunflower with thick, colorful, expressive strokes of paint. Of course, in addition to Einstein, van Gogh, and Darwin, there might be other gods on Mt. Creativity as well. Thomas Edison would likely be there tinkering with light bulbs, Pablo Picasso might be there, too, painting nudes from multiple angles, and around the corner we might find Johann Sebastian Bach, playing a fugue on an ethereal organ. In addition to these old timers, there would probably be a few newcomers on Mt. Creativity. Steve Jobs, for instance, might be there, perpetually giving a Keynote presentation, and Mark Zuckerberg might be there, too, writing code, friending people, wearing a hoody. One would hope that Mt. Creativity would not be an exclusive boys' club, and that there would be goddesses of creativity there as well. Perhaps we might find Emily Dickinson in a field not far from van Gogh, observing the world and writing poems. Perhaps we might find Georgia O'Keefe painting flowers and skulls (though in a much different way from van Gogh). We might also find Margaret Mead offering lectures on anthropology and sociology, Vera Rubin staring up at the sky, studying galaxy rotations and calculating dark matter, and Virginia Wolff taking notes for a new novel—Janis Joplin might be there, too—whoopin' up a song.

Mt. Creativity might become quite crowded after a while, due to the growing list of people that have been culturally deified as the gods and goddesses of creativity. And while I've been flippant about the deification of creative individuals, it's quite serious to see that, here on Earth, we do indeed place the most accomplished amongst us on pedestals, and discuss their achievements as being extraordinary acts of human invention.

There are several problems associated with the hero worship of creative individuals that derive from the influences of our culture of power. And this leads us to our seventh crisis of creativity in education: a misalignment of identity in the representation of creative icons. The first of these problems has been well discussed by now, and that is that celebrating seemingly lone innovators gives the false impression that creativity is an individual process. The second problem is related to the first, and that is the lionization of creative individuals suggests that these larger than life characters are in some way gifted more than the average individual.[23] For some young people, the feats of achievement associated with creative icons may serve as an inspiration to strive for great heights. Perhaps these young people arrive to the creative classroom being primed to believe that they too can accomplish great things if they just work hard enough, if they just follow their dreams. But for other young people, the larger than life narrative associated with many creative icons may suggest that achieving greatness is not for them, but just for the gifted few. For these young people, particularly those who have not been raised within the culture of power, this narrative therefore has the opposite effect; it makes creative achievement seem like a far-off feat that is simply out of reach. "If Mark Zuckerberg can create Facebook in his dorm room at Harvard, then anyone can come up with the next biggest thing," one student might say. "But wait a minute, how do you get into Harvard in the first place?" another student might ask. And though he might not say it out loud, another student might think to himself, "no one in my family has ever even gone to college," followed by the question, "how come we're not talking about race and class here?" In this way, achieving creative greatness slowly drifts further and further into the distance. Becoming the next Mark Zuckerberg becomes less and less of a possibility.

No matter the rags to riches stories that may be associated with particular innovators, certain young people simply do not see themselves in the posters of the popular gods and goddesses of creativity hanging on the walls of the creative classroom. And this brings up the third problem associated with celebrating creative icons; it is no wonder that many students do not see themselves in the images of the gods and goddesses of creativity—because too often these individuals literally do not look like them. I've been very intentional in my naming of the gods and goddesses of creativity up above. My goal was to make a point—that too often the individuals we deify as creative geniuses are white people. Indeed, this is not the case in every creative classroom.

Certainly, there are plenty of classrooms that celebrate creators of color—Langston Hughes, Gwendolyn Brooks, Dr. Martin Luther King, Jr., Frida Kahlo, Maya Angelou, Toni Morrison, Salman Rushdie, Jean-Michel Basquiat, John Mitchell, Jimi Hendrix, Stevie Wonder, Washington Carver, Malcolm X, Ibn al-Haytham, Wole Soyinka, Diego Rivera, Sherman Alexie, Ai Weiwei, Alvin Ailey; the list of people of color who can just as well be considered amongst the gods and goddesses of creativity goes on and on. Nonetheless, there is an inclination for the culture of power to draw upon examples from white culture when exemplifying the apex of creative achievement. My fear is that there is a distance that arises when young people of color are surrounded by creative icons that not only do not look like them, but also do not represent their cultural and social orientations to the world. This distance needs to be bridged by a concerted effort to truly understand who is present in the creative classroom, and where they are positioned within our culture of power.

My aim here is not to suggest that we need to diversify the inspirational posters that hang in the creative classroom. Instead, I find that the challenge to educators is to reduce the emphasis placed on the icon of the creative individual by broadening their models of creativity to include the distributed networks of people who come together to develop greater creative effects. Doing so may show young people of all stripes that there is a role for everyone to play in the creative classroom, and that creativity can look like them, too.

Crisis Eight: An Imbalance of Opportunity

In many of the ways that have been discussed above, the manner of teaching and learning that takes place in the creative classroom can be said to perpetuate the power structures that have been established by the dominant white, middle- and upper-classes. Through this process, cultural reproduction—which leads to social reproduction—takes place. This is a process Bourdieu and Passeron referred to as "the social reproduction function of cultural reproduction."[24]

As discussed above, this process of cultural and social reproduction within the classroom is a form of symbolic violence—the imposition of certain cultural forces over others, to maintain dominant social structures. The final crisis of creativity in education is perhaps the most obvious one, and the most symbolically violent one: our culture of power has set up a system where there is an imbalance of opportunity to participate in creativity that grossly favors those who come from the most dominant social classes.

Though there are many efforts to make creative learning experiences more accessible to young people of all backgrounds, here in the United States—and in many other countries—there has been a long tradition of restricting access to the creative classroom to the children of the middle- and upper-classes. A quick walk through the hallways of America's schools will reveal that there are far more doorways that lead to creative classrooms in private schools and public schools in wealthier neighborhoods than there are in the under-resourced schools that are found in inner-cities, rural districts, and poorer neighborhoods. As Mehta and others have noted, engaging in the types of deeper learning that take place in the creative classroom primes young people for success in higher paying professions, whereas students who have limited access to such learning experiences are more likely prepared for less lucrative professions.[25] Or, in other words, restricted access to the creative classroom perpetuates social reproduction.

The challenge for educators, administrators, and policymakers is to find ways to make the learning experiences offered in the creative classroom more accessible to young people from all social classes and cultural backgrounds. Throughout the United States, many educators, administrators, and policy makers are already taking on this challenge. Thousands of after-school programs, informal learning opportunities, and "artist-in-residence" type programs are in effect, working hard to open the doors to the creative classroom to young people who may otherwise have no access to creative learning experiences. While there are some very high quality programs that have designed deep dives into invention and innovation for young people living in some of the world's poorest neighborhoods, unfortunately, despite the best efforts of the individuals who have made access to the creative classroom their life's work, many of the creative learning experiences that young people from non-dominant social classes experience are fragmented and short lived.

Recognizing the complexity and immensity of this challenge has prompted me to wonder how we might think differently about providing young people access to what is learned in the creative classroom. Perhaps, beyond bringing the creative classroom to young people, we may also reconsider what it means to participate in creativity. It is my hope that reframing creativity as a participatory experience may, in some way, open up new opportunities for young people to engage in the work of creativity by viewing young people from non-dominant cultures from an asset-based perspective, and seeing them as already being rich in creative potential. Viewed from this perspective, the trick, then, is not to find the door to the creative classroom—with all of its shining tools and lush materials inside—but to make participation in the development of creative ideas the norm in all classrooms.

The Eight Barriers to Access and Equity in the Creative Classroom

In the Introduction to this book I defined access as having the opportunity to engage with creative learning experiences in an unbounded, uncomplicated, and unencumbered way. I further noted that creative classrooms that are most accessible to young people include those that are universally available in schools or through after-school programming free of charge, regardless of race, class, or address. To truly be accessible, a creative classroom must not only be universally available, but also welcoming to young people of all stripes, including those that represent a variety of cultural and cognitive profiles. Access—on these many different levels—is a key component to achieving equity in the creativity classroom. In the Introduction of this book, I compared equity with equality, and argued that beyond offering equal opportunity for all students to engage in creative learning experiences, we must also tailor those learning experiences to meet the specific cognitive, character-based, and sociocultural needs and interests of each unique student.

Though many well-intentioned educators and administrators strive to achieve access and equity in the creative classroom, several cultural barriers persist that impede this goal. In Chapter 3 I presented the five crises of creativity in education derived from our culture of individualism. In the current chapter, I presented three additional crises of creativity that emanate from our culture of power. Combined together, these separate though interconnected crises of creativity in education can be rearticulated as *the eight barriers to access and equity in the creative classroom*:

1. Maintaining an individual-based approach to creativity, and utilizing creativity tests, sets up an environment where educators and administrators may determine that some students are more creative than others, or worse, that some students are creative, and other students are not. This raises the potential for *creativity tracking*, where young people are placed into educational and career tracks that may fail to capture their full potential.
2. Utilizing creativity tests based on individual measures poses the risk of presenting young people with "creativity quotients" that function like IQ test scores. These standardized measures of creativity set up an environment where students may perceive their creativity as being a fixed capacity. Students who score poorly on creativity tests may therefore develop an anti-growth or "I'm just not a creative person" mindset that psychologically discourages them from participating in future creative experiences.
3. Maintaining an individual-based approach to creativity, and utilizing creativity tests, naturally privileges the cognitive capacities of some students, while alienating others.
4. Considering that all learning and development is social, it must also be true that all learning in the creative classroom is social. Maintaining an individual-based approach to creativity in these settings sets up an environment where children are denied the opportunity to create and invent with others.
5. The contemporary creative economy no longer favors individual genius, but rather seeks individuals adept at participating in interdisciplinary work groups that are capable of developing new innovations and solving complex problems together. Maintaining an individual-based approach to creativity therefore poorly equips young people for life and work in the decades ahead.

6. Our culture of power is present in the creative classroom in the same way that it is within any other classroom. Assuming creativity in education is socially and culturally neutral overlooks the forces of race and class at play in the creative classroom, leading to instructional design that favors students that are most adept at understanding the rules of the culture of power, while estranging others.
7. Heralding larger than life individuals (especially those who represent the culture of power) as exemplars of creative achievement further estranges students who fail to see themselves represented in these individuals.
8. Our culture of power exists to perpetuate itself. As a result, there is an imbalance of opportunity to participate in creative learning experiences that favors young people who have been raised in the culture of power.

If we are to truly fulfill the promises of constructivism, progressive education, process-based learning, and all that the creative classroom has to offer, we must then take seriously the crises of creativity in education stated in these past two chapters—and develop strategies to address the eight barriers to access and equity presented above. I believe that what is required to overcome these crises of creativity in education and to surmount the barriers to access and equity in the creative classroom that they present, is a conceptual change that will require a shift in thinking for educators, administrators, researchers, parents, policymakers, and even students. At the heart of this epistemological shift is moving from an individual-based conception of creativity, to a more distributed and participatory understanding of invention and innovation. More than a technical fix, this shift in thinking will require an adaptive change—a complete reorientation towards how we understand what it means to participate in creativity.[26] This shift will require us to look for creativity beyond the skulls and skin of presumably gifted individuals, and to recognize the distributed nature of creativity, and its more broadly participatory potential.

Making the shift from an individual-based understanding of creativity to a more distributed orientation towards invention and innovation may be difficult for some, but it is a necessary shift to make. As the crises of creativity discussed above suggest, maintaining traditional orientations towards creativity prompts educators and administrators to focus on the wrong unit of analysis. Rather than attempt to gauge creativity *within* young people, it is of greater value to identify the many ways that young people can *participate* in the development of creative ideas—and explore the learning that takes place along the way. To that end, the chapters ahead consider the central role of an *idea* as that which is creative, highlight the *participatory* and *distributed* nature of group-generated creative ideas, and explore the *dialectical learning* that takes place when young people collectively generate creative ideas.

The goal here is to reframe creativity as an educational experience students participate in, rather than something one either *is* or *has*. This reframing of creativity will relieve the stress of fostering creativity *within* individuals that many educators now face, and allow for the emergence of new pedagogical practices aimed at developing teaching and learning environments where creative ideas—and the broad spectrum of individuals who participate in those ideas—may flourish. Ultimately, this reframing of creativity has the potential to significantly shift thinking about pedagogy and instructional design, just as it may lead to new ways of thinking about how creativity can be understood and assessed in a variety of educational settings.

Notes

1. See Jal Mehta, "Deeper Learning has a Race Problem," *Education Week's Blog* (June 20, 2014). Retrieved from http://blogs.edweek.org/edweek/learning_deeply/2014/06/deeper_learning_has_a_race_problem.html
2. Ibid., para 2.
3. See Hanchett Hanson, *Worldmaking: Psychology and the Ideology of Creativity*, p. 211 (New York: Palgrave Macmillan, 2015), p. 211.
4. See Angela L. Duckworth, Christopher Peterson, Michael D. Matthews, & Dennis R. Kelly, "Grit: Perseverance and Passion for Long-term Goals," *Journal of Personality and Social Psychology*, 96, no. 6 (2007): 1087–1101.
5. See Hanchett Hanson, *Worldmaking*, p. 212.
6. See Michel Foucault, *Ethics, Subjectivity, and Truth, Essential Works of Foucault 1954–1984*, Paul Rabinow, ed. (New York: The New Press, 1997).
7. See Lisa D. Delpit, "The Silenced Dialogue: Power and Pedagogy in Educating other People's Children," *Harvard Educational Review* (1988), 58, no. 3 (1988): 280–298.
8. Ibid., p. 282.
9. Ibid., p. 283.
10. See Pierre Bourdieu and Jean-Claude Passeron, *Reproduction in Education, Society, and Culture* (Beverly Hills, CA: Sage, 1977).
11. Ibid., p. 11.
12. Ibid., p. 10. Note here that Bourdieu and Passeron's use of the word "arbitrary" is meant to suggest that the norms of a culture (symbolic system) are neither based on individual decisions nor on universal principles: "*The selection of meanings which objectively defines a group's or a class's culture as a symbolic system is* arbitrary *insofar as the structure and functions of that culture cannot be deduced from any universal principle, whether physical, biological or spiritual, not being linked by any sort of internal relation to the 'nature of things' or any 'human nature'*" p. 8 (emphasis in original).
13. Ibid., p. 5 (emphasis in original).
14. See Mehta, "Deeper Learning has a Race Problem."
15. For example, here in the United States we must consider the rise and fall of initiatives such as No Child Left Behind and the Common Core State Standards, amongst other initiatives, such as the charter school movement and the Partnership for 21st Century Skills, etc.
16. See Delpit, "The Silenced Dialogue," especially footnote 1 on p. 282.
17. For Feist's complete discussion of the personality traits of artists and scientists, see Gregory J. Feist, "The Influence of Personality on Artistic and Scientific Creativity," in *The Handbook of Creativity*, pp. 273–296, R. J. Sternberg, ed. (New York: Cambridge University Press, 1999).
18. Ibid., p. 290.
19. See Mehta, "Deeper Learning has a Race Problem," para 6.
20. See Delpit, "The Silenced Dialogue," p. 286.
21. Ibid., p. 282.

22. The reference to Howard Gruber and Sara Davis's essay "Inching Our Way Up Mt. Olympus" is playfully referenced here with respect for the concepts they present in this text. See Howard E. Gruber & Sara N. Davis, "Inching our Way up Mount Olympus: The Evolving Systems Approach to Creative Thinking," in *The Nature of Creativity*, ed. Robert J. Sternberg (New York: Cambridge University Press, 1988), and Gruber & Wallace, "The Case Study Method" in *Handbook of Creativity*, ed. Robert J. Sternberg (New York: Cambridge University Press, 1999).
23. See Alan H. Scheonfeld, "What's All the Fuss About Metacognition?" in *Cognitive Science and Mathematics Education*, A. H. Schoenfeld, ed. pp. 189–215 (Hillsdale, NJ: Lawrence Erlbaum Associates, 1987). As Schoenfled has discussed in terms of mathematics education, some students come to believe that "only geniuses are capable of discovering mathematics . . . and students who believe that mathematical understanding is simply beyond ordinary mortals like themselves, become passive consumers of mathematics, accepting and memorizing what is handed to them without attempting to make sense of it on their own" p. 198.
24. See Bourdieu and Passeron, *Reproduction in Education, Society, and Culture*, p. 10.
25. See Mehta, "Deeper Learning has a Race Problem."
26. See Ronald A. Heifetz, *Leadership without Easy Answers* (Cambridge, MA: Belknap Press/Harvard University Press, 1994).

Chapter 5

Making Creativity Visible
Introducing the Biography
of an Idea Methodology

The preceding chapters of this book make a theoretical case for the importance of reframing creativity as a distributed and participatory process, especially within the educational sphere. But, as noted in Chapter 1, the tractor beams of our individualistic culture are strong. Considering all of the cultural hype around creative geniuses that has long structured our common understandings of what it means to be an innovator and achieve greatness, it is no surprise that, from time to time, we may cast doubt on a social theory of creativity. The chapters ahead aim to illustrate and provide support for such a theory. To do so, it is important to first understand how creativity researchers have pursued the study of creative individuals from a more traditional, individual-based perspective—and then to provide an alternative, though similar, approach to studying creativity from a more distributed and participatory perspective.

For decades, creativity researchers have employed the biographical method as a means to tell the story of individuals who are often heralded as geniuses for their feats of greatness. Researchers have meticulously combed through journals, interviewed friends, relatives, and rivals, scrutinized artifacts, visited childhood homes, and pored over early sketches and doodles to painstakingly construct the biographies of our most celebrated inventors and innovators. What these researchers are in search of is the perfect combination of nature and nurture that has the capacity to yield creative genius. Of course, what they find is that—despite claims made about personality traits, neurological structures, social economic status, or even psychosis and mental illness—there is no one type of creative individual. Instead, the biographies of so-called creative individuals are as unique and diverse as the ideas those individuals are known for.[1] Without consistency across investigations, applying the biographical approach to the study of creative individuals does little more than provide us with some very interesting life histories—about some very interesting people. Nonetheless, the biographical method should not be entirely discarded as a valid research tool. It just needs a change in focus.

A Change in Focus, a Change of Locus

From a traditional perspective, the locus of creativity is thought to lie within the individual. From a more systems-based perspective, this same concept becomes socially rearranged and literally redistributed: individuals enact their agency throughout the creative idea development process, but no one individual or group has ownership over any one creative idea. This subtle but important shift moves away from a possessive view of creativity (i.e., creativity is something one either *is* or *has*), to a more participatory view (i.e., creativity is something one participates in, along with others).

In order to make this epistemological change in perspective, the concept of creativity must experience a change of address: creativity must be relocated from the neighborhood of the individual self, to a more social space. This remix of logic concerning the locus of creativity is, understandably, not an easy transition to make. As with any big move, it is helpful to have a vehicle to assist with this process. Here, a subtle tweak in methodology is meant to act as an epistemological moving van for creativity.

Retelling the Story of Creativity as the Biography of an Idea

Whether in the physical sciences, the social sciences, or the arts, understanding the pathway towards innovation almost always involves an element of storytelling. In order to truly understand surrealism, the civil rights movement, or heliocentrism, each of these concepts must be situated within a broader narrative that includes the various characters and contextual factors that influenced the development of each of these ideas. Sure, one can tell the story of Salvador Dali, Dr. Martin Luther King, Jr., and Nicolaus Copernicus, but just telling the stories of these individuals does not fully capture the greater narratives associated with surrealism, the civil rights movement, and the astronomical model that describes how the earth and the planets revolve around the sun. Nonetheless, for decades, many creativity researchers have aimed to do just that—tell the story of the individuals associated with creativity, rather than tell the story of creative ideas themselves.

The argument to be made here is for the reframing of creativity as the biography of an idea. Instead of constructing the stories—or biographies—of supposedly creative individuals, what might we stand to gain if we constructed the biographies of the ideas those individuals have become most known for? At its heart, this is a methodological question—a question that asks us to rethink the way we investigate and understand creativity.

Telling the biography of an idea is not an entirely novel concept. For nearly a century the study of the history of ideas has been a thriving branch of intellectual history, largely supported by scholars such as Isaiah Berlin and Arthur Lovejoy who have each been highly regarded for their work in this domain. From a different perspective, the public relations pioneer Edward L. Bernays used the title *Biography of an Idea* for his 1965 memoir, which outlined his experiences developing new approaches towards shaping public opinion throughout the first half of the twentieth century.[2]

In terms of creativity studies, reframing creativity as the biography of an idea combines social sciences approaches to the case study and biographical methods with narrative storytelling to detail how creative ideas emerge, with an emphasis placed on the social factors and chain of events that lead to invention and innovation. As discussed in Chapter 2, an idea may be understood as an ever-evolving conceptual throughline that takes shape over time. The biography of an idea, then, is the story of an idea's development as it wends its way in the world. As suggested above, one can use the biography of an idea methodology to tell the story of domain changing concepts such as surrealism, the civil rights movement, and heliocentrism, but one can also use the biography of an idea methodology to understand the work of young people in the creative classroom—as Chapters 6 and 7 will do. Whether at the domain changing level of invention and innovation (Big C creativity) or at the local level of discovery that happens on a regular basis in the creative classroom (little c creativity), it is not implausible to suggest that any feat of invention or innovation, no matter how solitary it may seem, can be retold as the biography of a socially distributed idea.

In an effort to make visible the socially distributed nature of creativity, this chapter presents the biographies of three ideas: the special theory of relativity, Grunge rock, and Hip Hop. The first two idea biographies are meant to highlight the author function that has been ascribed to key innovators associated with each idea, namely Albert Einstein and Kurt Cobain, and then to show how each of these ideas involved the participation of far more actors than these two individuals alone. The third idea biography takes a different approach, and instead emphasizes how the cultural phenomenon of hip hop is naturally understood as a distributed construct, despite there being many pioneers associated with its long history. While entire books can be written to describe the biography of each of these ideas in careful detail, due to restrictions of space, the narratives presented herein serve as mere sketches.

The Biography of Albert Einstein Retold as the Biography of the Special Theory of Relativity

When introducing the concept of participatory creativity to an audience, I have become accustomed to the idea that there will likely be at least one person in every crowd whom I can tell, based on the furrowed expression on his or her face, is just not buying it. To both honor and address this skepticism, I have found it helpful to use the biography of an idea approach to reconsider the creativity ascribed to one of the most widely known icons—if not the very poster child—of creative genius: Albert Einstein.

Numerous articles and books have been written about Albert Einstein, the physicist known for his theories of motion and gravity referred to respectively as the special and general theories of relativity. Many of the texts devoted to Einstein situate his scientific discoveries within a biographical narrative, while also framing the Nobel laureate as being one of the greatest minds of our time.

Simply put, in many narratives, the story of Albert Einstein is the story of a creative genius.

But what might be the benefit of retelling the story of Albert Einstein as the story of one of his most prominent discoveries? More specifically, what if we retold the biography of Albert Einstein as the biography of the special theory of relativity? If we did that, we would find that Einstein indeed played a key role in the development of the special theory of relativity, but that many other actors played a role in the development of this breakthrough in scientific understanding as well.

Retelling the biography of a creative individual as the biography of a historical creative idea may seem like a daunting task at first, but after digging into a few texts, the task at hand may start to come into view. It is helpful to start with a central text, and then to support the development of the biography of an idea with other texts. In many instances, those who have written biographies of creative individuals have already done much of this work, their inquiries just require some reframing. Here, Gardner's case study of Einstein in his book, *Creating Minds: An Anatomy of Creativity Seen through the Lives of Freud, Einstein, Picasso, Stravinsky, Eliot, Graham, and Gandhi* serves as an excellent place to start.[3]

Considering his focus on the individual as his unit of analysis, it is not surprising that Gardner's chapter on Einstein reads like the biography of a creative individual, but with a little effort the first half of this chapter can readily be reimagined as the biography of a creative idea, namely, the special theory of relativity: the theory which argues that all motion is relative to a reference point, that space and time are relative (as opposed to absolute concepts), and that no speed shall exceed the speed of light.

Quite logically, Gardner tells the story of Einstein in chronological order. Beginning with Einstein's early years in Munich, Germany, walking the reader through the young scientist's initial struggles with the rigors of German education, his flourishing at a progressive school in Aarau, Switzerland, his time spent at the Zurich Polytechnic Institute, and later to his job as a patent officer in Bern, Switzerland. Along the way, Gardner introduces his readers to a series of individuals and events that helped shape the young Einstein's thinking.

Early on in the story a compass given to him by his father captures Einstein's attention and stirs his curiosity. Later in the story a medical student by the name of Max Talmey who had regularly boarded with Einstein's family introduced Einstein to several scientific texts, including "popular books on force and matter," which helped equip Einstein with a scientific lens on the world—and established Talmey as one of the earliest contributors to the developing scientist's knowledge base.[4] Frustrated with his physics classes at Zurich Polytechnic Institute, Gardner noted that Einstein began to educate himself by reading the work of James Clark Maxwell, Heinrich Hertz, Hendrik A. Lorentz, Ludwig Boltzmann, Gustav Kirchoff, and Jules-Henri Poincaré. But, as Gardner explained, at this stage in his thinking, Einstein was perhaps most influenced by the work of August Föppl, a relatively unknown physicist. "Föppl helped Einstein to see that mechanics is a part of physics, and that an exploration of these topics extends to philosophical and epistemological questions that cannot be ignored," noted Gardner. "Einstein's classic paper of 1905, in which he laid out his principle of relativity, echoes much of the conceptual framework and even one of the thought experiments introduced by Föppl."[5]

Following this initial set up, Gardner spent seven pages describing the pre-development of the special theory of relativity in terms of the various scientists and mathematicians that preceded (and ultimately influenced) Einstein's thinking—showing the varied cast of characters who had contributed to the evolving scientific theories of motion and gravity long before Einstein came into the mix. Gardner began with a discussion of mechanistic physics conceived by Galileo and Newton, in particular focusing on Newton's concept of absolute motion, absolute time, and absolute space as foundational principles. Gardner then moved on to a discussion of Michael Faraday's principles of electromagnetic induction and James Clark Maxwell's mathematics, which "linked the theories of electricity and magnetism with the wave theory of light" and later led Maxwell to reject Newton's concepts of absolute space and time, "all our knowledge, both of time and space, is essentially relative,"[6] Maxwell declared.

As per Gardner's account, Einstein viewed Maxwell as a revolutionary and was deeply inspired by his work. Maxwell's theories problematized the use of mechanics as the foundation of physics, and later work by Heinrich Hertz and Ernst Mach further led Einstein to question the use of mechanics to explain physical phenomena. Like Maxwell before him, Mach also rejected Newtonian mechanics and argued that "all masses and all velocities, and consequently all forces, are relative."[7] Towards the end of the nineteenth century, the physicist Henrik A. Lorentz and the mathematician Jules-Henri Poincaré increasingly challenged Newtonian mechanics, and further set the stage for Einstein's special theory of relativity. According to Gardner's account, in 1898 "Poincaré had coined the phrase 'principle of relativity' to stand for science's failure to determine the earth's absolute motion."[8] Poincaré additionally suggested that physics would need to create a "new mechanics," much in the manner that Einstein would put forth in his 1905 paper "On the Electrodynamics of Moving Bodies."

Written from this perspective, Einstein's special theory of relativity was not a stroke of genius that came out of the blue but rather part of a greater arc of scientific theory, which consisted of many actors, each building upon the contributions that had been added before them. Each of these actors set the stage for Einstein to add his contributions to their previous thinking. In this way, Einstein can be considered more of a primary actor in the development of the special theory of relativity, rather than a solo performer guided by his own genius.

Beyond situating the special theory of relativity within a greater arc of scientific theory building, Gardner noted that when Einstein was writing the paper that launched the special theory of relativity in 1905, he received a great deal of intellectual and affective support from a variety of other individuals whom he knew intimately well.

Einstein regularly hosted scholarly discussions for a group of friends who referred to themselves as the Olympia Academy. Using a format of social discussion not unlike a contemporary book club, the Olympiads regularly met at Einstein's apartment to debate physics, philosophy, and mathematics, including the works of many of the theorists noted above, as well as scholars in other domains. In addition to their vibrant debate sessions, the group "would hike, camp, swim, and then converse feverishly as they made their way home."[9] Beyond the lively discussions he enjoyed with his Olympiad colleagues, Einstein further utilized the group as a testing ground for his nascent ideas—and his thinking advanced a great deal as a result of the feedback he received from this trusted cohort of friends. The intellectual development of Einstein's contributions to science were also supported by Michelangelo Besso, "a young engineering colleague with whom [Einstein] had constant discussions about his evolving ideas."[10] As Gardner has noted, in his 1905 paper Einstein explicitly thanked Besso for a particular conversation that prompted his thinking on the special theory of relativity. Einstein was also both cognitively and affectively supported by his wife Mileva Maric, a fellow physicist whom he met while they were both students at the Zurich Polytechnic Institute. As per Gardner's case study analysis, it is suggested that Maric may have contributed more than has been previously thought to the development of some of Einstein's most celebrated ideas.[11]

As this recounting of Gardner's case study of Albert Einstein as one of the primary creative minds of the modern era suggests, individual creativity is not so individual so long as one focuses on the idea as the locus of creativity, and is keenly aware of the various actors who contribute to the development of that idea along the way. Of course, it would be inappropriate to entirely remove Albert Einstein from the development of the special theory of relativity, but it would also not be appropriate to singularly assign him with author function for the idea, considering all of the many other actors who likewise contributed to its development. What can be done, then, is to discuss the unique *role* Einstein played in the development of the special theory of relativity. Through his analysis of Einstein as a creating mind of the modern era, Gardner's case study does this work as well.

Gardner described Einstein's thinking in multiple ways—some of which were explicit, and others that were more implicitly suggested. For example, Gardner explicitly referred to Einstein as the "perennial child" and more implicitly as a synthesizer of information. As Gardner noted, at the time that Einstein wrote his 1905 paper introducing the special theory of relativity, he was mature in his thinking, but not entrenched in any one particular school of thought. Instead, Einstein saw scientific problems through the fresh eyes of a child and was able to find a pathway beyond Newtonian mechanics in a manner that other theorists who had come before him could not quite yet see. Gardner further identified Einstein's "object-centered mind," his ability to concentrate, and visualize problems in multiple ways, and the interpersonal relationships he developed with friends and colleagues he would look to for support for many years as being elemental to his work. Gardner's synthesis of Einstein does not offer one way that the physicist participated in the development of the creative ideas he is known for, but many ways. Each describes a different role that Einstein played in the idea development process, and those multiple roles may be combined to form a complex profile of participation that was unique to Einstein and particularly suited to the work that he engaged in during the early part of the twentieth century.

By retelling the biography of Albert Einstein as the biography of the special theory of relativity, it is possible to see the broad scope of actors who contribute to the development of creative ideas. In this case, at any given time the contributing stakeholder group that participated in the development of the special theory of relativity certainly included Einstein, but also included the Olympiads, a variety of close friends, colleagues, and acquaintances, a boarder in the young Einstein's home, Einstein's wife Mileva, and a diverse cohort of scientific and mathematical thinkers whose scholarship stretched across two centuries.

The Biography of Kurt Cobain Retold as the Biography of Grunge Rock

A more contemporary retelling of the biography of a creative individual as the biography of a creative idea lies in the story of Kurt Cobain. From the late 1980s through to his suicide at the age of 27 in 1994, supported by bass player Krist Novoselic and drummer Dave Grohl, Kurt Cobain was the frontman, guitarist, and lead singer of the band Nirvana. Many music critics have asserted that, at the time of his death, Cobain was arguably the most famous rock star in the world. Cobain's fame and influence continued to spread beyond his death and the impact his work has had on alternative music and popular culture can still be felt today.

Retelling the biography of Kurt Cobain as the biography of an idea might seem like a tricky undertaking at first. As with many artists, one must ask what is the creative *idea* that Kurt Cobain is best known for? Is Nirvana's song "Smells Like Teen Spirit," the idea Cobain is most known for? Well, certainly Cobain is known for "Smells Like Teen Spirit," but according to the definition of an idea as presented above—an ever-evolving conceptual throughline that is embodied through a succession of innovative products—then "Smells Like Teen Spirit" is best understood as a creative product that is part of the process of greater idea development. Then perhaps Nirvana's 1991 diamond certified album *Nevermind* is the idea? Here, too, the *Nevermind* album is more of a product of the idea development process, and not the idea itself. An idea is bigger than the individual products that come together to contribute to its development. Products are artifacts of an idea as it takes shape over time. Here, both "Smells Like Teen Spirit" and Nirvana's breakthrough album *Nevermind* act as products of the greater idea of Grunge Rock—the musical genre that came to be associated with Nirvana and the 1990s' Seattle-based alternative rock scene.

It has been widely argued that Grunge Rock was responsible for bringing an alternative rock sound to popular music, and a new edge to popular culture. "The phenomenon of Grunge had become a monster that overtook everything in its path, including Kurt Cobain. It could not be corralled,"[12] wrote Charles R. Cross, a Kurt Cobain biographer and rock journalist who experienced the emergence of Grunge Rock first hand—and whose many books about Cobain and Nirvana serve well as jumping off points for retelling the biography of Kurt Cobain as the biography of the Grunge idea.

Before going further however, it is important to pause here to acknowledge that neither Kurt Cobain, nor many of the lead players of the Grunge Rock movement, originally subscribed to this label that was largely placed upon them by outside influencers. In fact, many would suggest that Grunge Rock was not a movement at all, because the variety of bands and personalities who were said to comprise this movement were so diverse, and that no particular *scene* was in place to drive the movement forward.[13] While Grunge may have been rejected as a movement by the very people who were said to be making it happen, the *idea* of Grunge Rock as a phenomenon was strongly developed by the media and the genre's growing fan base. Nonetheless, the actors who contributed to the Grunge phenomenon were indeed in pursuit of a new sound. Each successive product that bands like Nirvana contributed to the emergent genre (e.g., a song, an album, a live performance, etc.) further contributed to the pursuit of that new sound—giving shape to the Grunge idea. As a result, even though many of the musicians, DJs, and rock journalists on the ground in Seattle dismissed the Grunge Rock label at the time, to the rest of the world, Grunge was very real—and Cobain was viewed by the press as being the leader of this emergent movement or, as *Time* magazine put it, Cobain was "the John Lennon of the swinging Northwest."[14] "Kurt was the biggest star of Grunge," Cross has written, "and in many ways its unwilling poster boy."[15] In other words, Kurt Cobain was in large part assigned author function for the Grunge idea.

Though Kurt Cobain may have been seen by the press—and by many adoring fans—as the leading icon of Grunge Rock, he was certainly not the only person contributing to the movement. In Cross's 2014 biography *Here We Are Now*, a reflection on the two decades that had passed since Cobain's suicide, through the process of addressing the enduring impact of Kurt Cobain, Cross also introduced a variety of actors who, along with Cobain, participated in the development of the Grunge idea.

To set the scene for Grunge Rock, it is important to remember what mainstream rock music was like in the 1980s and early 1990s. During this time, "hair bands" were selling out stadiums, topping the charts, and their videos could be seen all over MTV. As Cross wrote,

Rock in the eighties had gone in a highly formulaic direction, dominated by soft rock ballads in which style was often put before substance. Almost every hit eighties song was about girls, cars, romance, heartbreak, and partying. . . . Mainstream rock was so bad in the eighties and early nineties that Nirvana enjoyed what was fortuitous timing: they had something to rebel against.[16]

Of course, it was not just Nirvana that had something to rebel against, so too did their Grunge rock compatriots. And, as Cross has noted, Seattle was just the place for a rebellion to happen. As Cross has described, the Seattle of the late 1980s and early 1990s was a blue collar, working class, contemplative town ripe for emerging musicians who rehearsed in basements and garages in between their shifts as baristas or book store clerks. Different from other thriving music cities, Seattle did not have a vibrant club scene at the time. When bands did play at one of the few local clubs, attendance was usually thin, and those who were in the crowd were most often members of other bands. "A tribe mentality existed that was insular but also nurturing," Cross wrote.[17]

Oddly enough, it was this very lack of opportunities for bands to play live performances that equipped so many of them for success in the early 1990s. "Since bands couldn't make money playing live, they retreated to basements to rehearse and imagined that recording a single or an album would be their ticket to stardom," Cross wrote. "It was the very fact that there was no chance of success and riches from playing live that forced these groups to aim higher, to go straight to making a record."[18]

In addition to being an authority on Nirvana and Kurt Cobain (he has written four books about the band and its tortured frontman), Cross was the editor of a popular Seattle-based music magazine called *The Rocket* throughout the rise of the Grunge movement. Cross conceded that the word "grunge" had been used as an adjective to describe a certain style of music many times before, but also offered a Seattle-specific description of the sound, how it was made, and when it first came into use to describe the work of local bands:

The word "grunge" first appeared in *The Rocket* in the late eighties as an adjective to describe a certain sonic musical style, a raw and unpolished sound with distortion, but usually without any other added studio effects. Grunge, pre-capitalization, was almost always applied to a Sub Pop band, and almost always to a band produced by Jack Endino . . . it meant a mix of garage rock and slowed-down punk. Sub Pop did most of their albums at a low-rent studio named Reciprocal. That studio's acoustics, combined with Endino's production aesthetics, created true capital-G Grunge albums by bands like Mudhoney, Tad, Blood Circus, and a dozen other groups who have now been lost to history.[19]

In this quote Cross outlined the triumvirate of actors (none of whom are Kurt Cobain) who contributed to the development of the quintessential Grunge sound in important ways. The Sub Pop independent record label, the aesthetic sensibilities of producer Jack Endino, and the acoustic qualities of the Reciprocal studio (not to mention all of the bands who were recorded in this space) converged to form the sound that typified the sonic qualities of Grunge Rock.

Whereas the Grunge sound was a response to the saccharine soft metal ballads of the 1980s, it was also an extension of the roar of Punk Rock that first sparked up in the UK during the late 1970s—and quickly carried over to the US. Punk purists will argue that the real *fuck-this-and-fuck-that* of Punk only lasted two years,[20] but many bands on both sides of the Atlantic—as well as in Australia—carried the Punk sound and aesthetic forward. By the late 1980s Punk had passed its prime in the UK, and British fans and rock journalists were hungry for the next big thing. As rock journalist Simon Reynolds has noted, "it's often implied that nothing real happened between punk and grunge, between *Never Mind the Bollocks* and *Nevermind*."[21] At this time, UK fans and rock critics began to pick up on the new sound emanating from the Northwest United States. It was here that Sub Pop bands were beginning to garner attention and where the Grunge label began to stick. As Cross has noted, "In a British newspaper, Mark Arm [of Mudhoney] described the streets of Seattle being 'paved with grunge.' Almost over night, 'grunge' became 'Grunge' as the British music press started using the name in headlines."[22]

In that same year, Nirvana's first album *Bleach* was produced under the ideal Grunge Rock conditions. It was released under the Sub Pop label and engineered by Jack Endino at Reciprocal. Suffice it to say, *Bleach* was the band's most Grunge sounding album. Overall though, Nirvana was not the grungiest of the Grunge. While some of Nirvana's earlier recordings can be said to adhere to the sonic aesthetics of Grunge, Nirvana also had a pop sound, influenced by Cobain's interest in popular bands like the Beatles. It was this subtle pop aesthetic that made the band's music edgy enough to feel raw and anti-mainstream, but still catchy enough to be attractive to a larger audience.

It would be two years later, in the fall of 1991, when Nirvana would explode onto the music scene. After leaving the indie Sub Pop record label and signing with the major record label, DGC/Geffen Records, Nirvana recorded their second album *Nevermind* in California. When "Smells Like Teen Spirit," the first single from the album, was released, with the support of DJs at a variety of alternative radio stations around the country, the band and its frontman were rocketed into stardom. Before long, Nirvana's "Smells Like Teen Spirit" video was all over MTV, the band's songs were being played on more and more radio stations, and the Northwest trio would soon be packing stadiums throughout the US with screaming fans—just like the "big hair" soft metal bands that had come before them.

Nevermind and the album's lead single "Smells Like Teen Spirit" have been heralded by many as being amongst the best of all time. *Rolling Stone* has declared *Nevermind* the number one album of the 1990s or, in their words, "the album that guaranteed the nineties would not suck."[23] "Smells Like Teen

Spirit," on its own, has been referred to as the anthem for a generation. And while Cobain played a chief role in composing both "Smells Like Teen Spirit" and the other eleven tracks on the original studio album, these products of the Grunge idea came about as the result of several other participants. Because Cobain had not fully worked out the song, the iconic "Smells Like Teen Spirit" is the only track on *Nevermind* that lists bandmates Grohl and Novoselic as co-authors. Furthermore, producer Butch Vig played a significant role in developing the sonic shape of the song. Musically, Cobain has noted that "Smells Like Teen Spirit" was an attempt to emulate the sound of the Pixies, a popular alternative rock band that paired soft verses with heavy choruses in much the same way that "Smells Like Teen Spirit" was structured.[24] Interestingly, the very name of the song "Smells Like Teen Spirit" was inspired by a phrase spray-painted on Cobain's bedroom wall by Kathleen Hanna, then frontwoman of the punk-inspired riot grrrl band Bikini Kill. Hanna's graffitied "Kurt Smells Like Teen Spirit" message was mistaken by Cobain to be a reference to anarchism and punk angst—themes that resonate throughout the lyrics of the song. In reality, Hanna was mocking Cobain, saying he smelled like Teen Spirit—which was a brand of deodorant his then girlfriend Tobi Vail (also of Bikini Kill) wore at the time.[25] Much to the chagrin of an unknowing Kurt Cobain, "Smells Like Teen Spirit" not only became the anthem for a generation—it also served as the best free advertising a deodorant company had ever known.[26]

While copies of *Nevermind* continued to sell worldwide, drawing inter-national attention to the Seattle music scene, yet another actor entered into the mix of the biography of the Grunge Rock idea. During the late summer of 1992 the movie *Singles* was released. Directed by Cameron Crowe, the romantic comedy was a riff on life as a twenty-something in Grunge-era Seattle. "The film was a worldwide success, spawned a hit soundtrack, and forever wedded Seattle to Grunge."[27] In one of the leading roles, Matt Dillon played the character Cliff Poncier, the frontman for the fictitious band Citizen Dick; Poncier was also a coffee shop attendant and a flower delivery guy. In the film, Poncier's long hair, worn shirts, and Doc Marten boots were meant to epitomize the Grunge aesthetic.[28] Beyond the caricature played by Dillon, Crowe was keen to cast several musicians who were actual members of the Seattle music scene. Among them, Chris Cornell from Soundgarden and Eddie Vedder from Pearl Jam. "By the time the movie came out," Cross wrote, "they had become major stars."[29] In fact, two years later Nirvana, Soundgarden, Pearl Jam, and fellow Seattle-area band Alice in Chains would all have chart-topping albums.

Though the Seattle-based Grunge scene would continue to rock for a number of years, like Punk before it, Grunge as a musical genre soon petered out—though its impact continued to affect alternative rock music and popular culture for decades to come. Interestingly, beyond the domain of music, one of the ways in which the idea of Grunge has continued to thrive is within the domain of fashion. As noted above, Matt Dillon's portrayal of Cliff Poncier in the movie *Singles* provided a foundation upon which the Grunge aesthetic has been built. And though Cobain can never be said to exactly fit this aesthetic, the tattered sweaters, flannels, and distressed jeans he wore have been replicated through the "anti-aesthetic" of Grunge couture—which Cobain has been granted author function for as well.[30] As Cross has noted, Cobain's look was based on necessity, an initial lack of money, and a minimal wardrobe that was repeated so often it was referred to as "the Kurt Cobain uniform, or, in a larger framework, the Grunge look."[31] Before long, designers began to capitalize on the Grunge aesthetic—selling distressed flannels and jeans (like the ones Cobain bought in thrift shops) for hundreds if not thousands of dollars each.[32] While contemporary alternative rock bands, and even Hip Hop artists have referenced Grunge, and in particular the work of Nirvana and Kurt Cobain, as influencers of their work, post-Nirvana, the aesthetic of Grunge has largely been perpetuated by designers aiming to keep the unkempt spirit of punk-infused angst in their apparel lines.

Though the temptation to deify Cobain as a tortured god of rock is strong, the goal for this retelling of the biography of Kurt Cobain as the biography of the Grunge Rock idea has been to shed light on the many actors who contributed to the Seattle sound and style of the early 1990s, while also stressing the socially distributed nature of a domain changing creative idea, in this case, the idea of Grunge Rock. Cobain was certainly amongst the stakeholders who contributed to the development of the Grunge Rock idea, but so too were a host of other individuals, including hundreds of musicians, rock journalists, producers, record company executives, designers, actors, filmmakers, friends, lovers, family members, and fans. That Grunge took on so many different meanings for so many different people may complicate it as a rock genre and cultural movement, but this diversity and range of interpretations are also what gave—and still give—Grunge its strength and cohesion as a social throughline, as an ever-evolving creative idea.

Certainly, one can also tell the story of Kurt Cobain the individual artist— but there too one will find a host of actors who have contributed to him becoming the man whom rock journalists and fans have come to praise so frequently and so well.[33] For example, as Cross and other biographers have indicated, Cobain came from a musical family, having both an aunt and an uncle who were semi-established musicians; he took drum lessons at an early age, began to play guitar when he was only fourteen years old, and had exposure to extensive record collections. Growing up as a young man, he hung out with a musical crowd, including members of the Melvins and a host of others. Dozens of members of his community, especially his band mates Dave Grohl and Krist Novoselic and his wife Courtney Love served as both cognitive and affective supports—many playing strong roles in influencing his musical sensibilities, while also contributing to the idea of Grunge Rock in their own ways, as well.

Ultimately, the idea of Grunge Rock was as much about an attitude, a worldview, a way of making meaning of one's experiences as it was about music, or fashion, or tragic rock deities. Grunge was a rebellion against the sentimentality of the 1980s, a return to the angst of Punk Rock, and an embrace of the apathy that legions of latch-key-kid Generation Xers had experienced as they groped their way through the haze of post-Baby Boomer culture. Grunge was an expression of frustration, but at the same time, it wanted to dance. And perhaps that is what made the idea of Grunge so attractive—and so influential—for so many young people. As a movement, Grunge was heavy, it never really promised to be hopeful, but it was often full of life. The same could be said about Kurt Cobain—the man who was so frequently given author function for the idea of Grunge, both then and now.

As the retelling of the biographies of Albert Einstein and Kurt Cobain as the biographies of the ideas they are most known for suggest, even narratives that support the seemingly individual genius of some of Western culture's most celebrated innovators can be reframed as stories that tell a much more socially distributed tale. But not every creative idea needs to be teased out of a dominant personal history. There are some ideas that are naturally understood as social phenomena, and their stories are often told in just such a way.

Hip Hop: The Emergence of a Collective Culture

> Every moment of major social change requires a collective leap of imagination. Political transformation must be accompanied not just by spontaneous and organized expressions of unrest and risk, but by an explosion of mass creativity.[34]
>
> Jeff Chang

Grunge Rock came howling out of the Northwest in a tumbling roar of feedback and tattered flannel, rattled Western culture and then, like Punk Rock before it, it was gone. Traces of Grunge and Punk continue to influence contemporary pop culture, and many diehards still live by the tenets of the Grunge and Punk movements but, for the most part, while there are still nuances to add (and revivals to be had), many will argue that the stories of the original Grunge and Punk epochs have largely been told.

The biography of an idea methodology is just as much an exploration of history and culture as it is of invention and innovation. From a historical and cultural perspective, it is possible to trace the biography of an idea far back into time, and widely through many cultural associations. But every idea has an apex moment when it is most ripe with change. For Punk Rock, that moment of time was the mid- to late-1970s and for Grunge Rock, the late-1980s and early-1990s. There are, however, certain creative ideas that experience much longer periods of cultural richness, of constant energy supported by rampant change. One such creative idea with a storied history, a vibrant present, and a promising future is the cultural phenomenon of Hip Hop.

Recounting the history of Hip Hop as the biography of an idea is a different task from either Grunge Rock or even the special theory of relativity. Different because, though there are indeed many luminaries who have achieved greatness throughout the long arc of Hip Hop's development as a cultural phenomenon, no one individual can be ascribed author function for Hip Hop in quite the same way that Kurt Cobain and Albert Einstein have been in the past. Without a doubt there have been many *pioneers* that have contributed to the evolution of Hip Hop—but no one primary contributor. This makes logical sense; with a cultural idea as broad and constantly changing as Hip Hop, there could not possibly be one person to point to as the author of it all. And while the diversity and range of contributors associated with Hip Hop make it an excellent subject to explore as a creative idea, the breadth of Hip Hop as a cultural phenomenon also makes it a daunting topic to study—one that will only briefly be touched upon here.

Fortunately, many others have studied the history of Hip Hop. One powerful text that serves as a starting point for understanding the evolution of Hip Hop as the biography of an idea is Jeff Chang's 2005 text *Can't Stop Won't Stop: A History of the Hip Hop Generation*.[35] Chang's recount of the history of Hip Hop is deep. In it a wide variety of characters play a role in the development of the Hip Hop idea—not just the musicians, MCs, dancers, DJs, and artists one would expect, but also filmmakers, politicians, gang members, community organizers and activists, poets, producers, publishers, and police—even baseball players play a role.

The story of Hip Hop is the story of various members of a community coming together, building on the work of one another, always in pursuit of developing something new. By its very nature, Hip Hop is a socially distributed phenomenon originally consisting of four elements: DJing, MCing, b-boying/b-girling, and graffiti writing. While each of these four pillars of participation has its own history, what holds them all together is the very idea of Hip Hop. What Chang has described as a "shared . . . revolutionary aesthetic . . . about unleashing youth style as an expression of the soul."[36]

The evolution of Hip Hop has been, by all means, "a collective leap of imagination" and "an explosion of mass creativity"[38] that has required the contributions of multiple actors each uniquely contributing to the idea of Hip Hop over time. But, as Chang has noted, there are still creation myths within that point to particular pioneers as being the originators of Hip Hop. In Chang's narrative, "the three kings, the trinity of hip-hop music" include DJ Kool Herc, Afrika Bambaataa, and Grandmaster Flash.

DJ Kool Herc, Afrika Bambaataa, and Grandmaster Flash were certainly pioneers of Hip Hop, but each had their own origins story, too. DJ Kool Herc (Clive Campbell) was said to be the DJ at what was perhaps the first Hip Hop performance—a back-to-school gathering hosted by his sister, Cindy Campbell, to raise money for her new school wardrobe. The event took place in the recreation room of their apartment building on Sedgwick Avenue in the Bronx on the last week of August in 1973. Herc played a mixture of dancehall, soul, and funk tracks, with an emphasis on James Brown.

Following the success of this event, DJ Kool Herc continued to DJ larger events with a massive sound system he borrowed from his father. Over time, Herc had begun to notice that the dancers at his events were waiting for certain parts of the songs he played. As Chang has written,

> The moment when the dancers really got wild was in a song's short instrumental break, when the band would drop out and the rhythm section would get elemental. . . . Herc zeroed in on the fundamental vibrating loop at the heart of the record, the break.[38]

"They always wanted to hear breaks after breaks after breaks," Herc said.[39] And so, DJ Kool Herc devised a way to mix two copies of the same record in a way that would loop the break section of a song. He called this technique the "Merry-Go-Round."[40] Through his Merry-Go-Round DJ sessions, b-boying and b-girling—dancing to the looped breaks of songs—began to emerge.

But DJ Kool Herc did not evolve his DJ style all on his own. Instead, Herc was influenced by his childhood on Jamaica where he experienced the development of Reggae and Dub culture as a young man. He was further influenced by the energy of other clubs in the Bronx and, of course, by responding to the dancers in the rec rooms, dance clubs, and outdoor spaces in front of him.

Like DJ Kool Herc, Afrika Bambaataa was also a Hip Hop pioneer known for his turntablism, but Bambaataa also brought an important sense of spirituality and a commitment to unity to Hip Hop as well. Once a warlord for the Black Spades, one of the most powerful gangs in the Bronx during the late 1960s and early 1970s, Afrika Bambaataa was known for expanding the Black Spades' turf, making them the largest gang in the city. But soon Bambaataa began to see that his talents as a gang warlord could be used to promote peace amongst the gangs. He became a boundary crosser, mixing with other gang members, walking in and out of the turf of rival gangs to establish positive relationships—and make peace.

According to Chang's narrative, Afrika Bambaataa recognized that music could be a means to bring people together, and move beyond gang tensions. And so he began apprenticing with a pair of DJs who were ex-Spades members. Before long, Afrika Bambaataa was DJing and hosting parties of his own. With all of his followers behind him, Bambaataa was always assured to have a full house. Afrika Bambaataa began to see that parties were a positive alternative to gang warfare. And so he established the Bronx River Organization, which he stressed was an organization, a family, not a gang. The Bronx River Organization later became the Organization, which helped serve as a means to promote the DJ sessions and parties Bambaataa would host. As Chang has described, soon after a life-altering trip to Africa and Europe, Afrika Bambaataa returned to the Bronx to found the first Hip Hop organization: the Zulu Nation.

As the leader of the Zulu Nation, Afrika Bambaataa became a "preacher of the gospel of the 'four elements' [of Hip Hop] DJing, MCing, b-boying and

Graffiti Writing," later adding knowledge, wisdom, and "overstanding" as a fifth element necessary to help Hip Hop achieve a greater sense of consciousness and cultural awareness.[41] Chang has referred to Afrika Bambaataa as the "Promethean firestarter of the hip-hop generation"[42] responsible for bringing a new social order to Hip Hop. As a DJ, "Bam's sound became a rhythmic analogue of his peace-making philosophy," wrote Chang. "He mixed up breaks from Grand Funk Railroad and the Monkees with Sly and James and Malcolm X speeches. He played salsa, rock, and soca with the same enthusiasm as soul and funk. He was making himself open to the good in everything."[43]

Like DJ Kool Herc, Afrika Bambaataa's background also influenced his contributions to Hip Hop. He was raised in a political household and discussions of the Black cultural and liberation movements were prominent in his Bronx home. Members of Afrika Bambaataa's family were Black nationalists and Black Muslims—their conversations informed Bambaataa's worldview—and their broad musical tastes, particularly his mother's record collection, helped shape his musical sensibilities. Aside from his family, other cultural forces contributed to Afrika Bambaataa's Hip Hop aesthetic. In particular, the 1964 movie *Zulu*, paired with his trip to Europe and Africa, informed Bambaataa's interest in community organizing—and later led to his establishment of the Zulu Nation.

As a young man growing up in the Bronx, Joseph Saddler "was less attracted to the street life than he was attracted to the broken radios in the street," wrote Chang.

> Back in his room with his screwdriver, soldering iron and insatiable curiosity, the kid who would later be named Grandmaster Flash was theorizing the turntable and mixer, pondering the presentation of the party, trying to figure out how to turn beat-making and crowd-rocking into a science.[44]

Though not equipped with the same sound system or rich record collections as DJ Kool Herc and Afrika Bambaataa, Grandmaster Flash was an innovator at the turntable, introducing new methods for cutting, scratching, and cross fading with a dramatic effect—and a large dose of showmanship. But Grandmaster Flash's music and showmanship were not everything. The burgeoning DJ was further supported by three, and then four, MCs who collectively became known as the Furious Five. Together, they rocked the parties Flash DJed, bringing energy and a new sense of style to their performances. The MCs' lyricism became frenetic and complex, and Flash's turntable style became increasingly dramatic—informed by guest appearances by others such as Grand Wizzard Theodore who, Chang has noted, invented a technique for scratching records by accident.

As a cultural phenomenon, one may argue that Hip Hop was born in the Bronx in the 1970s, heralded in by the contributions of DJ Kool Herc, Afrika Bambaataa, and Grandmaster Flash. But when considering the biography of

Hip Hop as a creative idea, the story of Hip Hop is much more complex and includes far more actors than the Herc, Bam, Flash trinity. And of course—the story of Hip Hop has gone on—and goes on—taking many different forms, and including the contributions of countless others.

From the perspective of participatory creativity, what is interesting about the cultural phenomenon of Hip Hop is its plurality of practice. Incorporating so many different genres of cultural participation (and sub-genres of cultural participation), there is no one way to engage with Hip Hop, but rather multiple ways to be a Hip Hop participant. At the same time, there is a cultural throughline that holds the many different strands of Hip Hop together, and which allows an innovation in one element of Hip Hop to influence an innovation in another element of Hip Hop. In fact, it would not be a stretch to make connections between Howard Gruber's individual-based concept of a network of enterprises, and the more socially distributed manner by which Hip Hop has likewise been established upon its own unique network of enterprises.

Hip Hop certainly has its luminaries and eminent figures, but as Chang and others have pointed out, the history of Hip Hop is not grounded in the contributions of any one individual, but rather based on the contributions of various cultural innovators over time. The continuance of Hip Hop as a healthy cultural phenomenon (and an ever-evolving creative idea) is therefore based on the health of its community. Many of the originators of Hip Hop have framed this community as a family. Like any family, Hip Hop has experienced its ups and downs, along with its conflicts of personalities. But ultimately, at its core, Hip Hop is a cultural bond that brings people together—a community where each member is encouraged to take care of the others. As DJ Kool Herc has stated, "Hip-hop is a family, so everybody has got to pitch in."[45]

The biographies of the special theory of relativity, Grunge Rock, and Hip Hop presented above emphasized the ways in which various actors contribute to the development of socially emergent ideas over time. Just as one can utilize the biography of an idea methodology to tell the stories of ideas that have deeply affected culture, so too can the biography of an idea methodology be used to describe how young people pursue invention and innovation in the creative classroom. In Chapters 6 and 7 the biography of an idea approach is used to describe how public high school students working in a Boston-based after-school program have worked together to develop socially distributed ideas at the intersection of the arts and sciences.

Notes

1. See Howard E. Gruber & Doris B. Wallace, "The Case Study Method and Evolving Systems Approach for Understanding Unique Creative People at Work," in *Handbook of Creativity*, ed. Robert J. Sternberg (New York: Cambridge University Press, 1999).
2. See Edward L. Bernays, *Biography of an Idea: Memoirs of Public Relations Counsel Edward L. Bernays* (New York: Simon and Schuster, 1965).

3. See Howard Gardner, *Creating Minds: An Anatomy of Creativity Seen through the Lives of Freud, Einstein, Picasso, Stravinsky, Eliot, Graham, and Gandhi* (New York: Basic Books, 1993).
4. Ibid., p. 91.
5. Ibid., p. 94.
6. See James Clark Maxwell quoted in Gardner, *Creating Minds*, p. 98
7. See Ernst Mach quoted in Gardner, *Creating Minds*, p. 99.
8. See Gardner, *Creating Minds*, p. 101.
9. Ibid., p. 102.
10. Ibid., p. 102.
11. Ibid., pp. 102–103.
12. See Charles R. Cross, *Here We Are Now: The Lasting Impact of Kurt Cobain* (New York: HarperCollins, 2014), p. 46.
13. Ibid.
14. See Bruce Handy, "MUSIC: Never Mind," *Time* (April 18, 1994). Retrieved from http://content.time.com/time/magazine/article/0,9171,980562,00.html
15. See Cross, *Here We Are Now*, p. 67.
16. Ibid., pp. 24–25.
17. Ibid., p. 116.
18. Ibid., p. 116.
19. Ibid., p. 46.
20. See Simon Reynolds, *Rip It Up and Start Again: Postpunk 1978–1984* (New York: Penguin, 2006). See also Jon Savage, *England's Dreaming: Anarchy, Sex Pistols, Punk Rock, and Beyond*, (New York: St. Martin's Griffin, 2001).
21. See Reynolds, *Rip It Up*, p. xi.
22. See Cross, *Here We Are Now*, p. 49.
23. See *Rolling Stone's* "100 Best Albums of the Nineties." Retrieved from www.rollingstone.com/music/lists/100-best-albums-of-the-nineties-20110427/nirvana-nevermind-20110517
24. See David Fricke, "Kurt Cobain, The *Rolling Stone* Interview: Success Doesn't Suck." *Rolling Stone* (January 27, 1994). Retrieved from www.rollingstone.com/music/news/kurt-cobain-the-rolling-stone-interview-19940127
25. See Everett True, *Nirvana: The Biography* (Cambridge, MA: De Cappo Press, 2007), p. 226; see also Cross, *Here We Are Now*.
26. See Cross, *Here We Are Now*.
27. Ibid., p. 44.
28. It should be noted that, though Doc Martens boots became a part of the Grunge aesthetic, according to Cross, Kurt Cobain doesn't appear to have ever worn a pair himself.
29. Ibid., p. 45.
30. Ibid., p. 68.
31. Ibid., p. 74.
32. Ibid.
33. Of course, the other popular idea Kurt Cobain is widely known for is . . . Kurt Cobain, the socially constructed idea of himself, separate from who he actually was. Certainly, the idea of Kurt Cobain has been constructed by a variety of actors—journalists, fans, publicists, record company executives, fashion designers, even myself as the author of this chapter. And while Cobain participated in the development of the idea of himself by living his life, in the process of doing so his fame morphed into a mythology of the self that became larger than life, and certainly bigger than the flesh and blood human being Cobain was when he walked this earth. While an investigation of Kurt Cobain as a construction of the self is indeed a worthwhile pursuit, it is unfortunately

beyond the scope of this chapter.

34. See Jeff Chang, "A New Deal for Culture," *The Nation* (May 4, 2009). Retrieved from http://cantstopwontstop.com/reader/the-creativity-stimulus/

35. See Jeff Chang, *Can't Stop Won't Stop: A History of the Hip Hop Generation* (New York: St. Martin's Press, 2005).

36. Ibid., p. 111.

37. See Chang, "A New Deal for Culture," para. 3.

38. See Chang, *Can't Stop Won't Stop*, p. 79.

39. See DJ Kool Herc in Chang, *Can't Stop Won't Stop*, p. 79.

40. Ibid., p. 79.

41. See Chang, *Can't Stop Won't Stop*, p. 90.

42. Ibid., p. 92.

43. Ibid., p. 97.

44. Ibid., p. 112.

45. See DJ Kool Herc's Introduction in Chang, *Can't Stop Won't Stop*, p. xiii.

Chapter 6

Biography of an Idea
BiodegradaBall

What does creativity look like? This is an important question to ask, but a tricky one to answer—especially if one maintains traditional beliefs about invention and innovation, which suggest that creative ideation is an internal psychological event. From this perspective, creativity may be thought to be invisible. This makes perfect sense. If creativity were to be understood as an internal mind–brain affair—then of course we can't see it. And if we can't see it—it must be invisible.[1]

In the same way that creativity has been traditionally understood as being an invisible, internal process, so too have thinking and learning been traditionally understood as internal, individual processes. The invisibility of creativity—and thinking and learning alike—have created a certain mystique associated with these processes that is both alluring and puzzling. At Project Zero, researchers have devoted a great deal of energy into demystifying the processes of thinking and learning by making them visible. Popular Project Zero initiatives like Making Learning Visible and Visible Thinking have used various approaches to documenting student work over time to shed light on the mechanics of student thinking and learning.[2] Some of the core findings of these projects are that students co-construct knowledge by working in groups, and that the documentation of student work not only tells the story of student learning, but can also be used as an assessment tool to gauge how individual students and groups develop important cognitive and non-cognitive skills and progress towards understanding complex ideas. In much the same spirit, the current and proceeding chapters aim to demystify the creative process in education by making it visible.

Whereas Chapter 5 utilized the biography of an idea methodology to illustrate the socially distributed nature of creative ideas that have impacted contemporary culture, Chapters 6 and 7 present the biographies of two ideas developed by young people in a creative classroom. The first of these two idea biographies makes the distributed nature of creativity visible, while also emphasizing the temporal aspect of creative idea development. The second idea biography covers this same ground, while also emphasizing how young people play various roles throughout the process of invention and innovation. Both idea biographies are based on data collected at the Boston ArtScience

Prize, a weekly after-school program available free of charge for local high school students.

As the name suggests, the Boston ArtScience Prize encourages young people to develop creative ideas at the intersection of the arts and sciences. As the name also suggests, the program is structured as a competition. Working within the parameters of a particular scientific theme, each year small teams of Boston-area public high school students collaboratively develop ideas utilizing the Idea Translation Process, an approach to idea development established by founder David Edwards.[3] Throughout their idea development process, young people in the Boston ArtScience Prize program receive feedback from their program mentors (instructors), peers, program staff, and various professionals in their field of study. Towards the end of the program, student teams pitch their ideas to a jury of field experts. A small amount of seed funding is awarded to the most innovative ideas.[4]

Biography of an Idea: BiodegradaBall

This chapter introduces BiodegradaBall as a creative idea—an innovative product design developed by Danny, Billy, and Hamza, three public high school students working at the Boston ArtScience Prize during the 2010 to 2011 school year, under the guidance of their program mentors Ethan and Jen.

The below biography of the BiodegradaBall idea was based on the analysis of a comic produced by the Boston ArtScience Prize to describe the structure of their programming to others (see Figure 6.1). After an extended interview with the BiodegradaBall project team, the storyboard and text for the comic was developed by ArtScience Prize program staff member Andrea Sachdeva and me, before then being illustrated by the graphic artist Craig Bostick.[5]

The BiodegradaBall comic narrative presented in Figure 6.1 is both a lot of fun while also being very helpful in shedding light on the distributed, participatory, and temporal nature of creativity. What the comic does well is tell the story of the development of the BiodegradaBall idea, including many of the twists and turns the idea took, as well as an introduction to many of the actors who participated in the idea along the way.

Beyond telling a good story, the biography of an idea approach for understanding the creative process can also be employed more specifically as a research tool, a reflection tool, and an assessment tool designed not only to make creativity visible—but also to make learning visible. Here, the BiodegradaBall comic serves as rich datum, ripe for investigation. To dig deeper into this work, it is necessary to peel back the layers of inherent complexity in idea development by deconstructing the neat narrative the comic presents. While there are many approaches to such an analysis, I find it helpful to develop a temporal map of the biography of an idea. Figure 6.2 presents just such a map.

While developing such an idea development map may appear to be merely telling the story of the BiodegradaBall idea development process in another

Figure 6.1 Biography of BiodegradaBall.

Source: Illustrations by Craig Bostick. Reprinted with the Permission of the Boston ArtScience Prize.

Figure 6.1 (Continued)

Figure 6.1 (Continued)

Figure 6.1 (Continued)

Figure 6.1 (Continued)

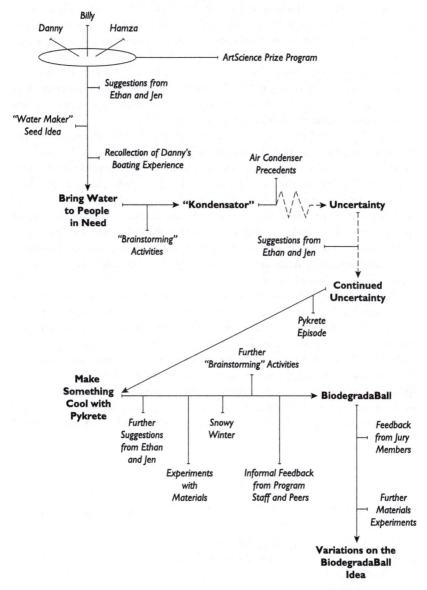

Figure 6.2 Mapping the Timeline of the BiodegradaBall Idea Development.

form, such a map is useful in breaking apart this process into core elemental pieces that can be investigated further. Here, the items in bold text represent the various *manifestations* the BiodegradaBall idea took along its path of development; the italicized items represent major *influencers* that contributed to the evolution of the idea; and the arrowed lines represent the *direction* of idea development.

Mapping out the biography of the BiodegradaBall idea makes visible the influencers that helped shape this idea at different turning points along the way. Often times these influencers are events, but sometimes they are actual people, acting on the idea themselves. Including these influencers is both intentional and important. For, it's one thing to understand the different forms an idea has taken over time; it's another thing to have an understanding of the reasons *why* the idea changed form, and *what* elements can be identified as being responsible for those changes in form.

While it is helpful to view this temporal map of the biography of the BiodegradaBall idea as a whole, for the purposes of analysis, it is also useful to break the map into smaller chunks, or *phases*, of idea development work. Figure 6.3 presents the first phase of BiodegradaBall's idea development, starting from the moment that Danny, Billy, and Hamza entered the ArtScience Prize program, to the time they first arrived at the general idea of making some sort of device that could potentially bring water to people in need. Focusing on the influencers present during this phase of idea development (the italicized text), helps us to understand the multiple layers of actors involved in this early phase of work.

This analysis begins with the boys themselves. Danny, Billy, and Hamza don't arrive at the door to the ArtScience Prize as clean slates or empty vessels waiting to be filled; rather, they arrive as all young people do—rich with experiences, personal interests, and unique worldviews. They also arrive with what R. Keith Sawyer has referred to as a host of past collaborations to draw upon.[6] In other words, previous interactions with others that have helped develop the basis of each young man's knowledge, skills, character, and outlook on the world. Some of these collaborations may have taken the form of direct instruction, such as a teacher–student relationship, and some of these

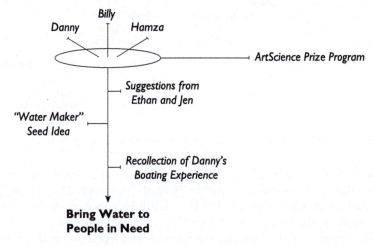

Figure 6.3 Mapping the Timeline of the BiodegradaBall Idea Development—Phase One.

collaborations may have been more cultural by nature, such as adhering to the norms of society on both a grand scale, but also on a very local level. In whatever form these past collaborations may have taken, the important point to be made is that as individuals, Danny, Billy, and Hamza do not enter this work alone, they bring all of their past collaborations and experiences with them.

The second influencer on the temporal map of the BiodegradaBall idea biography is the ArtScience Prize program. As the BiodegradaBall comic suggests, even before Danny, Billy, and Hamza came together in Ethan and Jen's class, there were already structures in place that were contributing actors to the development of the BiodegradaBall idea the boys would later develop. Many actors—such as the program's administrative staff, leadership, funders, and curriculum development consultants—who do not appear in the project comic—helped develop these structures and, in that way, those individuals indirectly contributed to the development of the BiodegradaBall idea. The structures of the program themselves are also contributors to the development of the BiodegradaBall idea. One of the specific structures that the comic mentions during this early phase of idea development is the scientific theme that guided the students' work, the "Future of Water," which intentionally placed creative constraints on the students' idea development by narrowly focusing on this one topic area. Without these structures being in place—or the people who designed them—Danny, Billy, and Hamza would not have come together in the first place.

The next influencers represented on the temporal map of the biography of the BiodegradaBall idea are the early suggestions offered by Ethan and Jen as a way of providing the boys with an entryway into the problem space. Like the boys themselves, Ethan and Jen did not enter their work with the program alone; they, too, brought all of their past collaborations and experiences with them—including their past collaborations and experiences working with one another as a teaching team. So, indeed, Ethan and Jen were contributors to the BiodegradaBall idea, but so too were their past collaborators.

As the BiodegradaBall comic notes, to help students kickstart their thinking, the ArtScience Prize additionally offered *seed ideas* as potential starting points designed to help students find a way into the opportunity space framed by the program's annual scientific theme. Danny, Billy, and Hamza were particularly drawn to a seed idea called Water Maker:

> There is only so much water in the environment. . . . Might you imagine ways to create water? Hydrogen plus oxygen makes water. Is there enough hydrogen and oxygen in the environment to make a lot more water?[7]

Indeed, this seed idea had an influence on the overall arc of idea development that was illustrated in the BiodegradaBall comic, but so too did the individuals who helped develop this, and many other, seed ideas. Months before the program began, the ArtScience Prize hosted a brainstorming session composed of field professionals who collectively offered teaser *what if . . .?* ideas that were later synthesized into the program's seed ideas. In this way, these individuals (and all of their past collaborations and experiences), also served as indirect contributors to the BiodegradaBall idea.

While the Water Maker seed idea itself can be seen as an influential contributor to the boys' initial interest in developing some form of water making device, it is important to note that the boys were primarily drawn to this seed idea because of Danny's personal experience being stuck on a boat in Boston Harbor with a dwindling supply of potable water—where just such a device would have been helpful. This is an excellent example of the role past experiences may play in influencing the later development of related ideas.

But here it is important to point out an interesting moment in the creative process. While both the Water Maker seed idea and Danny's boating experience played a role in pushing the team's thinking forward, neither of these influencers would have been sufficient in having this effect on their own. New ideas occur when the elements of past experiences coalesce. The Water Maker seed idea was *activated* by Danny's unfortunate experience at sea. According to the narrative illustrated in the BiodegradaBall comic, it was the interaction of these two influencers that brought Danny, Billy, and Hamza to the first manifestation of their idea: developing some sort of device that would bring water to people in need. While this initial manifestation of their idea development provided the boys with some footing to stand on, it was still more of a question than a firm concept: "How can we produce water in environments where it is really needed?" While this question may not be much of a step forward from the original Water Maker seed idea, the admixture of Danny's experience brings a nuance of urgency to the question that the original seed idea did not have.

After they arrived at this initially vague notion of developing a way to bring water to people in need, the biography of the BiodegradaBall idea entered its second phase of development. During this phase of work, the boys made an effort to provide an answer to the question they posed for themselves, and in their roles as program mentors Ethan and Jen did their best to help them out. As Figure 6.4 illustrates, this phase of work shows the idea taking three different forms. It begins with the general notion of providing water to people in need, advances to a more specific idea that the boys referred to as a "Kondensator," before then collapsing entirely and arriving at a state of uncertainty.

With the foundational idea of making some sort of water making device in position, Danny, Billy, and Hamza began to engage in "brainstorming" activities to come up with exciting new directions for their idea. As with many concepts related to creativity and innovation, there is a lot of positive hype around brainstorming, but the formal research on the actual benefits of brainstorming is mixed—with many researchers arguing that individuals are more likely to come up with creative solutions to complex problems on their own, than are groups who are put to the task of developing creative solutions

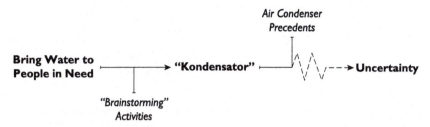

Figure 6.4 Mapping the Timeline of the BiodegradaBall Idea Development—Phase Two.

to similar problems in laboratory-based brainstorming experiments.[8] Like others, I am moderately skeptical about the impact of brainstorming as a formally structured activity, but do indeed support the informal practice of groups of individuals organically riffing ideas off of one another in an intentional way. The frames at the bottom of page one and the top of page two of the BiodegradaBall comic show (pages 112–113) Danny, Billy, and Hamza engaged in just such a process. It is during this process that the boys make the shift from the general idea of making a device that can bring water to people in need, to the more specific idea of developing "a sort of condenser that could pull water from the air . . . for personal water making devices."

Before moving forward, it is helpful to pause here to consider what takes place throughout the brainstorming process. As media theorist Steven Johnson reminds us, "A good idea is a *network*."[9] During the process of group ideation the networked effects of idea development are multiplied. Instead of one individual calling upon his or her past collaborations to develop new ideas, now multiple people combine their past collaborations to develop new ideas. In the moment, one may have seen Danny, Billy, and Hamza riffing ideas off of one another under the guidance of Ethan and Jen, but what was not visible in that instant were the thousands of past collaborations and experiences the boys were drawing on throughout this process.

In the end, the brainstorming process led Danny, Billy, and Hamza to arrive at their idea to develop a Kondensator, a personal device that condenses water molecules in the air in emergency situations. Wisely, Ethan and Jen encouraged the boys to look up precedents for their idea, to both inform their work going forward and to see if this path had been trod down before. Much to their dismay, Danny, Billy, and Hamza became crestfallen when they found many similar precedents to their Kondensator idea. As the comic suggests, the boys had even felt that other inventors had stolen *their* idea—even though the precedents the boys discovered online had been patented years ago.

Though these related inventions were disappointing for the boys to encounter at the time, what they could not have realized then was that the discovery of these precedents, and indeed the inventors who had originated them, were indirectly contributing to the boys' later idea development by prompting a shift in thinking away from their initial false start idea. In other

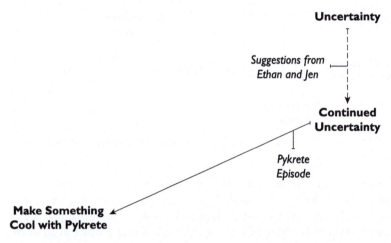

Figure 6.5 Mapping the Timeline of the BiodegradaBall Idea Development—Phase Three.

words, without discovering the precedents that crushed the team's water condenser idea, their later interest in developing biodegradable golf balls would have never come to be.

Nonetheless, at the time, the boys were stuck. In need of support and perhaps a new direction, the status of the boys' idea was floating in a state of uncertainty. As Figure 6.5 indicates, phase three of the BiodegradaBall idea development process begins in this state of uncertainty, but then takes a dramatic turn.

In the third phase of the development of the BiodegradaBall idea, the primary influencers represented on the temporal map of the idea are Ethan and Jen's efforts to engage the boys in a series of experiments to provide them with fresh ideas pertaining to the Future of Water theme. Though Ethan and Jen had made several attempts to push the boys forward, none of the concepts the program mentors introduced had a significant effect on the team's thinking. But, as the narrative suggests, this all changed very soon.

After seeing a segment about an experimental World War II shipbuilding material called *pykrete* on *MythBusters*,[10] Ethan shared what he had learned about this peculiar material with Danny, Billy, and Hamza. For reasons entirely unrelated to their interests in developing a water condenser, the boys found pykrete to be really cool!

This was an important moment in the development of the BiodegradaBall idea. Introducing the concept of pykrete helped the boys zag away from their previous idea, and placed them on the path towards their ultimate pursuit of developing biodegradable golf balls. When establishing the biography of an idea, it is helpful to call out such pivotal moments, and then to analyze these moments for their significance. What we learn here is that the boys' original interest in developing a water making device by condensing water particles from the air was too abstract, and too technically complex for the team to take on. Conversely, pykrete—generally understood as 18 percent wood pulp and 82 percent water—was an accessible material the boys could make on their own. The fact that the team could easily make a potentially bullet-proof material themselves was not only cool, it also opened a new possibility space with broad applications.

The information Ethan had gleaned from the *Mythbusters* episode on pykrete switched the perspective of Danny, Billy, and Hamza's thinking, and provided the boys with the basic material concept that would serve as the foundation for the BiodegradaBall idea. Other than responding to the cool factor of this idea, the boys themselves had very little to do with what became a major turning point in their idea development. The boys certainly asserted their agency in the next phase of this work, but at this stage there were several other actors who played more significant roles in contributing to the development of the BiodegradaBall idea. Ethan was certainly among those actors but, as the comic suggests, Ethan appears to be little more than a messenger. While this may seem to be the case in the BiodegradaBall comic, Ethan was actually being a thoughtful and responsible instructor, sensitive to the interests of his students, relaying valuable information that he perceived as having great potential. In particular, Ethan was keenly aware that Danny, Billy, and Hamza would benefit from some hands-on experiments with this new-found material. Though he was certainly not physically in the room at the time, Geoffrey Pyke (who died in 1948) can be understood as an indirect contributor to the BiodegradaBall idea as well—along with all of the influencers of his time that drove him to develop pykrete, and propose its use in the construction of naval vessels.

While the introduction of pykrete brought much needed energy back to the project team and offered an important zag in thinking, at the end of this third phase of work, Danny, Billy, and Hamza had still not arrived at a concrete idea to pursue. Instead, the boys were back to asking big questions: "What's something cool that we can make with pykrete?"

As Figure 6.6 illustrates, during the fourth phase of the development of the BiodegradaBall idea, multiple influencers helped move the boys from vaguely considering what they could do with pykrete, to firmly establishing an interest in developing biodegradable golf balls made of this interesting material.

Further suggestions from Ethan and Jen, hands-on experiments with the pykrete material, the snowy New England winter, additional brainstorming, and informal feedback from ArtScience Prize program staff and the students' peers all served as influencers on the BiodegradaBall idea during this phase of work. Each of these influencers, of course, can be connected to several other actors. Many of these actors have been discussed before, such as the past collaborators and experiences of the three boys and their program mentors, but some of these influencers are new to this story. For example, up until this point, the BiodegradaBall comic does not suggest that the boys engaged in hands-on experiments with materials. Instead, their idea development process

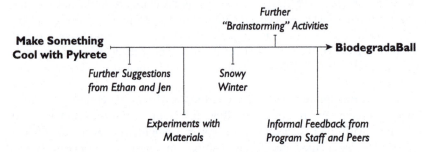

Figure 6.6 Mapping the Timeline of the BiodegradaBall Idea Development—Phase Four.

had mostly been based upon the abstract consideration of possible ideas, combined with Internet research. But now, the boys had actual stuff they could get their hands on. The concept of pykrete itself, including all of the materials the boys used to make it, became a contributor to the development of the BiodegradaBall idea. So, too, did the snowy New England winter, as the comic suggests. While one may not ordinarily consider the weather to be an influencer in idea development, in this scenario, the overwhelming snow the boys confronted on a regular basis provided new problems for the project team to solve, and a living laboratory for them to test out some of their pykrete-based prototypes. Now that they had a concrete idea that they could talk about, the boys also began to receive feedback from ArtScience Prize program staff and from their peers. This informal feedback further served as an influencer of the BiodegradaBall idea.

Oddly enough, it's while wrestling with a New England winter that the idea to create golf balls made of pykrete occurred to the team. Given the circumstances, this may seem like a huge "creative leap." But it's important to pause here to take a closer look at what's going on. As the center frame on the top row of the fourth page of the BiodegradaBall comic suggests (page 115), the origination of this idea came from Danny (and was later expanded upon by Hamza in the next frame). But what really happened was that Danny was once again pulling on past collaborations and synthesizing information from various sources.[11] Danny's suggestion, "What if we used pykrete to make golf balls?" is less a stroke of insight, and more a piecing together of information. Without being exposed to the concept of pykrete—or the concept of golf for that matter—Danny would never have suggested using an ice-based material to develop balls for a sport associated with green grass, sun visors, and short-sleeved collared shirts. Beyond Danny's synthesis in this moment, it's also important to note the contributions of Billy and Hamza. At the time that Danny pronounced this synthesis—yet another landmark moment in the development of the team's idea—the boys were riffing ideas off of one another in a manner where one idea led to the next. In this way, Danny's synthesis was both psychological and social. Danny may have been the first to say it, but the idea was formed by the ideas the group was throwing out in quick succession.

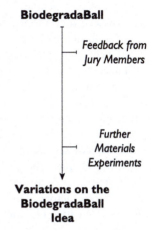

Figure 6.7 *Figure 6.7* Mapping the Timeline of the BiodegradaBall Idea Development—Phase Five.

All of these ideas, of course, were informed by the team members' past experiences and collaborations.

Figure 6.7 illustrates the fifth phase of development for the BiodegradaBall idea. At this point, Danny, Billy, and Hamza had a firm grasp on the concept they were developing and were now engaged in bringing nuance to their idea. As the temporal map of the idea indicates, two influencers played a role in the development of the idea at this stage: the feedback the boys received from a panel of experts during an ArtScience Prize sanctioned presentation event, and the further materials experiments the boys engaged in to bring further shape to the BiodegradaBall idea. As the BiodegradaBall narrative wraps up, it's exciting to see that the idea to develop biodegradable golf balls continued to evolve and develop beyond the final frame of the comic.

As one can see from the biography of the BiodegradaBall idea, neither Danny, nor Billy, nor Hamza came up with the idea to invent a biodegradable golf ball on his own. Though they also played key roles, the concept can neither be solely attributed to Ethan or Jen. In fact, it's misleading to refer to the BiodegradaBall concept as "their idea" as I have in many places in the above analysis. There is no doubt that Danny, Billy, Hamza, and their program mentors participated in the development of the BiodegradaBall idea, but a careful look at the biography of this idea reveals that far more actors were in the mix, making it problematic to use possessive language that suggests the idea *belongs* to them. What is to be learned from this analysis is that in this specific case, the idea to develop a biodegradable golf ball emerged socially, and included a wide range of contributors.

While many thoughtful educators and administrators would like to believe that young people are creative, as this analysis of the BiodegradaBall idea biography illustrates, clearly they are not—at least not in the traditional sense.

Instead, young people *participate* in creativity in various ways. Throughout the process, they adopt a wealth of knowledge and skills that they may then apply to future instances of creative participation. From this perspective, ideas are the entity that are identified as that which is creative. A biodegradable golf ball made of pykrete is a creative idea, but that idea is not the possession of any one individual, and to suggest that a single group has ownership of that idea is complicated because of the expansive nature of direct and indirect contributing actors. Of course, ideas cannot have agency on their own. Instead, ideas are enacted by human actors who participate in their development, sometimes directly, sometimes indirectly, in various ways.

In this chapter, the analysis of the biography of the BiodegradaBall idea illustrated how creativity is socially situated and distributed amongst many contributing actors. This idea biography further emphasized the temporal aspect of creative idea development, showing that the BiodegradaBall idea evolved over time through a succession of products. The following chapter returns to Jenny, Maria, Reggie, and Danny, the young people who were introduced in the Introduction of this book, to explore the biography of yet another idea—Static Fashion. Throughout the discussion and analysis of this idea biography, there is an emphasis placed not only on the distributed nature of creativity, but also on the various roles young people play throughout the creative process—and what they learn along the way.

Notes

1. Even though neuroscientists have made claims about seeing certain parts of the brain "light up" during moments when people are presumed to be creative, from a systems-based perspective many neuroscience assertions about creativity are challenged when one considers that (a) creativity is a social, not an individual process, (b) creativity takes place over time, not in solitary flashes of insight, and (c) there is no one way to be creative, but rather multiple ways to participate in creativity. That being said, the emergent field of *social neuroscience* holds much potential for integrating what we know (and are learning) about the brain with what we know (and are learning) about the social nature of human invention and innovation.
2. For more information about the Making Learning Visible project see www.pz.harvard.edu/projects/making-learning-visible; for more information about the Visible Thinking project see www.pz.harvard.edu/projects/visible-thinking
3. See David Edwards, *ArtScience: Creativity in the Post-Google Generation* (Cambridge, MA: Harvard University Press, 2008). See also David Edwards, *The Lab: Creativity and Culture,* (Cambridge, MA: Harvard University Press, 2010).
4. For more information about the Boston ArtScience Prize see www.artscienceprize.org/boston/
5. See ArtScience Labs, *ArtScience Prize Program Replication Manual* (Boston, MA: ArtScience Labs, 2011), pp. 46–54.
6. See R. Keith Sawyer, *Group Genius: The Creative Power of Collaboration* (New York: Basic Books, 2007).

7. See ArtScience Labs, *Program Replication Manual*, p. 51.

8. See Paul B. Paulus & Vincent R. Brown, "Enhancing Ideational Creativity in Groups: Lessons from Research on Brainstorming" in *Group Creativity: Innovation Through Collaboration,* pp. 110–136, eds. Paul B. Paulus & Bernard A. Nijstad (New York: Oxford University Press, 2003).

9. See Steven Johnson, *Where Good Ideas Come From: The Natural History of Innovation* (New York: Riverhead Books, 2010), p. 45 (emphasis in original).

10. See *MythBusters*, episode 115, Alaska Special II, "Pykrete Peril" (2009).

11. Interestingly, when Hamza rejected Billy's suggestion to make pykrete shovels in the top left frame of the fourth page of the BiodegradaBall comic (page 115), saying "It would be too hard to mold them." Having watched the *MythBusters* episode on pykrete and done additional research, the boys would have known that the original idea to construct a fleet of aircraft carriers out of pykrete was aborted in 1942 for much the same reason.

Chapter 7

Biography of an Idea
Static Fashion

As the biography of the BiodegradaBall idea notes, during the 2010–11 academic year, the theme of the Boston ArtScience Prize was the *Future of Water.* Two years later the program opted for a related theme: *Energy of the Future.* It was during this academic year that I had the privilege to observe young people engaged in the idea development process. Specifically, each Thursday afternoon I was a participant observer in the ArtScience Prize workshop sessions facilitated by two program mentors, Shaunalynn Duffy and Rosalie Norris.[1]

Shaunalynn and Rosalie worked with ten students who later formed two distinct idea development teams. One team referred to themselves as Reverse Outlet. The other team referred to themselves as Static Fashion. The Static Fashion team aimed to develop kinetic clothing that captured human-generated static electricity and transformed it into usable energy. Ideally, this energy would be both generated and stored in the garments the team designed and then later used to power a host of personal electronic devices such as smartphones, tablets, and laptop computers.

There are many similarities between the BiodegradaBall and Static Fashion idea development processes, but it is important to draw a few distinctions between the two idea biographies as well. First off, while both idea biographies make visible the distributed nature of the creative process, the Static Fashion idea biography places a greater emphasis on the ways in which the individuals associated with this project idea drew upon their strengths, skills, and personal interests to uniquely participate in the creative idea development process.

Second, while the biography of BiodegradaBall illustrated the many twists and turns an idea may take as it comes into being, the biography of Static Fashion is more of a straight shot. As the below narrative suggests, the Static Fashion idea became increasingly nuanced and complex as it progressed, but the core principle being developed did not change as dramatically as the BiodegradaBall idea did. This is not to suggest that one idea was more or less creative than the other, but rather that the development of Static Fashion had more to do with solving a complex problem that a team of young people had set for themselves and less to do with the constant reorientation that took place throughout the development of the BiodegradaBall idea.

The third distinction between the two idea biographies is methodological in nature. Whereas the biography of BiodegradaBall was developed *post facto*, the biography of Static Fashion was developed *in vivo*. In other words, the biography of BiodegradaBall was constructed after Danny, Billy, and Hamza had concluded their work as a project team. While the interviews conducted with the boys and their program mentors Ethan and Jen provided a thorough account of the highlight moments leading up to the development of the BiodegradaBall idea, many of the finer details of the idea development process were likely lost to memory, or glossed over in the process of the team and their program mentors recounting their experiences from a distance. Conversely, I had the privilege of being embedded within Static Fashion's idea development process. Not only was I able to document and observe each phase of the Static Fashion team's idea development process in real time, I also had ongoing access to each team member—as well as their program mentors—and was therefore able to engage the team in constant dialogue concerning the development of their idea.

As one may imagine, the *in vivo* process of developing the Static Fashion idea biography yielded far more data than the *post facto* approach to developing the BiodegradaBall idea biography. (It would not be an exaggeration to say that I accrued enough data to write an entire book about the development of the Static Fashion idea.) While the biography of BiodegradaBall provides a start to finish illustration of the idea development process, I have instead chosen to emphasize a key period in the development of the Static Fashion idea that highlights the various roles the individuals associated with this idea played along the way. More specifically, the below biography of an idea offers an in-depth look at the central part of the Static Fashion idea development process, while only providing a brief overview of the earlier and later stages of idea development.

Introducing the Key Players in the Biography of the Static Fashion Idea

Emphasizing the roles that individuals play in a systems-based idea development process inherently brings a distributed focus on invention and innovation back to the level of individual agency as enacted through the roles one plays. Considering this reorientation towards the unique roles that individuals play in systems-based creative processes, I find it helpful to introduce some of the key players in the biography of the Static Fashion idea. These individuals include the teenagers who comprise the core members of the Static Fashion team—Jenny, Danny, Maria, Reggie, and Dana—along with their adult program mentors, Shaunalynn and Rosalie. While there are many actors who indirectly contribute to the development of ideas in various ways, in the case of Static Fashion, Jenny, Danny, Maria, Reggie, Dana, Shaunalynn, and Rosalie were most deeply invested in the idea of kinetic clothing that could harness the power of static electricity. In this way, they can be referred to as the *primary stake-holder group*.

During my time spent in Shaunalynn and Rosalie's workshop space, Jenny, Danny, Maria, Reggie, and Dana were 16–17-year-old students who attended Boston-area public high schools. Each of the students identified as Latino/a or Hispanic American, three of the five students spoke fluent Spanish, and one student, Maria, had recently immigrated to the United States and, as a result, was in the process of learning English.

Shaunalynn and Rosalie were working together as a Boston ArtScience Prize program mentor pair for the second year in a row. Rosalie had come to this work with a theater, performing arts, and social services background, whereas Shaunalynn had a background in environmental engineering, creative writing, and community music. In addition to their regularly scheduled workshops, the duo also offered optional workshop sessions for the Boston ArtScience Prize community—including a bicycle generator night that challenged students to hack a bicycle and a simple motor to generate electricity.

After the presentation of the biography of the Static Fashion idea on the pages ahead, this chapter concludes with a discussion of the many ways Jenny, Danny, Maria, Reggie, and Dana—and their program mentors Shaunalynn and Rosalie—contributed to the development of this idea. In particular, this chapter considers how each member of the team's primary stakeholder group developed their own unique profile of participation.

Tracing the Origins of an Idea

As with the Boston ArtScience Prize's 2010–2011 theme of *The Future of Water*, the program's 2013–2014 theme of *Energy of the Future* emanated from the planning and intellectual contributions of various stakeholders, including outside field experts, organizational leadership, and administrative staff members. Shaunalynn and Rosalie were a part of this programmatic structure, in much the same way that Ethan and Jen had been in years past. Similarly, whereas Ethan and Jen brought their unique talents, skills, experiences, and cultural perspectives to the development of the BiodegradaBall idea, so too did Shaunalynn and Rosalie bring their unique talents, skills, experiences, and cultural perspectives to the development of the Static Fashion idea. As with the BiodegradaBall narrative, this early scaffolding suggests that a great deal had already been done to set the stage for the development of the Static Fashion idea before the young people who would later work together to cultivate that idea had even entered into Shaunalynn and Rosalie's workshop space.

Beyond the structure of the Boston ArtScience Prize program and the backgrounds of Shaunalynn and Rosalie, the formal development of the Static Fashion idea can be traced back to a conversation that Jenny had during a car ride with her father, soon after she had signed up to participate in the program and learned of the annual theme. It was during this car ride along a highway road that Jenny and her dad first began to brainstorm potential project ideas together. Her father noted that there are lots of lost opportunities to develop renewable energy in the world. For one, he suggested installing small wind turbines on highway medians to generate energy from passing cars. Jenny liked her father's idea, but she was more interested in pursuing a project that was associated with the human body. Her first thought was to develop a pillow that somehow captured the electricity produced by the brain while the body was asleep at night. It was Jenny's understanding that synapses are constantly firing in the brain, which in turn develop electrical charges. Conceptually speaking, Jenny's idea was to figure out a way to power one's devices with the energy generated by one's dreams. As she talked this idea through with her dad he asked, "Why stop there? Why not create clothing that captures energy from the body all day long?" Jenny then incorporated the use of static electricity into her father's suggestion of developing clothing that captured human-generated energy. This was the idea Jenny brought to her work at the Boston ArtScience Prize.

In the weeks that followed, Jenny became a member of Shaunalynn and Rosalie's Thursday afternoon workshop sessions. While the two program mentors provided learning experiences for the students that both educated them about the program's annual theme and surfaced student interests, Jenny frequently offered the idea of developing clothing that captured the energy released by static electricity as a potential project idea. As the program mentors consistently exposed their students to various project ideas they could pursue under the Energy of the Future program theme, slowly the ten students in

Figure 7.1 Biography of Static Fashion: Jenny and Her Father Brainstorm Ideas.

Source: Illustration by Craig Bostick.

Shaunalynn and Rosalie's Thursday afternoon workshop sessions began to cluster around particular ideas. Several weeks into the program Jenny and Maria—who had previously expressed an interest in fashion design and the arts—began to engage in Internet research that helped build a core knowledge base concerning the basic principles of static electricity.

Developing a Project Team

Shaunalynn and Rosalie's workshop space was in a large open room that had, at one end, a small stage area that could be curtained off with thick black velvet theater curtains. Building on the interest Jenny and Maria had shown in pursuing a static electricity based project, during a late November workshop session Shaunalynn took the two young women up into the stage area and then closed off the space with the black-out curtains while Rosalie showed the rest of the students videos about potential concepts they might pursue in the large open workshop area. Before long, an exclamation of "that's so cool!" emanated from behind the thick velvet curtains. There was laughter, some giggles, and then a dramatic *pop!* followed by a scream—and then more laughter. The enthusiasm emanating from behind the curtain piqued Danny's interest so much, he could barely focus his attention on what was happening in front of him. When Jenny called out "Danny get in here" Danny was happy to receive the invitation, and eager to act on his curiosity.

Figure 7.2 Biography of Static Fashion: Early Experiments with Static Electricity.

Source: Illustration by Craig Bostick.

Moments after Danny had joined Jenny, Maria, and Shaunalynn behind the curtain another *pop!* emanated from the stage area, followed by more screams and laughter. After some discussion, a very focused Jenny emerged from behind the curtain and, walking quickly, left the workshop space with a clear sense of purpose. In minutes Jenny returned carrying an armful of scarves, hats, mittens, and other assorted fuzzy materials. In a flash, Jenny had disappeared into the dark of the stage area. Before long there was another loud *pop!* and a scream, followed by more laughter. As his voice—including his screams and laughter—combined with those of Jenny and Maria, it soon became clear that Danny had signed onto Jenny and Maria's emergent team.

Soon after, Reggie began to express an interest in joining Jenny and Maria as well. In a side conversation with Rosalie, Reggie acknowledged that an important part of developing creative ideas was the ability to compromise and learn from others. And so, during a moment when Jenny had stepped out from behind the curtain of the stage area to get more supplies, Rosalie and Reggie approached her together. Rosalie started by saying, "Jenny, Reggie has something he'd like to ask you."

"Sure," Jenny replied, giving Reggie her full attention.

Using what appeared to be his most sincere voice, Reggie then asked, "Would it be ok for me to join the team with you and Maria?"

"Ok, sure." Jenny said. And that was it. Reggie was in.

By now all of the *pops!* screams, laughter, and excitement emanating from the darkened stage area behind the thick velvet curtains had piqued my curiosity, too. While Shaunalynn and Rosalie were swapping facilitation roles, I made my way behind the curtain onto the dark stage area to see what all of the excitement was about. Once there, I came to realize that the group was rubbing a balloon on different surfaces to generate a static electric charge, and then touching the balloon to the end of a four-foot-long fluorescent light bulb to make it light up. The flash, which extended from the bi-pins at the end of the fluorescent tube where the balloon touched the bulb, was faint, but it was enough to show evidence that the students could indeed generate static electricity—and then discharge it in a way that was visible. The occasional *pops!* were the sounds of balloons breaking when they were touched to the end of the fluorescent light bulb with either too much force—or too much haste.

In the time since he had joined the group, Danny had become the chief balloon charger while Maria, whom the students likened to Zeus throwing lightning bolts, had taken charge of holding the fluorescent tubes. To charge the balloon, Danny used a variety of surfaces and materials, but mostly rubbed the balloon on different parts of his own body. This was a very performative role for Danny, who made a show out of rubbing the balloon all over himself, and then touching the charged balloon to the light bulb. While rubbing the balloon intensely back and forth over his short hair, Jenny began to call Danny the team's "test monkey." Danny quickly adopted this character role by making monkey noises as he playfully rubbed the balloon on himself—and everything else within the dark stage area. For her part, Jenny was dictating

Figure 7.3 Biography of Static Fashion: The Static Fashion Team Takes Shape.

Source: Illustration by Craig Bostick.

to Danny where to rub the balloon and for how long. She would then record the effects of each test charge in the team's project idea notebook—a simple journal the program mentors had previously given to Jenny and Maria to track the progress of their ideas. Reggie soon became interested in developing more calculated measurements and began recording the time Danny spent rubbing the balloon on different surfaces, and the general result it had on the fluorescent light bulb. Reggie would call out his measurements to Jenny, who then recorded them in the team's notebook.

In a follow-up conversation with Shaunalynn and Rosalie, the program mentors noted that during their previous Thursday afternoon workshop session, Jenny had identified an Internet site that listed an experiment for generating static electricity. The experiment was complicated and required specialty materials that would have to be ordered online. While they were excited to see that Jenny had identified an experiment she could use to test out her interest in generating static electricity, they also felt that what she had found was not only too complicated and required too many specialized materials, but that the effects would be too abstract—and not dramatic enough to have an impact on the students' understanding of static electricity. Instead, the two program mentors began scouring the Internet to find an alternative, more interesting experiment for Jenny and Maria to pursue.

Around this time, Shaunalynn and Rosalie also had an interesting interaction with Dishon Mills—the director of the Boston ArtScience Prize. While casually visiting their workshop space, Dishon playfully asked the two mentors,

"Doesn't it annoy you to be working in a room with so many burnt-out fluorescent light bulbs?" Shaunalynn and Rosalie had never noticed that many of the fluorescent light bulbs in their space were indeed burnt out, but they were appreciative when Dishon offered to have them replaced. Soon after, the mentors made a connection between their need to find an experiment that exhibited the effects of static electricity and the spate of burnt-out fluorescent light bulbs that would soon be at their disposal. As Shaunalynn explained,

> Jenny had done some research . . . finding this kind of complicated thing that lit up a light with static electricity. And, it required all this stuff, and it was a YouTube video, so it didn't have the materials listed. So, . . . I was Googling for Jenny and Maria, and I was just like, "how [can they] power a light with static electricity?" And, I just read the first three pages of Google results. And one of the experiments was, "rub a balloon on your head, and stick it onto a fluorescent bulb."

By drawing Shaunalynn and Rosalie's attention to the fluorescent light bulbs, unbeknownst to himself, Dishon helped the two program mentors find a way for their students to experiment with static electricity in an easily accessible and visible way. He also became an indirect actor in the emergent student project team's idea.

Conducting Experiments and Sketching Designs

Shaunalynn and Rosalie's next Thursday afternoon workshop session took place on the eve of the Ideas in Progress Exhibition—an important pro-grammatic event where young people shared their ideas in progress and received feedback from the public. With the Ideas in Progress Exhibition only 24 hours away, this workshop session was all about getting down to business. And part of getting down to business included naming each project team. More than a casual way to refer to the project, Shaunalynn and Rosalie viewed naming each project team as an important part of develop-ing group identity and defining a project idea. It was on this day that Shaunalynn and Rosalie proposed the name Static Fashion to the students—and it stuck.

As with the week before, Shaunalynn and Rosalie had done a great deal of planning to ensure the success of their students during the scant time they had to work on the project ideas together. For the Static Fashion team the two mentors provided ample balloons, fluorescent light bulbs, and two laptop computers for the team members to use. Their workshop space was also equipped with an assortment of art supplies, craft materials, and hand tools that were always available to students. Shaunalynn and Rosalie also made cer-tain to have print outs of various fashion design templates for the team to work with. During this session the individual Static Fashion team members began to separately gravitate towards the different materials available to them.

Almost immediately Jenny began developing a poster for the team's exhibition, Danny and Reggie used a laptop to set up shared documents for the team to use, and Maria sat down with the fashion design templates and a box of colored pencils and began sketching colorful women's jackets.

Once Jenny had created the general outline for a poster, she interrupted Maria's design sketching and asked her to fill in the poster with the data they procured the week before. As Maria used different colored markers to attend to this task, Jenny switched her attention to Danny and Reggie, who were getting ready to conduct more tests on stage with the balloon and the fluorescent light bulb. Whereas last week they used descriptors such as "more," "less," "low," and "dim" to describe the flashes of light they saw in the fluorescent light bulb, this week the group was interested in being more scientific. To do so, Reggie suggested the team draw measurement lines on the light bulb. Once this was done, the entire team stepped behind the velvet curtain.

Reggie looked on as the team repeated the balloon/light bulb experiment. But Reggie was not just casually watching, he was trying to figure out patterns from one flash of light to the next. Indeed, the results from these experiments were inconsistent. It was hard for the team to get the same results twice, no matter how carefully they repeated the amount of time they rubbed the balloon, what they rubbed the balloon on, and how they touched the balloon to the fluorescent light bulb. After multiple iterations, the team broke from the darkened stage area to resume work on other tasks. As Maria went back to her

Figure 7.4 Biography of Static Fashion: Attempting to Measure Static Electricity.

Source: Illustration by Craig Bostick.

work sketching colorful jacket designs, Reggie asked Shaunalynn, "Do you have a multimeter that we can use?"

During this recent round of experiments Reggie began to wonder whether or not the light that the students were seeing within the fluorescent bulb was an accurate portrayal of the charge that was being emitted by the balloon. And so, rather than continue to measure the light they saw, Reggie wanted to see if he could directly measure the charge that was being emitted.

By asking Shaunalynn for a multimeter—an electronic measuring device used to gauge various units of electricity—Reggie was pulling on his previous knowledge from attending the optional bicycle generator night that Shaunalynn and Rosalie had hosted for interested students. Reggie had learned a lot that night through his work detecting circuits with a multimeter.

Soon after Reggie's request, Shaunalynn returned to the workshop space with a multimeter in hand. She then sat down with Reggie to remind him how to use the device to detect a circuit.

When the team returned to the stage area for a second round of experiments with the multimeter, Maria stayed behind to continue work on her design sketches. As the team's experiments went forth, Reggie struggled to get consistent readings with the multimeter. He worried that the charges being emitted by the balloon were either too weak to detect, or that there was some other variable present that was skewing the experiment, making it difficult to measure the charge emitted by the balloon with a degree of accuracy.

Jenny and Reggie took this work very seriously. Danny, however, occasionally let his performative self get the best of him. Danny's clowning around was meant to be playful, not disruptive, but nonetheless Jenny was stern with Danny, and was certain to rein him in when his goofing about began to distract the team from its work. Nonetheless, whenever Jenny reprimanded Danny, there was always warmth—and never hostility—in her voice. Jenny's goal was to always manage the team and move the work forward. This included negotiating Danny's playful spirit in a manner that made the work fun and productive at the same time.

Outside the curtain, Maria was continuing with her design sketches. Many of the students had complimented her on her work. While Maria graciously accepted her peers' compliments, she did not let the flattery distract her from her sketching. When Shaunalynn sat with Maria to ask her about her drawings, Maria said she had big ideas for the designs. She had a particular interest in hardware, and emphasized the role of buttons and zippers in her designs. This emphasis in fasteners affected the cut of her proposed jackets. Shaunalynn further asked Maria about the materials Maria had in mind based on the textures present in her drawings. Maria responded by saying that—though the properties of different materials were a consideration—she was drawing what she thought looked beautiful. Maria expressed that she was most concerned about designing clothing that people would want to wear. Therefore, her decisions about potential fabrics were based on aesthetic principles more than anything else. While Jenny, Danny, and Reggie continued

Figure 7.5 Biography of Static Fashion: Early Design Sketches Emphasizing Buttons and Zippers.

Source: Illustration by Craig Bostick.

to work on the scientific elements undergirding Static Fashion, Maria was busy bringing an artist/designer's eye to the group's work. By the close of the workshop session, Maria had made over a half dozen design sketches for the Ideas in Progress Exhibition.

While this appeared to be a successful project development session for the Static Fashion team, it also had its challenges. Dana, who had expressed an interest in movement and dance, drifted in and out of working with Jenny and Maria in the past and was now technically a member of the Static Fashion team. Despite her affinity for movement and dance, Dana's interest in the idea of developing kinetic clothing that could harness the power of static electricity had been tenuous, and on this evening, she was deeply disengaged from the work of her peers. After floating about the space for the earlier half of the workshop session, Dana ultimately decided to leave early. Before departing, Dana told both Shaunalynn and Rosalie that this would likely be her last day, suggesting that the program had become less interesting to her as her peers' project ideas developed.

How Not to Disburse Electrons throughout Your Body

The next evening, dozens of parents, siblings, teachers, and friends of the program filled the space to see the Ideas in Progress exhibition. Each visitor was eager to see and hear how the student project teams were interpreting this year's scientific theme: *Energy of the Future*. Unlike other student project displays—which were set up in traditional science fair style—the Static Fashion exhibition was spread out over three separate but connected stations. Maria's design sketches were framed and prominently hung in a neat column against a brick wall, which was situated at the entrance to a darkened room where the lights were out and a handful of other student projects that relied on the dark were also on display. The poster the team had made the day before was mounted above a table in one corner of the room and the team's balloon/fluorescent light bulb experiment was set up behind a temporary wall in the opposite corner of the space.

Maria stood by her design sketches and captured people's attention with her drawings. She then led interested exhibition-goers into the room where Jenny presented the team's poster and provided more detailed information about their project idea. Jenny then led guests behind the temporary wall where Danny and Reggie were demonstrating the team's balloon/light bulb experiment. Danny was in charge of rubbing the balloon while Reggie both held the fluorescent bulb and attempted to gain a reading on the multimeter. Danny was happy to live out the performative aspects of the work, while Reggie scrutinized the process to see what the team could learn from their experiments. Dana, however, was not to be found.

After visitors experienced Danny and Reggie's demonstration, Jenny asked guests three brief questions as they exited the space:

1. What kind of clothes are you comfortable in?
2. What other ways can you get energy from movement?
3. What do you want to use the energy for?

Jenny then recorded guests' responses to the team's questions on a large piece of sketchbook paper, and asked if they had any further questions or comments for the team.

As I left the darkened room, I checked in with Maria in the main exhibition space. She was standing in front of her design sketches. I complimented Maria on her drawings and asked her to describe her work to me. She said that she was very interested in clothing, and paid particular attention to materials and fabrics, and how garments were fastened. I noticed this emphasis in her drawings, as a variety of textures were used to represent different types of fabrics, and assorted styles of zippers and buttons were incorporated into her designs. The varied arrangements of zippers and buttons Maria had drawn uniquely affected the shape and the cut of each garment. Being that most of Maria's drawings appeared to be sketches for winter coats, I asked Maria if she had an interest in other pieces of apparel. She noted that she was interested in designing pants, shoes, and tops in addition to the jackets she had already drawn—but the team had a focus on winter clothes and active wear because these apparel pieces were likely to generate the most static electricity.

Figure 7.6 Biography of Static Fashion: The Ideas in Progress Exhibition.

Source: Illustration by Craig Bostick.

Later in the evening I returned to check in with the Static Fashion team. They were even busier than they had been before. Maria was standing in front of her drawings in the main space talking to several people. In the darkened back room, Jenny was engaged in describing the team's project idea to yet another group of people. When I turned the corner to enter Danny and Reggie's demonstration space, I found the two engaged in their experiment as I had expected—but this time they were wearing latex gloves.

I asked Danny and Reggie why they were wearing latex gloves. Reggie explained that a guest had spent some time with Danny and Reggie and observed that neither of them had insulated themselves from the static charge they were producing. This individual suggested that the reason the students could not get a consistent flash of light or a firm reading from the balloon touching the light bulb was because the charge from the balloon was being irregularly distributed through their bodies. The latex gloves would help insulate them from the balloon and the light bulb, and potentially provide more consistent results. And indeed, it did.

During the week of the Ideas in Progress Exhibition the team's idea developed in both form and content. Utilizing the design templates that were provided by Shaunalynn and Rosalie, Maria experimented with designs that advanced the students towards considering winter jackets as a likely application of their ideas—which provided the team with a visualization of what their final

Figure 7.7 Biography of Static Fashion: Incorporating Latex Gloves for Insulation and Increased Accuracy.

Source: Illustration by Craig Bostick.

products may potentially look like. These images, the first visual artifacts of the Static Fashion team, served as an important draw during the Ideas in Progress Exhibition. The team worked as a unit to figure out the science behind the flash of light they were able to produce within the fluorescent bulb that the two program mentors had provided for them. Whereas the team's first experiments were based on their visual observations, Reggie now employed a multimeter to see if he could get more specific readings. The suggestion to wear latex gloves that the students received from a visitor at the Ideas in Progress Exhibition not only helped the students be more careful when they conducted their experiments, but also sparked an idea within Jenny concerning how to generate static electricity within multiple layers of fabric, without unintentionally discharging electricity to the person wearing their clothes.

Welcome to the Bat Cave ...

When the Boston ArtScience Prize resumed programming after a brief holiday break, the Static Fashion team had a lot of information to process from their experiences at the Ideas in Progress Exhibition. To get started, Jenny, Danny, Reggie, and Maria huddled up to determine what to do during today's workshop session. The four core team members began by talking about what they learned from the people they spoke with at the Ideas in Progress Exhibition. Their discussion focused on the concept of positive and negative electrical charges, with an emphasis placed on what sorts of fabrics hold what sorts of charges. One of the team members said that someone they spoke to suggested that cotton was a neutrally charged material. The team began to consider how they could work with this information.

In response to what the team learned about cotton being neutrally charged, Jenny shared a diagram she drew, which depicted two materials that were likely to conduct static electricity when rubbed together, sandwiched between two outer layers of cotton that were meant to act like insulators. The idea behind Jenny's design was to build up static electricity within an internal layer of clothing without discharging it to the person wearing the garment.

Responding to Jenny's drawing, Maria began working on a laptop to research materials that had different levels of conductivity. Jenny sat next to Maria transcribing notes from the Ideas in Progress Exhibition into the team's project notebook. As Maria identified potential materials to use, she shared this information with Jenny. Amongst the materials Maria identified were lead, rabbit fur, aluminum, and silk. Jenny wrote each of these materials down in the team's notebook.

Meanwhile, Reggie began to set up the stage area to conduct further experiments with Danny. Reggie had a new idea. He wanted to use alligator clips to connect a multimeter to each end of the light bulb (as opposed to one

Figure 7.8 Biography of Static Fashion: Developing a Layered Fabric Model.

Source: Illustration by Craig Bostick.

end of the light bulb or the other, as he had been doing previously) to see if he could get a more accurate reading. His hypothesis was that by connecting the multimeter to each end of the light bulb he would make a complete circuit that electricity could flow through more easily. But before the two boys could begin their experiments, they needed latex gloves to insulate themselves from the static electricity Danny would be generating with a balloon.

While Shaunalynn made her way downstairs to get gloves for Reggie and Danny, Rosalie left the room to talk to Dana outside of the workshop space. Dana was not in attendance at the Ideas in Progress Exhibition, and the last time the two program mentors saw her, Dana had told them she probably would not be back. While Dana's return suggested a willingness to continue to engage with the program, Dana distanced herself from the Static Fashion team and expressed no interest in conducting experiments or discussing the effects of different electrical charges on various materials.

About the same time that Shaunalynn arrived back in the space with latex gloves for Reggie and Danny, Dana returned to the workshop space, sat near the Static Fashion team, and began tapping away on her cellphone. Now ready to enter the stage area to conduct their experiments, Reggie and Danny gathered up their materials and prepared to begin. But before closing the thick velvet curtains around themselves, Reggie invited Dana to join them on the stage area to help record information. Dana accepted the invitation. As she

Figure 7.9 Biography of Static Fashion: Welcome to the Bat Cave.

Source: Illustration by Craig Bostick.

stepped up onto the stage, Danny dropped his voice as low as it could go and said, "Welcome to the bat cave . . ." and then drew the curtains around them with a playful *mwuhahahahahaaa* . . . sci-fi villain's laugh.

Though it seemed like just a small gesture, Reggie's invitation to Dana was significant. The core members of the Static Fashion team—Jenny, Maria, Reggie, and Danny—had returned from the Ideas in Progress Exhibition with much momentum and an eagerness to advance their work. But the more the foursome advanced their ideas, the more distant Dana had become from them as a group. Reggie's invitation to participate in his experiments with Danny provided an entry point for Dana to engage with the team. Once Dana accepted Reggie's invitation, Danny literally welcomed her in. The sinister references he used were deeply ironic—and were ultimately meant to make Dana's re-entry into the team's work *less* scary, and more playful.

Before Reggie, Danny, and Dana began their work, Jenny slipped into the stage area to review their goals for this experiment session: to mix and match different materials, and then write down the resulting effects each produced on the light bulb. After ensuring that Reggie, Danny, and Dana understood their task, Jenny exited the stage and then, before resuming her own work, asked Maria if she would like to join the group conducting the experiments, too. Maria said no, that she was more interested in continuing her research on the laptop. Indeed, based on her level of focus, it certainly appeared that Maria was onto something.

Considering these exchanges and other interactions she had with her teammates, it occurred to me that Jenny had adopted a pronounced leadership role within the group. Jenny appeared to bring structure to the team by establishing goals, delegating tasks, documenting information, and checking in with her peers. While she frequently told her peers what to do, she was tactful and personable, and never bossy or demanding of her teammates. Based on the way that they responded to Jenny's management of their work, it seemed that the group appreciated having Jenny play this part.

In addition, the relationship between Jenny and Maria seemed to strengthen from one workshop session to the next; the two young women increasingly worked together on specific tasks, and regularly riffed off of one another's ideas. During this session Maria had been deeply focused on the idea Jenny surfaced earlier: how *not* to discharge the static electricity they generated into the body. To pursue this line of inquiry, Maria was searching the Internet to better understand the roles that positive and negative charges played in the generation and distribution of static electricity. After several minutes of browsing the Web, Maria posed a question to Jenny: "Is there a way to develop an indicator that displays the static electricity within the clothes?" she asked. "Yes!" Jenny responded. However, Jenny failed to see the underlying question *beneath* Maria's question. Then it clicked. What Maria was trying to understand was how to measure the static electric *potential* within an object before it discharged a flash of electricity and thereby neutralized itself. For example, how could they measure the static electric charge of the balloon without releasing that charge to the light bulb? It had just become clear to the young women that it was less important to measure the electricity they saw discharged into the light bulb, and more important to measure the charge they could build up within an object or material. Essentially, what they needed to do was to develop some sort of fabric that could function like a renewable battery; a fabric that could build a charge and then hold that charge until it was needed. The light bulb experiment appeared to have the opposite effect. When the team touched the balloon to the light bulb and saw a flash, they were releasing the static electric charge that had accumulated on the surface of the balloon.

With this realization in mind, Jenny jumped onto a laptop computer to look up different methods for measuring static electricity—but the Internet led her astray. A webpage she found explained that static electricity could be measured in volts, based on the length of a spark that was emitted when a negatively charged object or material neutralized itself when it transferred its excess electrons to another object. Talking this through with Reggie and Maria, Jenny argued that the team needed to make a spark. Danny inquired whether or not it would help to rub two balloons and hold one at either end of the light bulb. "We can't keep using light bulbs," Jenny said. The light bulb experiment had been helpful up until this point, but Jenny deduced that it was not the best way for them to gauge static electricity. Unfortunately, Jenny did not have a sense of what to do as an alternative experiment.

Shaunalynn had been observing this exchange and, noting a shift in thinking, asked the group, "What are your big questions right now?" Jenny explained what the team now understood about how static electricity worked: that an excess of electrons is transferred from one object or material to another, which creates a spark. The length of the spark, Jenny argued, indicated the voltage of the electrical charge. Maria spoke up at this point, saying that she had a different approach in mind. Jenny was excited about her own idea; but she paused to hear what Maria had to say. Maria tried to explain her idea, which was to deliberately choose a material that attracted electrons and a material that easily lost electrons, and then to rub the two together. However, Maria did not want to create a spark or discharge the built up static electricity in any way; she wanted to figure out how to accumulate this potential energy, store it, measure it, and be intentional about its later use. The team began to understand Maria's idea but in the course of her explanation, Maria lost her words and struggled to reach past the limits of her English vocabulary. Jenny listened closely, asked questions, and tried hard to understand her. It became clear to Jenny that Maria's idea was different from her own, but they were both based on a similar concept.

At this point, however, Shaunalynn and Rosalie's workshop session had come to a close—and Jenny was already late for her next after-school activity. As the students filtered out of the space, Maria lingered a bit, explaining her emergent understandings to Shaunalynn and Rosalie. "We need to do this different," she said, gesturing to the materials Danny and Reggie had been

Figure 7.10 Biography of Static Fashion: A New Insight Emerges.

Source: Illustration by Craig Bostick.

using to conduct their balloon experiments. Shaunalynn and Rosalie heard her out, until Maria, too, had to leave. The program mentors assured Maria that they would try out her ideas next week.

An Absence of Leadership

The following week the only Static Fashion team members in attendance at Shaunalynn and Rosalie's Thursday afternoon workshop session were Reggie, Danny, and Dana. Both Jenny and Maria were absent. The two program mentors began this session with a check-in activity and then announced that in a few weeks the students would be presenting their ideas to a panel of field leaders at the Boston ArtScience Prize's next big programmatic event. This event would provide the students with an opportunity to get feedback on their ideas from a panel of experts and to articulate what they would do with up to $200 in prototype funding.

The two program mentors announced that during this session each project team would begin to consider a set of questions to help them prepare for their upcoming presentations. Shaunalynn began by introducing Reggie to a page on the Edmund Scientifics website that promoted a static electricity powered light bulb. Meanwhile, Rosalie sat at a table with Dana on her own. Holding a balloon in his hand, Danny sauntered over to where Shaunalynn and Reggie were working on a laptop. Reggie asked Shaunalynn specific questions about the role resistors play in light bulbs. Shaunalynn stood up and began to sketch out what she knew about resistors by drawing a schematic for a simple electrical circuit on a nearby whiteboard. At this point Danny jumped in by asking what body parts might be best to use to generate static electricity. Reggie responded quickly and with confidence, stating that the armpits might make the most sense because of all of the friction they produced.

Reggie then continued to talk the project through with Shaunalynn from a very technical perspective. He was curious about the role of resistance in their work. Reggie then showed Shaunalynn a website he had found about the transferability of electricity between different materials that conducted heat. The website was essentially a succession of spreadsheets that formed a dense matrix of statistical data. Still holding a balloon in his hand, Danny passively looked on.

Noting that Reggie and Danny had diverging interests in the work of the project, Shaunalynn tried to figure out an activity the two boys could do together. She proposed two different options: they could choose materials to experiment with using their fluorescent light bulb technique and then start developing a spreadsheet that tracked their results, or they could continue

Figure 7.11 Biography of Static Fashion: Balancing Diverse Student Interests.

Source: Illustration by Craig Bostick.

research online with the goal of organizing a list of materials they would like Shaunalynn and Rosalie to bring in for next week. Danny was indifferent. He said either direction would be fine for him. His response was flat, and lacked his regular energy and enthusiasm. He then said, "We shouldn't order materials without Jenny and Maria. We're not qualified to make those decisions." Danny continued by questioning the direction of the project. He once again referred to Jenny by saying he thought her vision was to develop clothes for dancing. Where they were now—talking about resistors and voltage—felt a long way from the dance clothes element of the project. "I'm feeling lost and I don't know where the project is going anymore," he added.

Shaunalynn affirmed that the project was still going in a positive direction. She noted that Maria appeared to have a deep interest in design and Jenny seemed to be interested in developing the materials that would best suit the project's core concepts. Nonetheless, Danny's mood continued to plummet. Slumped in a chair with the skin of a popped balloon stretched over his hands, with downcast eyes Danny said he felt weird and tired today. As he poked holes in the deflated balloon with a pin, Danny said that he was afraid that all of his ideas were wrong.

A heavy pause hovered in the air for a moment before Shaunalynn jumped back into the conversation. "Your ideas are not wrong at all," she assured him, "they're exciting! They bring life and laughter to the team's work." She then asked if he would be interested in trying some of his ideas right now by making a quick prototype of a wild dance club outfit. "Reggie could help by going crazy with the tech side of your designs," Shaunalynn suggested. But, despite her best efforts, Danny just slumped deeper into his chair.

From across the room, Rosalie picked up on the low energy Shaunalynn was experiencing with Danny. The two program mentors then decided to switch. Rosalie came over to work with Danny and Reggie and—after offering some additional words of encouragement to Danny—Shaunalynn went to work with Dana.

Rosalie pointed out that one of their goals was to figure out what they would do with $200 in prototype funding. She then suggested that, considering their conversation from last week, Maria would probably like having a bunch of different fabrics they could use in their experiments. Danny said he had seen shoes and shirts that light up. Maybe that was something they could look into.

Danny's suggestion gave Rosalie an idea. Recalling some of the projects her colleagues were working on with other students, Rosalie engaged Danny and Reggie in online research that ranged from clothing dyes that changed color in response to one's body temperature to sneakers that used piezoelectricity— energy derived from pressure—to light up LEDs. While Rosalie and Reggie discussed the potential of piezoelectric technology and light-up sneakers, Danny looked up YouTube videos about heat-sensitive clothing dyes. He even found a video that illustrated how to use such a dye to make color-changing temporary tattoos.

Figure 7.12 Biography of Static Fashion: Experiencing a Moment of Uncertainty.

Source: Illustration by Craig Bostick.

Rosalie had successfully turned Danny's spirits around, but the two program mentors were still confounded as to how to fold Dana into the conversations Danny and Reggie were having about different fabric technologies. Noting that Dana was not interested in engaging with Reggie and Danny, Shaunalynn and Rosalie had begun to prepare Dana for their next activity, which was to use an iPad app to develop short promotional videos for each project team. Throughout this workshop session, Dana had been sitting alone with either one or the other program mentor, watching videos on an iPad. Dana laughed loudly at the videos she watched and seemed to be enjoying herself—but she was also distracting to the other students in the space who were trying to work on their project ideas.

In order to bring their students back together and to return some much needed energy to the group, at this point in the workshop session Rosalie and Shaunalynn decided to play a full group theater game. Their plan worked. By the time the students had finished this theater exercise, there was a new sense of energy in the room. Shaunalynn and Rosalie built on that energy by giving each student team an iPad and the task of making short videos that promoted their project ideas.

Figure 7.13 Biography of Static Fashion: Finding New Energy.

Source: Illustration by Craig Bostick.

The promotional videos that Danny, Reggie, and Dana made together were based on lively shots of Dana dancing—with arms pumping and feet stomping—while Danny yelled "Static Fashion, yo!" in the background. The videos were effective at bringing the three students together to work on an activity, but did little to advance the greater goals of the project team.

Jenny and Maria's absence from this workshop session caused a considerable disruption in the development of the Static Fashion project idea. Whereas Reggie had no problem finding self-directed, technically oriented work, Shaunalynn and Rosalie struggled to incorporate both Danny and Dana into productive group work. Nonetheless, the connections Rosalie made between Danny's interest in light-up clothing and heat-sensitive dyes would prove effective at moving Static Fashion's ideas forward in the weeks ahead.

Confronting Critical Issues of Peer Participation

The following week Jenny and Maria were once again in attendance at Shaunalynn and Rosalie's Thursday afternoon workshop session, and the Static Fashion team was back in full effect. Shortly into the workshop session, while Reggie was explaining how he was using a Styrofoam cup and an aluminum tray to make an electrophorus, Dana announced that she needed to leave early. After her departure, Maria, Jenny, and Danny fell into a deep discussion about

Dana's role on the project. Shaunalynn and Rosalie soon joined the conversation. It had become clear that the team was distressed about Dana's lack of participation. Maria was particularly vocal. "If she were a closer friend," Maria said, "I would tell her 'come on, stop goofing around and being lazy and get to work!'" Jenny made the case that Danny was able to be a part of the team and still have fun, and that Dana should be able to do the same. "Danny likes to make sound effects and be silly," she said, "but his goofing around is always in service of the team. If [Dana] wants to apply her interests in dance, that would be cool, but she has to make an effort." By now Reggie had joined the group and Jenny asked, "Reggie, what's your opinion?" Reggie simply said, "I don't think she understands she's part of our group." Danny then said the team should give Dana another chance. "Let me talk to her," he said, "she'll know where I'm coming from."

Figure 7.14 Biography of Static Fashion: Voicing Social Concerns.

Source: Illustration by Craig Bostick.

The conversation concerning Dana's participation continued for some time, and then concluded with Rosalie suggesting that the team would have a conversation with Dana next week. She and Shaunalynn would begin the discussion, but Rosalie suggested it would be important for Dana to hear from her teammates.

Attending to Group Dynamics and Making Connections

After a week off due to a snow storm that covered the city, the entire Static Fashion team was in attendance at Shaunalynn and Rosalie's next Thursday afternoon workshop session. As soon as the team got situated, they immediately set to addressing Dana's participation on their team. After Shaunalynn and Rosalie facilitated a tense conversation about the importance of teamwork with an emphasis placed on each member of the group participating in equal measure, Dana assured the group that she would be more of an active participant in the weeks ahead. The two program mentors did most of the

Figure 7.15 Biography of Static Fashion: Addressing Tense Group Dynamics.

Source: Illustration by Craig Bostick.

talking during this meeting, but Danny was also quite vocal, "We think you're one of us," he said to Dana, "You're cool and you're funny and we really want you to spend more time working on ideas with us."

As soon as it seemed appropriate, Shaunalynn shifted the team out of this difficult but important discussion about group participation and into a conversation about their project work. Shaunalynn prompted the group to consider what were some of the big questions the team had at this moment. Jenny offered: "What's the most active part of the body? How much electricity does it take to light up a light bulb?" Reggie jumped in by asking: "How do you transfer electricity from DC to AC?" Jenny then argued the group needed to work more with fabrics. She asked "What fabrics generate the most static?" Danny asked "What types of clothes are we interested in making?" While all of these questions were being bounced around, Jenny took notes in a sketchbook while Maria did the same by using the team's project notebook. Reggie continued to offer new questions: "What are the efficiency levels of different fabrics that our static electricity will pass through?" and "How much energy do we want to generate?" Danny then asked "What types of light bulbs do we want to work with? What color LEDs should we use?" Reggie offered that red LEDs are pretty bright. Jenny wrote down "target consumer?" and then asked "Who will really buy this?" Figuring out their target consumer, she argued, would shape their design. All the while, Dana sat at the table, attentive, and before long, contributed a few ideas of her own to add to those of her team members.

Figure 7.16 Biography of Static Fashion: Brainstorming New Ideas.

Source: Illustration by Craig Bostick.

After some time spent brainstorming key project questions, the team shifted into a more concrete discussion concerning how to operationalize the ideas they had for making clothing that could conduct usable static electricity. Reggie moved the group in this direction when he explained to Danny how a breadboard—a device used by hobbyists for prototyping small electronic projects without the use of solder—worked. It was at this point that Reggie revealed to the team—and the program mentors alike—that he had been using breadboards and other light electronics equipment at The Saturday Thing, a series of open studio workshop sessions that were held each week at MIT.[2]

Each Saturday morning, following the team's work on Thursday afternoons, Reggie would bring what he had learned from his work with the Static Fashion team to the scientists he engaged with at MIT. He would ask their advice on what scientific, technological, and engineering concepts to take into consideration in order to move his project team's ideas forward—and the MIT scientists would respond by offering their expert opinions. It was here that Reggie got the idea to focus on the armpit as the body part likely to generate the most static electricity, and also here that Reggie began to have discussions about how to accumulate and store static electricity, particularly through the use of resistors and other electronics components. Following this important reveal—which introduced a whole new host of indirect actors into the mix of the Static Fashion idea's development process—Reggie casually went on to describe the functionality of a breadboard, sharing what he knew about how circuits worked. Reggie's discussion of circuitry made something click for Danny, who referenced Circuit Scribe, a Kickstarter campaign video Shaunalynn and Rosalie had shown their students nearly two months ago when they were bringing the students up to speed on the program's theme, Energy of the Future.

Circuit Scribe was a product under development by a start-up called Electroninks. Utilizing a water-based conductive ink, the inventors of Circuit Scribe had created a ballpoint pen that made tinkering with circuits as easy as drawing and doodling. "Could we use this in the fabrics we're developing?" Danny wondered. "Keep going," Jenny said, urging Danny to expand on his ideas. But it was Reggie who spoke next. "Maybe the conductive ink could be used to transport static electricity produced in one part of the clothes to where we need to store it in another part," he suggested.

"I like where this is going," Shaunalynn said. She then told the group that she wanted the team to continue to work out the possibilities. Encouraging the students to think in terms of experiments they could try, Shaunalynn added, "Maybe you can make a conductive ink circuit and then use static from the balloons to see if you can get it to power a light bulb?"

"Would the ink be waterproof?" Reggie wondered. Recalling the heat-sensitive dyes that he had looked at a few weeks ago with Danny and Rosalie, Reggie worried that the conductive ink might have the same problem—it would become less and less effective with each additional washing.

At this point, Shaunalynn asked, "Have you guys heard about conductive thread?"

They had not.

Shaunalynn gave the group a quick overview of what conductive thread was, and how it was similar to the conductive ink that they were talking about—and then told them to "look it up!"

Managing their social unit slowed the progress of the Static Fashion team for several weeks, but the team was nonetheless able to make progress on their consideration of circuits as a means to carry static electricity throughout their proposed garments. It was during this session that several influences from past sessions (e.g., conductive ink, heat sensitive dyes, etc.) came to the surface. Additionally, Reggie was able to incorporate his experience developing circuits at the Saturday Thing into his work with his Static Fashion colleagues. At the conclusion of this session, the consideration of using conductive thread to develop circuits within fabrics seemed like a promising step forward for the team.

Figure 7.17 Biography of Static Fashion: Considering New Materials.

Source: Illustration by Craig Bostick.

Inductors, Capacitors, LEDs, Diodes, and some Input from Field Experts

The next week of the program, Shaunalynn and Rosalie's students had the opportunity to participate in their Formal Idea Meetings—a programmatic event that provided each project team with the opportunity to present their emergent ideas to a panel of field leaders, and then to receive feedback. Static Fashion was scheduled to present their ideas towards the end of the session. This gave the team members some time to continue work on their ideas.

During the early part of this session I was sitting next to Reggie while he was working in his notebook. I noticed that he had four words written down on a single piece of paper: "Inductor, capacitor, LED, and diode." I asked Reggie what these words meant. He then told me that he had continued to talk through the team's idea with the scientists he worked with at the MIT Saturday Thing and that they had helped him identify these electrical elements to consider in his work with Static Fashion. Reggie said the capacitor would help change voltage and the diodes would help change electrical resistance.

Before Reggie was able to explain these electrical elements to his teammates, Static Fashion was called upon to present their ideas to the expert panel. During their presentation, all five of the Static Fashion team members discussed a different aspect of the team's work. The experts were impressed by the team's idea, and after some clarifying questions, offered some suggestions. Primarily, the panel members suggested that the team consider two approaches—first, to consider carrying on with their idea of making winter clothes that incorporated the multiple layers the team's new fabric technology would need to generate static electricity and to capitalize on the static electricity that naturally occurs during the colder winter months. Second was to develop some form of athletic clothing that capitalized on the friction generated by the body's movement during a kinetic workout activity—and to tap into the growing market of athletic gear designed to hold an individual's smart phone or media player during a work-out.

After their presentation the panel applauded the team, complimented them on their presentation, and expressed their support of the Static Fashion project idea. At the close of their discussion with the field experts, Dishon said, "Good work. We want to see you keep going. We're going to give you $200 to move your idea forward. Congratulations."

The Further Development of an Idea

The Static Fashion team's presentation to a panel of field experts marked a shift in the after-school program's arc of experience. After a mid-winter break, the Static Fashion team returned to their work in Shaunalynn and Rosalie's Thursday afternoon workshop sessions to enter into a new phase of idea development. It was at this point that—just as she was starting to find her place within the team—Dana was transferred to a new high school and, as a result, no longer attended the program's after-school sessions, leaving Jenny, Danny, Maria, and Reggie to continue their work as a quartet.

In the weeks ahead, the students continued to explore ways in which they could not only generate energy by sandwiching conductive fabric layers within insulating layers of fabric, but also store the electricity they generated. The science and technology behind the students' idea development was continuously supported by Reggie's interactions with the MIT researchers at the Saturday Thing. Each week, Reggie arrived at Shaunalynn and Rosalie's workshop space with a new idea to try, and each week he left their workshop space with a new problem to bring to the MIT scientists. Reggie's engagement with the scientists at MIT began to focus more on the importance of figuring out how to convert alternate current electricity into direct current electricity, which suggested that Reggie and his teammates needed to incorporate the use of a capacitor to switch from one form of electrical current to the other in order to make their idea a reality.

Whereas Danny and Reggie had originally collaborated together to engage in experiments and test ideas, as Reggie's experiments with different electrical components became more sophisticated, Jenny became more interested in working with him, and recording findings from the circuitry experiments he conducted. Before long, these experiments incorporated the use of the inductors, capacitors, and resistors he had mentioned previously, and soon also included conductive thread that could be woven into various fabrics. Maria continued to be interested in the aesthetic dimensions of the team's project work, and frequently collaborated with Danny and Jenny, oftentimes draping Danny in elaborate layers of fabric as he played the role of the team's "fashionista." But beyond the aesthetic and design aspects of the team's work, Maria also had a strong interest in better understanding what types of fabrics could act as conductors of electricity, and what types of fabrics might play a more insulating role. The team ultimately decided to use their $200 of prototyping money in two ways. First, to buy electronics components for Reggie and others to experiment with, and second, to purchase a variety of fabrics for Maria to experiment with.

A landmark experience in the team's late-stage idea development took place when the students took a field trip to a local fabric store. During this excursion, the team kindly asked one of the women working at the fabric store a question she had likely never been asked before: "Excuse me miss, but can you show us what fabrics you have that are good for conducting electricity, and what other fabrics you have that aren't good for conducting electricity?" Puzzled at first, the fabric store attendant asked a few clarifying questions that helped her understand what the students were looking for, and directed them to look into certain fabrics. After conducting some in-store experiments and making a few important aesthetic choices, the Static Fashion team left the fabric store with several yards of fabric—and a handful of zippers. These fabrics were later incorporated into the team's experiments with circuitry and conductive thread, to further prototype the team's ideas.

A month later, at the conclusion of the program's school year arc, the Static Fashion team developed ideas to support a line of athletic gear that could be worn by runners to charge their personal electronic devices while they trained and competed in long distance events. Ultimately, the team proposed to design apparel for Boston Marathon runners to wear that would help them concept test their ideas, while also providing the runners with a power source for their devices that they could use during the race.

Though the Static Fashion team was well regarded by their peers and received high marks from the program's jury, in the end, they were not awarded full funding to continue to pursue their work. The formal story of the Static Fashion may seem to conclude here but, in truth, the idea to develop kinetic clothing that can harness the power of static electricity lives on and takes new forms as the students recall their past collaborations with one another and carry their Static Fashion experiences with them.

What Roles do Individuals Play When They Participate in the Development of Creative Ideas?

Similar to the biography of the BiodegradaBall idea presented in Chapter 6, the biography of the Static Fashion idea presented above was a distributed process that included the unique contributions of several actors. The goal for the previous chapter's analysis of the BiodegradaBall idea was to make visible the various actors who contributed to the development of that idea. While a similar idea development map can be drawn to illustrate the development of the Static Fashion idea, the goal here is to make visible the various *roles* individuals played when they participated in the process of developing the Static Fashion idea.

Before digging into the individual roles that the members of the Static Fashion team played during their idea development process, it is important to pause here to reiterate a core tenet of participatory creativity theory introduced in Chapter 2. Simply put, though individuals may play different roles throughout the idea development process, those roles are neither fixed nor unidimensional, but rather dynamic and multiple in nature. In this way, individuals do not merely play roles when they engage in the development of creative ideas, they develop *profiles of participation*.

Identifying Profiles of Participation

While a wide breadth of actors participated in the development of the Static Fashion idea as described above, it is helpful here to focus in on the primary stakeholder group, or core members of students and adult facilitators, who most closely shaped the idea. Taking a closer look at the biography of the Static Fashion idea reveals that the individual members of the Static Fashion

Table 7.1 Observed Moments of Significant Participation (Student Participants).

Role	Dana	Danny	Jenny	Maria	Reggie	TOTAL
Connector	1					1 Moment
Critic				2	1	3 Moments
Designer				3		3 Moments
Experimenter		5	2	2	9	19 Moments
Ideator		2	3	1	3	9 Moments
Listener			1			1 Moment
Performer	2	7			1	10 Moments
Project Manager			8			8 Moments
Researcher			4	3	2	9 Moments
Social Negotiator		3	1		2	6 Moments
Spokesperson		2	4	2	1	9 Moments
Synthesizer		1	3	3	3	10 Moments
Technician				2	13	15 Moments
TOTAL:	**3 Moments**	**20 Moments**	**26 Moments**	**18 Moments**	**36 Moments**	**103 Moments**

team—Jenny, Maria, Danny, Reggie, and Dana—and their program mentors Shaunalynn and Rosalie, played a variety of roles throughout their process of idea development. To illuminate the roles that these individuals played, I carefully reviewed the field notes I took during my time spent in Shaunalynn and Rosalie's Thursday afternoon workshop sessions, and then coded what I referred to as the *observable moments of significant participation* throughout my notes. Of course, whenever a member of the Static Fashion team merely showed up to Shaunalynn and Rosalie's workshop session, it could be argued that they were technically participating in the work of the project team just by being there. However, my analysis showed that, beyond merely being present, there were several instances in which individuals significantly participated in the development of the Static Fashion idea in observable ways. These visible moments of significant participation indicated not only when a member of the team was participating in the process of idea development, but also *how* they were participating. Of course, there were many unobservable moments of significant participation in the work of the team members—such as ways in which they were contributing to the development of the Static Fashion idea outside of Shaunalynn and Rosalie's Thursday afternoon workshop space—but here, the focus is on the young people's observable participation within that environment.

Overall, I recorded 103 observable moments of significant participation by the core members of the Static Fashion team, which helped me to develop profiles of participation for each of the group's members. As Table 7.1 illustrates, each of the Static Fashion students played unique roles throughout their participation in the biography of the Static Fashion idea, but these roles were neither fixed nor unidimensional. Below, I discuss the roles each student in the Static Fashion team played throughout their process of idea development, by triangulating my observations with the students' own perceptions of the roles they played, as well as with the perceptions of their program mentors, Shaunalynn and Rosalie.

Danny: More than a "Test Monkey"

As I learned from my field notes, Danny exhibited twenty moments of observed significant participation spread out amongst six different roles. Mostly, Danny's participation in the development of the Static Fashion idea was in the role of a performer, experimenter, and social negotiator. Interestingly, Danny regularly combined his performer role with his experimenter role. Danny's decision to join the Static Fashion team came from his interest in working with the light bulb and balloon experiment, wherein he spearheaded the rubbing of the balloon across his body, and made a show of the experiment as he did so. This led Jenny to nickname Danny the team's "test monkey." This moniker can literally be understood as the coming together of Danny's experimenter role ("test") and his goofy, performer role ("monkey"). Indeed, when I asked Danny what role he played on the Static Fashion team, he said "probably the

test monkey." Though he objected to the terminology, Reggie also understood Danny's role in this way:

> Jenny calls Danny [the] test monkey. I mean, I don't want to use that
> term, but, yeah. He pretty much finds a way to help everyone. He volun-
> teered to be the fashionista when the clothing is actually fitted. And, he
> also helped out with the experiment that we did about turning the static
> electricity with the balloon. How he just kept rubbing himself all over the
> place.

As Reggie's assessment of Danny's role suggests, there is something more to
what Danny contributes to the group than "test monkey" implies.

When asked about Danny's role, Jenny was quick to say, "He's definitely the
test monkey," but she also expanded upon what this role entailed in a very
thoughtful way. When pressed for what she meant by the term "test monkey"
Jenny responded:

> Well when I mean it I don't mean it in like a silly way, [Danny] definitely
> does help a lot, because he helps like, when we're like "can you help test
> this, can you do this?" And he's like "yeah sure, I'll do it." So it's not so
> much in like in one way joking, but definitely in a way, [being the test
> monkey is] definitely more of a responsibility than it sounds because he
> really does help to push the idea forward and like, when we're like "does
> this make static?" He's like, "well I'll try it out, I'll help you guys do it."
> So he's definitely very gung ho about, like if we're ever stuck on something
> and we don't know what to do and we need help with that experiment,
> he's always ready to do that.

Shaunalynn and Rosalie do not dispute Danny's role as a performer/
experimenter, but they also resist holding such a narrow view of Danny.
Indeed, my observations of the Static Fashion team's process suggest that
more than any of his peers, Danny also played the role of a social negotiator.
During one of our interview discussions, Shaunalynn and Rosalie affirmed this
observation:

> Shaunalynn: [Danny's] like really dedicated to making the social experience
> of the team positive . . . because what he wants out of it is a positive
> social experience, he's invested in making sure that he's not getting that
> at the disturbance of other people, he's getting that with everyone on his
> team.
>
> Rosalie: Right—and in that conversation where they asked Dana to step
> up her game, Danny was like, the most willing to say something positive
> about her and like, tell everyone "it's ok, I'm going to call her and make
> sure that she's ok. I'll call her and smooth everything over."

As this analysis suggests, Danny played multiple roles throughout the Static Fashion idea development process. His profile of participation is largely composed of his roles as a performer/team personality, experimenter, and social negotiator.

Jenny: A Reluctant "Leader"

My observational data suggested that Jenny played as many as eight different roles throughout her participation in the biography of the Static Fashion idea. However, she overwhelmingly acted as the team's project manager—fulfilling this role more than twice as much as any other. In our interview discussion, Jenny acknowledged this position, reluctantly referring to herself as the team's "leader":

> I feel like in a way I'm kind of the "leader" [air quotes] . . . like when people get confused and wonder what's happening with the idea, they definitely come to me to figure out like, "is this what we are supposed to be doing?" like, "where should we go next?" . . . I mean, I help other people I make sure things are just running smoothly because that and I like to make sure that everyone is active, that we're all doing something to help push the idea further. So if we're not running experiments I want to be looking at new options and just kind of like make sure to give everybody that extra push. Making sure that we're ready to go forward with our idea.

Indeed, Jenny (along with Maria) was viewed by her team members as the leader of the group. "Jenny is the leader," Reggie said. Danny concurred, saying, "And, I kind of think of Jenny and Maria as the leader. They give me directions and I follow them." Examples of Jenny playing a leadership role can be found throughout the biography of the Static Fashion idea, particularly in her delegation of tasks to others, her constant checking in with team members, and her maintenance of the team's project notebooks and other forms of documentation.

When asked about the roles people played on the Static Fashion team, Maria pushed back. "I don't feel like [we play separate roles] because we all like work together," she said, "even though [we all] work on different things, you know, we talk together, we know like what [each other] are doing." Pressed further for *how* differently members of the team worked together, Maria noted a close alliance with Jenny. "Jenny and I, we always work together," Maria said "We search on the Internet. We think about how to conduct electricity and create designs." While Jenny may be seen as acting in the role of "leader" or project manager by others, the distributed nature of a project manager's work, combined with her close tie with Jenny, helped Maria see Jenny not as the "leader" of the team as Reggie and Danny expressed, but rather as a peer who assumes the multiple roles necessary to participate in the development of a creative idea.

Maria: Designer, Researcher, Synthesizer— and Chief Skeptic

Maria developed the first visual artifacts for the Static Fashion team, and was the only person to draw designs for the project. As a result, many members of the team relegated Maria to the role of the team's artist and designer. As Reggie noted, "Maria is pretty much the fashion sense [of the team]." While I recognized this sensibility within Maria as well, my field notes told a more complex story. Of Maria's eighteen moments of significant participation, her time was largely distributed across her work as a designer, researcher, and synthesizer. But she also significantly contributed to the team's idea development work as a critic, experimenter, spokesperson, and technician.

Shaunalynn and Rosalie confirmed that Maria's role stretched beyond her work as a designer. "I think of Maria as swapping between being someone who is very interested in aesthetics," Shaunalynn said, "but she's not interested in occupying that role all the time. I think of her kind of as like a synthesizer." Shaunalynn added that Maria is the team's chief skeptic, and Rosalie affirmed Maria's ability to synthesize disparate information, and challenge the flow of the team's project work. "[Maria's] great at articulating her skepticism at any given moment," she said, "you know, no matter how much Danny wants things to be positive and Jenny wants to have a solid, perfect idea, Maria's the one who is going to find a hole in it and talk about it."

Reggie: Technical Problem Solver

My observational data suggest that with thirty-six observed moments of significant participation, Reggie participated in the biography of the Static Fashion idea more than anyone else. Reggie's thirty-six moments of participation could be categorized into nine separate roles, but he mostly contributed to the work of his project team in the role of a technician and an experimenter. Interestingly, though the two had much different approaches to their participation in the Static Fashion idea, I saw many connections between Reggie and Danny. Both young men spearheaded the team's experiments and, in this capacity, they frequently worked together. Whereas Danny brought his performative self to the team's experiments, Reggie brought his technical self to this work. "I think of Reggie as like, the IT guy," Shaunalynn said, and then continued:

> I feel like he started out with ideas of his own, and at some point that boiled down to "what I'm really interested in is doing an electronics project and if it is not exactly the thing I came up with on my own, that's ok." . . . I feel like he took all that passion and interest he had and was like, "ok, now the problem I'm trying to solve using electronics is this one, that this team has articulated, and I'm like 100 percent bought in." And I feel

like a lot of his creativity isn't about articulating the idea but about solving that technical problem.

Colloquially, creativity is often understood as the ability to develop novel ideas. But here, Shaunalynn indicates that the way that Reggie participated in his team's creative process was by pursuing and solving technical problems. The divergent thinking usually associated with creativity was not a core element of Reggie's creative participation. Instead, Reggie applied his interest and skills as a technical thinker to help move the Static Fashion team's ideas forward.

Jenny likewise positioned Reggie as the team's technician—but also expanded on this role, positioning Reggie as an important thought partner as well:

> Reggie's definitely like, he's like co-developer because he helps with a lot of the electronics and stuff . . . but then he definitely like, when I'm confused about something we're doing and I'm like, "how can we make this a circuit?" I'm like, "Reggie how can we do this?" so me and him kind of work together technically and kind of figure out the technical side of stuff, and Reggie's very good with that, he's very good at knowing what to do and how to create it.

Interestingly, when asked about his role on the Static Fashion team, Reggie said,

> I mean, I guess I'm pretty much the person that gives out information and ideas. I don't see myself as the type of stylist, as Maria and Jenny. I'm more towards math and science. Which means that I just use my knowledge from there to help out with trying to create the process of using kinetic clothing to make electricity.

When I asked Shaunalynn and Rosalie what they thought about Reggie being the information and ideas guy, Shaunalynn said, "I bet he means a different thing by 'ideas'" suggesting that Reggie's conception of being the ideas person was deeply rooted in figuring out, quite literally, how an idea can be activated by understanding the technical components that support it.

Dana: A Difficult Fit?

The story of Dana's participation in the development of the Static Fashion team's idea is an interesting one. Though her participation in the biography of the Static Fashion idea was variable, Dana was indeed considered a member of the Static Fashion team until she was ultimately transferred from one school to another and, as a result, ended her participation in Shaunalynn and Rosalie's Thursday afternoon workshop sessions. As the above idea biography illustrates, Dana's participation in the Static Fashion team was inconsistent, and this inconsistency led to social tensions within the group. As a result, Jenny, Danny, Maria, and Reggie became frustrated with Dana's lack of participation and wanted her to engage more with the work they had become so invested in.

When I asked Jenny, Danny, Maria, and Reggie what role they thought Dana played on their team, each student acknowledged Dana as having been a member of the team but, in their own way, each student said that Dana never adopted a particular role. Though it is true that Dana participated less in the idea development process than other members of the Static Fashion team, it cannot be said that she didn't play a role at all. When I asked Dana what role she thought she played on the team, she referenced her experience creating iPad videos with Danny and Reggie, and spoke of herself in a sort of performer role. "I do the singing and dance," she said. Indeed, as Table 7.1 indicates, Dana was identified as having engaged in three moments of significant participation, one as an experimenter, and two as a performer.

It is true that neither Dana, nor Shaunalynn and Rosalie, nor the other students engaged in the Static Fashion team were able to find a consistent role for Dana to play in their idea development process—though everyone, including Dana, certainly tried. Was Dana just not a good fit for the team? Looking closely at the biography of the Static Fashion idea, and each student's participation along the way, yields some interesting questions to consider concerning Dana's engagement—as well as the social nature of creative idea development. First, Dana identified herself as a performer, and indeed she contributed to the team in this way. But within the structure of the team, Danny had also established himself as a performer, and a very bold and outgoing one at that. Could it be the case that the team simply didn't need a second performer? This is a possibility, but is also unlikely as there were several duplicative roles that the Static Fashion team members played, and even some instances in the team's work when it was a great help to have more than one student playing the same role at the same time. Could it then be the case that Danny's brand of performance was more in line with the needs of the team's idea development work, or that Danny's character and sense of humor were more in synch with the tenor of the team? Whereas Dana was interested in movement and dance, Danny's performance abilities were more rooted in comedy. Danny's comedic contributions often built off of the work at hand, or brought a comedic element to that work. In this way, Danny's brand of performance was more aligned with the work than Dana's brand of performance, which had the possibility to be applicable to the work (movement and dance have great potential to generate static electricity!), but was never incorporated into the team's idea development in a significant way.

A third possibility is that, whereas the other members of the Static Fashion team contributed to their idea development work in multiple ways, despite her brief contributions to the team as an experimenter, Dana had not yet tapped the variety of ways that she could potentially engage with the team's work, other than a focus on movement and dance. A final consideration, of course, is that Dana may have been struggling with personal issues that had little to do with her participation in Shaunalynn and Rosalie's workshop sessions, but that distracted her attention from that work.

We may never know how things may have turned out differently if Dana was a more engaged participant in the Static Fashion idea, but what is clear is that Dana's limited participation marked a loss of opportunity for the team. As will be discussed further in Chapter 8, the more an individual participates in the development of a group-generated creative idea, the more that individual learns from the group, and the more the group learns from that individual's unique contributions. As a result of this individual and group learning, the idea itself becomes more sophisticated, and more complex. But the opposite is also true. The less an individual participates in the development of a creative idea, the less they have to learn from their limited engagement with the group, and the less the group learns from that person's limited participation. As a result, the idea being developed is likely to be less sophisticated than it may have been. Overall, though, what we learn from Dana's limited participation in the Static Fashion team's idea development process is that, even when creativity is framed as a distributed and participatory process that is meant to make access to invention and innovation open to all students, it is still difficult to find a role for all students to play in the creative classroom.

Understanding the Roles of Instructors in the Creative Classroom

In their roles as program mentors, Shaunalynn and Rosalie also participated in the development of the Static Fashion idea and can therefore be considered members of the team's primary contributing stakeholder group. Considering the two program mentors' roles in the development of the Static Fashion idea not only provides a deeper understanding of how socially distributed ideas develop, but also sheds light on the many roles that educators may play in the idea development process. Table 7.2 illustrates the variety of roles Shaunalynn and Rosalie played throughout the Static Fashion team's idea development process.[3]

Table 7.2 Observed Moments of Significant Participation (Shaunalynn and Rosalie).

Role	TOTAL
Connector	8 Moments
Facilitator	6 Moments
Project Manager	7 Moments
Researcher	1 Moment
Social Negotiator	17 Moments
Synthesizer	8 Moments
TOTAL:	**47 Moments**

As Table 7.2 indicates, Shaunalynn and Rosalie largely played a social negotiator role throughout the Static Fashion Team's idea development process, while also acting as connectors, synthesizers, project managers, and facilitators. Though behind the scenes they conducted a great amount of research for their students, in class, Shaunalynn and Rosalie's role as researchers was much less pronounced.

One many not consider these to be traditional roles played by educators in the creative classroom, but considering the above biography of the Static Fashion idea, the roles played by Shaunalynn and Rosalie make a great deal of sense. To begin, it should not be surprising that if one were to take a socially distributed approach towards innovation and invention, then one should expect that all of the tensions that arise in social settings will emerge. This was certainly the case in the biography of the Static Fashion idea, wherein Shaunalynn and Rosalie needed to help the project team negotiate their social misunderstandings, and find balance. Though Danny was sensitive to social tensions and frequently actively pursued social harmony amongst his teammates, the situation was such that Shaunalynn and Rosalie likewise needed to step in in this capacity.

Reviewing the Static Fashion idea biography, it is perhaps not surprising that Shaunalynn and Rosalie acted in the roles of connectors, synthesizers, project managers, facilitators, and researchers to lesser extents. A reason for this is that their students acted in these roles, and therefore needed less assistance in these capacities.

What is interesting to note are the roles that Shaunalynn and Rosalie needed to play when particular students were not present. For example, considering the dominant role that Jenny played as a project manager on the Static Fashion team, one may be perplexed as to why Shaunalynn and Rosalie needed to act in this capacity for this group. An explanation for this was revealed during one of my conversations with the two program mentors. "Even today when she wasn't here, I was thinking 'I really want this group to have a successful day,'" Rosalie expressed after one of the days that Jenny had missed class. She then continued,

> I don't want it to be like, "oh . . . wet blanket because Jenny's not here," that's just—I feel like no one should have that kind of effect on their team. And I understand why it's there and it's no one's fault but like, I just don't want to have a class where one person being absent means three people have a bad time. So when I was working with them I was like, "how can I [bring] a similar energy to [the Static Fashion team] that Jenny offers to them?" Because I feel like that is a dynamic that they have all been successful in. And so I was like, delegating the whole time. I was just delegating the whole time.

As Rosalie notes, the Static Fashion team had grown accustomed to having Jenny present in the role of a project manager. In her absence the team struggled to find their bearings. As a result, Shaunalynn and Rosalie were forced to step in and direct the group. A glaring example of such an occurrence can be found during the week when both Jenny and Maria were absent, and the Static Fashion team lost much of its forward momentum. Recognizing the various roles that each of the Static Fashion team members played within the greater dynamic of the group—and development of the idea—helped Shaunalynn and Rosalie figure out the roles they needed to play to support the group, when certain team members were absent.

Just as telling the story of the development of BiodegradaBall in Chapter 6 helped illuminate the distributed narrative of creative idea development, so too did telling the story of Static Fashion illustrate the many roles that young people and adults play throughout the creative process, and the unique profiles of participation that develop for each individual along the way. These two idea biographies aimed to make clear two core aspects of participatory creativity. First is that creativity is a socially distributed process that relies on the unique contributions of various individuals. Second is an understanding that while the ways that young people (and adults) participate in the creative process are unique, it is important not to pigeonhole individuals into particular roles that may limit their full potential. Instead, it is necessary to understand that, just as each individual possesses his or her own unique profile of intelligence, so too do individuals develop their own unique profiles of participation throughout the idea development process. Chapter 8 builds on these two core concepts to better understand what is learned throughout the process of invention and innovation within the creative classroom.

Notes

1. In this chapter, all adults are mentioned by their actual names, whereas the names of all young people are pseudonyms.
2. For more information on the Massachusetts Institute of Technology's "Saturday Thing" program, please see https://edgerton.mit.edu/k-12/academic-fieldtrips-mit/saturday-thing
3. Though Shaunalynn and Rosalie participated in the development of the Static Fashion team's idea development process as individuals, due to the larger focus on their students' engagement in this work, their participation as program mentors was coded jointly. An interesting future study would be to carefully code the individual contributions of teacher pairs throughout the idea development process.

Chapter 8

Participatory Creativity, Learning, and Development

There is a widely held belief that the most important thing to be learned within the creative classroom is how *to be* creative, innovative, or inventive. A participatory understanding of creativity, however, takes a difference stance and instead suggests that one of the primary outcomes of engaging within the creative classroom is learning how *to participate* in creativity. The difference between *to be* and *to participate* may seem semantic, but this shift in understanding can in turn have major effects on how learning experiences may be designed to engage the widest array of young people in the process of invention and innovation.

This final chapter on participatory creativity, learning, and development is roughly divided into three parts. The first part considers what learning takes place when young people engage in participatory creativity. The second part proposes a framework for participatory creativity, learning, and development, and the last part considers the implications for education associated with a participatory reframing of creative learning experiences.

What Types of Learning Take Place During the Development of Socially Distributed Creative Ideas?

Participating in creativity may help equip one with new understandings about the world, one's self, and others. To gain a greater sense of how young people are enriched by engaging in the process of developing socially distributed ideas, it is helpful to once again look more closely at the experiences of the Static Fashion project team. As was mentioned in Chapter 7, not only did I have the privilege of observing the Static Fashion team's idea development *in vivo*, I also had the opportunity to casually interview the Static Fashion team members—including their program mentors Shaunalynn and Rosalie—throughout their process. Part of what was discussed during these semi-structured conversations was what each member of the project team was learning. Ultimately, the biography of the Static Fashion idea—and the team's reflection on their participation in the development of that idea—teaches us that three key things are learned by engaging in the process of socially distributed idea development: *content-area knowledge and skills, intrapersonal and interpersonal skills*, and *a sense of self as a creative participant.*

Developing Content-area Knowledge and Skills

The Static Fashion team members entered the ArtScience Prize idea development space with a great amount of enthusiasm—but with very little content-area knowledge and skills in the domains of practice within which their ideas were situated. As Shaunalynn noted, it was essential for the team to develop a general understanding of the principles of static electricity in order to realize their ideas:

> Maria, Jenny, and Reggie spent a lot of time thinking about what is static actually, what is electricity actually, and what is the difference between charge and electricity? That exploration is where a lot of the [team's] shared vocabulary came from . . . so that they could better understand the project.

Amongst the content the students came to understand is that "Static is a charge being collected on different surfaces and the transfer of electricity is [the charges] being attracted to one another," Shaunalynn said. Students also came to understand that "cold weather and humidity [affect] static electricity," Rosalie added. Referring to the concepts of alternating and direct current, Jenny further articulated how her work with the Static Fashion team helped her better understand these two different forms of electrical current and the impact this understanding would have on their project development:

> I can't remember off the top of my head, but there is one current that is just constant [direct current] and then there's the one that changes a lot and that's the one that goes through the wires and walls and across lines [alternating current], but then when you plug it into the wall it turns into the straight one, and static runs on the straight one and that's the one we actually need, and I got confused with those concepts and I thought we actually had to turn it into the other one, but it's actually not that case so I definitely learned things about static and how static can like produce a lot more energy than I thought it could. At first when we started going with this idea I thought that at a point it's like "oh static can't produce that much [electricity]" but since then I've learned like, "oh it can produce that much, it can be used for this, and if we do this, and with the capacitor to hold it, then we can actually collect it, and that's something I never thought was possible.

In our interview discussions, Maria noted how difficult the scientific aspects of the team's work had been for her; "The most hardest parts are to think about how to conduct electricity," she said. When she began her work in Shaunalynn and Rosalie's workshops, Maria had no background in either electricity or apparel design. "I didn't think anything about conducting electricity through clothes," she said, "[to] turn on a lamp with static is something I never [thought] of." When asked about his learning experiences in Shaunalynn and Rosalie's workshop sessions, Reggie said that he learned "more about static electricity . . . and how it's easier to transfer electrons than I actually thought it was." Shaunalynn articulated that one of the concepts the Static Fashion team learned from its experimentation is that it is difficult to store static electric energy:

> They've learned more about [how] static energy gets created. But, it's not stored, then it's like, there's this additional level of what the design needs to include in order to store enough energy to power something. Because, you can't just touch your phone to your clothes. Your [phone] won't get powered by a zap.

Indeed, wrestling with the idea of storing static electricity had been an issue the team continued to address throughout their idea development work. As Jenny noted,

> We figured out you can create static, we figured out you can generate static, but then we couldn't figure out how to get it away from the balloon and the light bulb and how to make it so that it is actually a circuit . . . getting from the whole premise of collecting static to making an actual circuit and something that could go in clothing was kind of the wall we hit.

Maria tackled this problem when she asked Jenny if it was possible to develop a device that could measure the static electricity potential within the clothing they proposed to make. Asking this question prompted the Static Fashion team to consider not only how they could generate static electricity, but also how they could store it. The team never figured out this puzzle, but they learned a great deal about the science of static electricity, circuitry, and fabrics/materials along the way. In the end, the students not only learned about the nature of static electricity, throughout the course of their work together they also developed increased content-area knowledge and skills related to circuitry, electrical current, and electrical potential of various fabrics and materials.

Developing Intrapersonal and Interpersonal Skills

When I spoke to the Static Fashion team members about their learning experiences, many of them mentioned the content-area knowledge and skills they had acquired, but they spoke a great deal more about the ways in which the idea development experience helped them develop intrapersonal and interpersonal skills. While developing intrapersonal and interpersonal skills may seem to be learning outcomes that live on the opposite ends of a spectrum from one another, the Static Fashion team members I spoke with frequently talked about the two in tandem. Largely speaking, the students indicated the many ways in which their social experiences indeed helped them develop interpersonal skills, but also helped them develop important intrapersonal skills ranging from empathy and perspective taking, to confidence and leadership skills. This suggests that both intrapersonal and interpersonal skills are benefits that build character, and accrue to the individual.

During one of our discussions, Danny emphasized how engaging with the work of the Static Fashion team helped him both develop aspects of his character, as well as develop important social skills. "I learned to correct my mistakes, build up confidence, and . . . be supportive of others," Danny noted. He then went on to comment on the value of working with others. "Working with teammates and, getting support," was important to Danny. "After [receiving] the support from teammates and mentors," he said, "you feel like you can do anything."

In one of our interview discussions, Maria said that she was selective when it came to deciding whom she spends her time with, "but in here," she said, "I have to learn to like different kinds of personalities, because like, Danny's a different person, and Jenny's different, Reggie's different, I'm different. Like, I learned a lot [about] the characteristics of people."

Though her fluctuating participation posed challenges for the Static Fashion team, Dana likewise emphasized the social aspects of idea development as being the richest part of her learning experiences. "I'm learning how to be in a group, as a community. How to work as a teammate," she said. "Because, not everywhere people like to work with people they don't know, and create a community of people they don't know, either."

In a discussion with Shaunalynn and Rosalie, the two program mentors articulated how the science and the social experience of working on the Static Fashion team have uniquely overlapped for Reggie. As the following transcript excerpt indicates:

ROSALIE: The other thing that feels like a little victory for Reggie is that his own curiosities and personal [technical commitment] towards going in his free time to [work on the] capacitor also gives him some social credibility when he joins back into the group. . . . I often wonder how much social cred he has generally in his life experience, and I'm just seeing him be more and more socially playful in the way that he talks to people. I feel like earlier in the year he was very sort of calculated in the way that he spoke to people and like incredibly polite.

SHAUNALYNN: Yeah, earlier today he laughed out loud at Danny and—it was a moment when Danny clearly wanted people to laugh at him—but like, I remember earlier in the year Reggie would like, not laugh and I felt like it was part of his politeness, and when I saw him cracking up at Danny I was just like wow—things have changed!

As Rosalie nicely summed up, through Reggie's participation in the development of the Static Fashion idea, and specifically in his role as the team's primary technician, "he's finding his place in the world among people."

The intersection of the science and the social component of the Static Fashion work had also been an enriching experience that helped Maria improve her English language skills. Shaunalynn explained to me that increasing her English language skills was a very specific learning outcome for Maria, which, on the surface, may appear to be individually based, but in reality was socially driven:

> Talking to Maria at different times I know that learning that is specific to her is speaking English. And I think, she's articulated to me and I've noticed both the idea of increasing confidence in [speaking], developing . . . the sensibility inside yourself to say, "I could not speak now, but I'm going to speak," and just being more—she speaks in a completely different way now than she did at the beginning of the year. Part of that is social and part of that is that she is developing some amount of vocabulary around the project.

In my conversation with Maria, she said, "I'm so afraid to talk to people. I'm so shy." But Maria's shyness, rooted in her initial insecurity in her English language skills, was mitigated by her work on the Static Fashion team. Maria pointed to her experience at the Ideas in Progress Exhibition as an important learning experience:

> Yeah. That's the thing that changed now because the day of the exhibition I had to talk to people and smile and speak up, and at first I was like, "oh my god," but then I felt like, "forget about it, go for it!" I changed. I was smiling. . . . I was enjoying it, I was so proud of myself.

Maria also made the case that participating in the development of the Static Fashion project idea had broadened her perspectives and changed her thinking.

> For me, at the beginning, I was like, I don't know what to do. I didn't have any idea[s] . . . . And then I met people that I liked and they [came] with ideas different from mine and they combine[d] them together and I think that is incredible. It's really cool. It's a lot different than how I think. My thinking has changed because sometimes now I have different ideas which at the beginning I didn't come to.

Ultimately, participating in a socially distributed idea development process helped the Static Fashion team members develop important intrapersonal and interpersonal skills, which in turn contributed to the development of each student's character, and their confidence in working with others. While the individually based outcomes of this learning experience are significant, it is important to note the value of the social skills the students developed—especially considering the premium placed on social skills and social intelligence in the contemporary innovation economy.[1]

Developing a Sense of Self as a Creative Participant

In one of the conversations I had with Maria, she mentioned that she never saw herself as being a creative person, and when she signed up to participate in the ArtScience Prize, she did not have a real sense of what she was doing. When it became clear that she had signed up for a program that was all about creativity and innovation, Maria became nervous. But, over time, as Maria engaged in the work of idea development with her Static Fashion teammates, she found that there was a place for her in the idea development process. Even though she did not consider herself to be a creative person, she soon came to realize that she had talents and skills that were important to her teammates and essential to move the group's work forward. It no longer mattered whether or not she viewed herself as *being* creative, Maria had learned how to *participate* in creativity.

Though developing content-area knowledge and skills and intrapersonal and interpersonal skills were important learning outcomes for the Static Fashion team members, perhaps the most significant benefit from participating in the idea development process for each student was establishing a sense of oneself as a creative participant. For each student, creative participation took a different form. As the tasks of developing a fabric that could potentially harness the power of static electricity placed new demands on the students, they rose to the challenges of those demands in different ways. In the end, each student had developed a unique profile of participation that did not place a number or a score on their creative potential in a narrow way, but rather offered a doorway into how he or she could participate in creativity in ways that they were already good at—or in ways that tapped talents and expertise they had not yet realized they had. This was a particularly palpable experience for Jenny, who came to see herself as having the potential to participate in creativity in a leadership role. As she noted during one of our discussions:

> I definitely have learned how to like, take a leadership role, because like I'm usually the one who follows behind somebody else's idea and I definitely have been that way like all my life, but with this now I feel like I've developed the skills with how to like talk to people and explain my ideas in a very articulate way and then also make sure that people stay on task and that I also can help facilitate things for people, and those are skills I've developed because I didn't really know how to do that before like—helping other people was something I've always liked to do, but I've never had to run something, which is very different.

Jenny's realization of her talents as a leader and a project manager came out of necessity. Through the process of participating in a socially distributed idea development process, Jenny not only developed new skills, she also came to realize how she can participate in creativity in ways she had not expected. As the Static Fashion team members' profiles of participation began to take shape, each of them came to understand that there were many ways that they could contribute to the development of creative ideas. In this way, the Static Fashion team members began to see how their individual agency could be uniquely enacted through a project that demanded the collective efforts of a larger and more distributed group.

Based on my field notes and interviews with the Static Fashion students and their program mentors, the learning outcomes that accrued to these individuals through their participation in a socially distributed idea development process included content-area knowledge and skills related to static electricity, fabrics, and materials, coupled with intrapersonal and interpersonal skills that built character within individual students while showing them how best to work with others, leading to each student establishing a sense of him or herself as a creative participant. While the specifics of these learning outcomes may be unique to the experiences of the Static Fashion team members, within this particular case study of student learning lie more generalizable notions about what's learned through engaging in a participatory and distributed idea development process.

Establishing a Learning and Development Framework for Participatory Creativity

As described above, the back and forth between individuals and groups and the strong social component of the creative process served as key markers of the learning experiences associated with the work of the Static Fashion team. To establish a framework for learning and development based on a participatory and distributed model of invention and innovation, it is therefore helpful to refer to the socially oriented work of Lev Vygotsky as interpreted by Vera John-Steiner and her colleagues.[2] These scholars have utilized Vygotsky's cultural-historical theory and dialectical method to "argue that development and creativity are dialectically interrelated processes,"[3] wherein the word *dialectical* is used to suggest a reciprocal effect.

Vygotsky's cultural-historical theory states that the processes of *internalization* and *externalization* exist in a dialectical relationship with one another, wherein internalization involves the individual's transformation and reorganization of cognitive information in response to engagement with social groups and externalization involves the individual conferring new information outwards into social groups in the form of ideas or inventive new products. In this way, the individual learns from society and, by generating new ideas and products, the individual reciprocally contributes to the development of society. "This internal/external movement becomes cyclical. . . . Creativity, then, depends on development, and development depends on creativity."[4]

This model of the individual affecting culture and culture affecting the individual is resonant with Mihaly Csikszentmihalyi's sociocultural model of creativity (see Chapter 2). Not unlike Csikszentmihalyi's sociocultural theory, John-Steiner and her colleagues' Vygotskian theory of creativity and development is also a theory of learning. As a cultural domain develops, the individuals who participate in that domain are transformed—they learn from new developments in culture, just as they spawn new cultural developments through the contributions they make to particular domains of practice. John-Steiner and her colleagues have suggested that Vygotsky's cultural-historical theory brings a temporal element to Csikszentmihalyi's sociocultural model. Thus, their interpretation of Vygotsky's theory of creativity incorporates a cyclical component "connecting past to future . . . contribut[ing] to a community's history and culture."[5]

A reframing of this process of innovation and development from a participatory creativity perspective quite literally adds a new twist to John-Steiner and her colleagues' cyclical model. Building on the structure presented by these theorists, participatory creativity can be described as a *double-loop* process of dialectical learning and development.

A Dialectical Approach to Creativity, Learning, and Development

In order to establish a participatory creativity-based framework for learning and development, it is important to first scale back John-Steiner and her colleagues' theory from the cultural level to the local level, and then to add a distributed contributing stakeholder group into the mix. Having done this, it is then possible to build a framework for learning and development that extends from individuals to groups to ideas—and then back again.

As suggested above, this framework consists of two loops. The first loop can be described as the dialectical relationship between individuals and a contributing stakeholder group. As Figure 8.1 illustrates, as individuals enact their agency by collectively participating in the co-construction of new ideas, they form localized groups of actors—the contributing stakeholder group. Through this process, individuals externalize their knowledge, expertise, background experiences, and cultural perspectives, which then become internalized by the contributing stakeholder group. As a result, group learning takes place and the contributing stakeholder group becomes more complex. As the contributing stakeholder group becomes more complex as a result of the various contributions of its group members, it externalizes the new information it has absorbed, which is then internalized by its individual participants. In this way, individuals learn something new from the other individuals in the group—and become more complex themselves—as a result of their group participation.

Of course, if the goal of the contributing stakeholder group is to develop new and innovative ideas, then the knowledge, expertise, and cultural

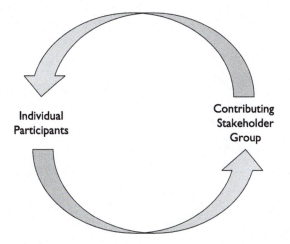

Figure 8.1 The Dialectical Relationship between Individual Participants and a Contributing Stakeholder Group.

Note: When individuals participate in creativity by enacting their agency and externalizing their knowledge, skills, background experiences, and cultural perspectives, the contributing stakeholder group they are participating in internalizes these attributes, and becomes more complex. In this way, group learning takes place. At the same time, through the process of participation, the group redistributes the diverse attributes of its many participants through a process of externalization. In turn, the individual participants of a contributing stakeholder group internalize these diverse attributes. In this way, individual participants in a contributing stakeholder group learn from their peers.

perspectives described above do not stay within this closed loop. Instead, a contributing stakeholder group externalizes its knowledge and expertise to the idea it is developing, the idea internalizes this information and, as a result, the focal idea under development becomes more nuanced and complex. As this focal idea becomes more complex it externalizes new information, in the form of new challenges and opportunities, to the contributing stakeholder group, which then internalizes this information, resulting in group learning and making the contributing stakeholder group more nuanced and complex (see Figure 8.2). This second loop can be described as the dialectical relationship between a contributing stakeholder group and a creative idea.

When these two loops come together, a figure eight forms (see Figure 8.3), providing a framework for participatory creativity that is structured as a double loop process of learning and development. In summary, as ideas develop and become more nuanced and complex, so too do the contributing stakeholder groups who develop those ideas become more complex. In this way, group learning takes place. And when group learning takes place, the individual actors associated with a group acquire knowledge and develop skills along the way. It is also true that as individual actors contribute new information to their contributing stakeholder group, the group learns from these individuals. The

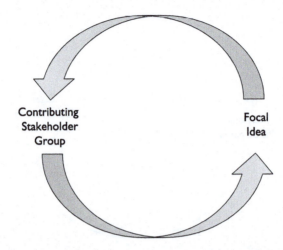

Figure 8.2 The Dialectical Relationship between a Contributing Stakeholder Group and its Focal Idea.

Note: As a contributing stakeholder group externalizes the attributes of its individual participants in the pursuit of developing a focal idea, the focal idea internalizes those attributes and becomes more nuanced and complex. In this way, idea development takes place. As a focal idea becomes more nuanced and complex, it externalizes new opportunities and challenges to its associated contributing stakeholder group. As the contributing stakeholder group addresses these new opportunities and challenges through a process of internalization, the contributing stakeholder group builds new knowledge skills and in turn becomes more complex. In this way, group learning and development takes place.

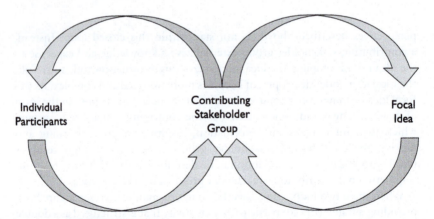

Figure 8.3 Participatory Creativity and the Double Loop Process of Learning and Development (Local Level).

Note: When individuals participate in socially distributed groups (a contributing stakeholder group), the group becomes more complex and, as a result, the focal idea the group is developing becomes more nuanced and complex. As a focal idea becomes more nuanced and complex, the group developing that idea further becomes complex. As the group developing a focal idea becomes more complex, the individuals participating in that group develop new knowledge and skills. In this way, learning and development take place locally on the individual, group, and idea level.

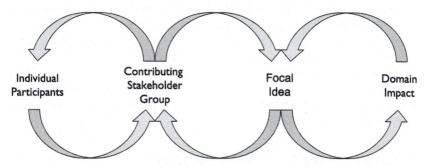

Figure 8.4 Participatory Creativity and the Triple Loop Process of Learning and Development (Cultural Level).

Note: In the triple loop process of learning and development that takes place when idea development on the local level has a broader impact on a domain, learning and development take place on the individual, group, idea, and cultural level.

more a group learns, the greater potential that group has to bring further complexity to the ideas it is developing.

This model for learning and development stresses the importance of individual participation. If an individual ceases to participate in the contributing stakeholder group that is engaged in the development of a creative idea, then that creative idea will cease to learn from that individual's contributions, and the idea will be diminished by the lesser complexity of the contributing stakeholder group as a result.

As mentioned above, the entire cycle described by this double loop process of learning and development exists on the local level. If one were to consider a creative idea's effect on a domain of practice (culture) as suggested by John-Steiner and her colleagues (and Csikszentmihalyi), then the double loop model for learning and development can be expanded to a triple loop model of learning and development, as Figure 8.4 suggests.

Implications for Education

While the above model presents a sound theoretical theory to describe the dialectical nature of the learning and development associated with a participatory reframing of creativity, it is also important to translate theory into tangible practice. Throughout this book I have frequently underscored the importance for teachers, administrators, and other professionals working within the sphere of education to make the shift from traditional, individual-based understandings of creativity to more socially distributed and participatory orientations towards invention and innovation. I have also emphasized the cognitive dissonance that such a change of mindset may entail. Having made this epistemological leap, one may wonder: what's a teacher or school administrator to do?

There are many implications for education that may be drawn from a participatory and distributed reframing of creativity. In fact, I imagine an entire book can be devoted to the topic on its own. The challenge I find for myself here is to discuss the implications for participatory creativity in a way that is neither too prescriptive nor so abstract or theoretical as to be inactionable. With the idea in mind that there are many more applications to practice to be discussed, below I offer a baker's dozen of general implications for education that I find to be most salient.

1. Foreground the Social Nature of Ideas

Central to a theory of participatory creativity is the notion that ideas are social, not psychological, events. In the creative classroom it is important to foreground the social nature of ideas, and to make visible the ways in which ideas evolve over time and take shape through the contributions of others. Even when it appears that an idea has emerged as the result of one person's individual thinking, it is important to recall that even when young people and adults appear to be acting independently, their process of ideation can always be traced back to past collaborations. Mapping out the social origins of ideas is helpful in understanding how an idea has evolved over time, and who has participated in its development along the way.

2. Provide Opportunities for Young People to Connect and Learn from Others

As emphasized in the dialectical model of participatory creativity presented above, learning and development is enhanced and ideas become more nuanced and complex when young people and adults are given the opportunity to work with and invent with one another. Not only should young people and adults have the opportunity to collaborate with one another within the creative classroom, it is important for individuals participating in the idea development process to remember that they may find many influential collaborators outside the walls of the creative classroom as well. External knowledge and information sourcing and seeking out the perspectives and expertise of others are practices that will not only benefit young people and adults working within the creative classroom, but will also serve as valuable skills throughout one's life and work.

3. Follow Students Wherever they Lead, and Help them Make Connections Wherever they Go

Traditionally, the work of teaching and learning has often taken the form of a structured experience designed by a knowledgeable educator—perhaps with some twists and turns along the way—but generally consisting of relatively well defined start, middle, and end points. The creative classroom should be a different place—and the role of the educator within that space should be understood differently as a result. It is likely that, given the opportunity to develop innovative ideas that are personally meaningful to oneself and others, groups of young people and adults may find themselves on a path that leads beyond the expertise of the educator in the room. Though an educator may feel understandably nervous when following students beyond the comfort zone of their own knowledge base, within the creative classroom it is important for educators to follow students where they lead, to learn with them along the way, and to help them make connections to new sources of knowledge and expertise as they continue down their pathway of group discovery.

4. Stress that Creativity is Neither a Spark nor a Flash of Insight—Creativity is Purposeful Work

As mentioned above, creativity is not a psychological event—such as a flash of insight—but rather a social affair, crafted over time by the contributions of many people. It is also important to emphasize that creativity is work. It requires intentional effort and time. The work that takes place in the creative classroom should be no easier nor less rigorous than the work that takes place in any other classroom. Though it may not always be easy, if the ideas being developed by groups of young people and adults are meaningful and relevant to themselves and others, then the effort required of creative idea development will always be work worth doing.

5. Recognize that a Social Theory of Creativity is not Immune from the Tensions that may Arise through Social Interactions

As a participant in a socially distributed idea development process, one should not assume that things will always run smoothly. Inviting multiple players into the creative idea development process invites multiple personalities into that process as well—and personalities do not always get along. The practice of participatory creativity is just as susceptible to the tensions that arise when groups of people get together as is any other social setting. In this way, social negotiations become an important part of the idea development process. As difficult as it may be to smooth out social tensions, participants in the creative classroom should keep in mind that the ability to navigate choppy social waters is a highly prized professional skill—and it can never hurt to have some practice developing one's skills of social negotiation.[6]

6. Honor and Encourage Individual Student Agency within the Collective Idea Development Process

While participatory creativity is based upon a distributed model of idea development, one should never lose sight of the role of individual agency throughout the pursuit of social efficacy. Ideas do not develop on their own, but rather through the actions of others. Educators in the creative classroom should encourage their students to enact their individual agency throughout the creative process in ways that capitalize on the best that each individual has to bring to the process. While the work of the creative classroom should focus on the ideas that individuals develop together, each participant should be able to see him or herself in the pursuits of the greater collective.

7. Creativity is who Young People Already Are, not Someone New they Must Become

As in any classroom, participants enter the creative classroom with a wealth of talents, skills, background experiences, and cultural perspectives. A participatory approach to creativity does not suggest that young people and adults need to be shaped or reinvented to be creative in a contrived way. Instead, the creative learning experience itself is shaped by what young people have to bring to the process. This is not to say that young people will not learn something new about themselves through the idea development process (the hope is that they most certainly will) but rather that it is important to start with the richness young people and adults already bring with them when they walk through the door of the creative classroom, and build up from there.

8. Resist the Urge to Pigeonhole Students and Place them into Boxes

When students participate in creativity, they naturally take on particular roles that are best suited to the demands of the task at hand and their own strengths. But as the roles that students play in the creative classroom come into greater relief, it is important for educators to remember that young people and adults are multi-dimensional. Rather than narrowly define students and place them into participatory boxes, it is important to understand how each participant in the creative classroom contributes to the idea development process in multiple ways. Identifying the profiles of participation for each student in the creative classroom further avails educators the opportunity to understand the dimensionality of their students and to tap students' potential—or challenge students to stretch beyond their comfort zones—in unexpected ways.

9. Make Students' Profiles of Participation Visible

If young people and adults in the creative classroom are to reach their full potential, then it is important that each individual understands and explores his or her unique profile of participation. While a particular individual's profile of participation may be clear to a researcher or careful observer in the creative classroom, recognizing one's own profile of participation may not be so obvious. For this reason, it is important that educators in the creative classroom not only recognize and understand each student's profile of participation, but also for educators to support their students by making their profiles of participation visible. Understanding one's own profile of participation may help young people and adults develop a deeper sense of themselves as a creative participant, which may in turn lead to greater confidence and self-efficacy both within the creative classroom, and throughout one's life and work.

10. Utilize the Tools of Documentation and Narrative to make Creativity Visible

In addition to making individual students' profiles of participation visible, it is also important that educators in the creative classroom utilize the tools of documentation and narrative to make the overall creative process visible. In Chapter 5 the biography of an idea methodology was presented as a tool for telling the emergent story of creative idea development. Through the process of telling the story of creative ideas, one may see the various actors who contribute to an idea along the way, important interactions that take place during an idea's development, essential turning points that have affected the development of an idea, and perhaps most importantly—what young people and adults learn when they participate in the process of invention and innovation.

From a teacher's perspective, one may view the biography of an idea methodology as a form of assessment. The biography of an idea both chronicles how individual students participate in idea development, and what individual students and groups learn throughout this process. Astute educators will note that the biography of an idea methodology may not only serve as a form of *summative assessment*, but that its real power lies in its potential as a form of *formative assessment*. In other words, the biography of an idea need not only be a story told at the end of the learning process, but instead used throughout the learning process to help students understand where they have been, how they got there, what pitfalls they have fallen into in the past, what information has benefitted their process and where that information came from, and what might be some promising ways forward. Of course, the biography of an idea does not need to be a traditionally text-based story, but may also include documentation of all sorts, including audio, video, still images, sketches, 3-D models, prototypes, or even elements of live performance.

11. Break Down the Barriers to Creative Participation Wherever they are Found

A driving theme throughout this book has been the importance of making creativity more equitable and accessible to all students. In any creative learning environment, educators should celebrate the students they have to work with and provide the most valuable learning experiences for those individuals. At the same time, educators must also be aware of who is *not* in their creative classroom—and why. If we endeavor to live in a world shaped by innovation and cultural richness, then—as educators, administrators, and others involved in the practice of education—it is important that we ensure that all students have access to creative learning experiences, and that those learning experiences are as equitable as possible. In some instances, this may literally mean that young people and adults know how to find their way to the creative classroom, and that there are no financial or cultural barriers to entry once they are there. In other instances this may mean that the language and sociocultural norms of the creative classroom must be as accessible as possible for all students, so that each young person and adult may equally benefit from their time spent in that space.

12. All Classrooms have the Potential to be Creative Classrooms

Part of making creativity more equitable and accessible to all students is recognizing that all classrooms have the potential to be creative classrooms. It has long been argued that creativity should not be the sole province of disciplines like the arts, or that creativity is not just something one engages in within the makerspace or during a design thinking workshop but, instead, the potential for young people and adults to engage in the development of socially distributed ideas should be a practice that takes place in all learning environments. This includes the mathematics classroom and the physics lab, but it also includes the kitchen table, the local park, and the town square. Opportunities to engage with others to develop creative ideas can be found—and should be found—everywhere. To restrict creativity to certain times, places, and spaces, is to keep creativity on too short a leash. There is great value in having dedicated spaces to do important creative work, but a truly systems-based approach towards understanding invention and innovation must not be bounded by time or physical space.

13. Don't Forget Joy

Creativity is purposeful, sometimes difficult work and the process of socially distributed idea development will undoubtedly surface uncomfortable social tensions from time to time. Furthermore, access to creative learning experiences in our contemporary culture is riddled with unjust barriers. Making the creative classroom more equitable and accessible is indeed an uphill battle. Nonetheless, despite the rigor of work associated with creativity, the social drama that may arise in the creative classroom, and the struggle to make creative learning experiences more equitable and accessible to all young people, it is important for educators, administrators, and all of the participants and stakeholders associated with the creative classroom to remember that to pursue invention and innovation is to pursue joy. Participatory creativity is, by all means, serious business, but throughout the process of developing new ideas in the company of others—whether those individuals be near or far—one should never forget the humanity associated with the creative process. One should never forget joy.

Educators and administrators know their students and their learning environments best. While the above implications for education are meant to serve as general guidelines, how one structures a creative learning experience—and where—is a task each person will tackle in their own unique way. While not being too specific, I hope that the implications for education that I have provided above are substantive enough for educators and administrators to see the potential to establish a wide array of creative learning experiences for the many individuals they work with every day—and for the new faces they may meet tomorrow.

Notes

1. See David J. Deming, "The Growing Importance of Social Skills in the Labor Market," Working paper 21473 (Cambridge, MA: National Bureau of Economic Research, 2015). Retrieved from: www.nber.org/papers/w21473
2. See Vera John-Steiner & Holbrook Mahn, "Sociocultural Approaches to Learning and Development: A Vygotskian Framework." *Educational Psychologist*, 31, no. 3–4 (1996): 191–206. See also Seana Moran & Vera John-Steiner, "Creativity in the Making: Vygotsky's Contemporary Contribution to the Dialectic of Development and Creativity," in *Creativity and Development*, pp. 61–90, ed. R. Keith Sawyer (New York: Oxford University Press, 2003).
3. See Moran and John-Steiner, "Creativity in the Making," p. 63.
4. Ibid., p. 65.
5. Ibid., p. 63.
6. See Deming, "The Growing Importance of Social Skills."

Conclusion: Taking Responsibility for the Creative Classroom

An excerpt from the recent Project Zero book *Visible Learners* illustrates a palpable tension that exists between the realities of our twenty-first century lived experiences and conventional thinking about the nature of teaching and learning within schools:

> Globalization and the new economy of the twenty-first century demand the ability to learn and function as part of increasingly diverse groups. In an interconnected and rapidly changing world, our knowledge of ourselves as individual and group learners becomes more important. Yet the acquisition of knowledge is still primarily viewed as an individual process. Thinking and learning are generally considered individual rather than social or communicative acts. Virtually all assessment and many aspects of instruction still focus on promoting individual performance and achievement.[1]

As the Project Zero researchers state, there is a disconnect between the globally interconnected world in which we live, and the ways in which young people are educated within many formal and informal learning environments. This misalignment between sociocultural experience and curricular practice extends beyond the realm of general education and into the creative classroom, where—in many instances—a culture of individualism continues to reinforce traditionally held beliefs about creativity and creative learning experiences.

A participatory reframing of invention and innovation aims to address this misalignment by presenting a new way of looking at the ways in which ideas develop in the world—with an emphasis placed on changing the way we think of creativity in education. As discussed in Chapter 2, the theory of participatory creativity puts forth an epistemological shift that argues that individuals are not creative, ideas are creative—and that by shifting the locus of creativity from individuals to ideas opens up the opportunity for all young people to participate in creativity in ways that most naturally suit their talents, skills, background experiences, and cultural perspectives. A systems-based theory of creativity does not strip individuals of their agency. Quite the contrary. Through the process of developing socially distributed ideas, young people enact their individual agency and develop unique profiles of participation. This experience of individually participating in the development of group-generated ideas empowers young people not only to excel on their own terms within the creative classroom, but also throughout their experiences in life and work in the wider world.

As educators, researchers, administrators, parents, and policymakers invested in the outcomes associated with the creative classroom, I believe that we are responsible—in several ways—for that learning space. Our first responsibility is to structure and support creative learning experiences that empower all young people to develop a sense of themselves as creative participants in the world. Key to this mission is recognizing that there is no one way to participate in creativity, but rather multiple ways for a variety of young people to bring the best of themselves to bear on their engagement in the creative classroom. In this sense, creative learning experiences should be open to all that young people have to offer.

But having an open door policy on what it means to participate in creativity is just one part of our responsibility for the creative classroom. We also have a responsibility to break down the barriers that keep so many young people from either stepping foot in the creative classroom or from being their best selves once they arrive there. As is discussed in Chapter 4, in addition to a culture of individualism that causes us to uphold traditional, narrowly focused conceptions of creativity in education, our cultures of power further limit who has access to the creative classroom in a quite literal sense, but also in terms of how certain sociocultural norms are favored over others within our most progressive creative learning environments. Both access and equity are at issue here—and attending to these issues is our responsibility.

But there is yet another responsibility we have for the creative classroom that, as of yet, has not been explicitly discussed in this book. Just as we have a responsibility to make creative participation more equitable and accessible for all young people, we also have a responsibility to address the ethical dimensions of invention and innovation within the creative classroom.

On April 15, 2013, during the 117th annual running of the Boston Marathon, two brothers detonated homemade bombs made of pressure cookers in close proximity to the marathon's finish line. Their act of terror killed three people and seriously injured over two hundred others. The press quickly regarded the Boston Marathon Bombing as an act of homegrown terrorism, but one can also make the case that this horrific event was an act of malicious creativity of the very worst kind. It is not a pleasant thing to think about, but one can argue that the two brothers who planned the attack formed their own contributing stakeholder group, sourced information from others, and developed the idea to launch a domestic terror campaign, of which the Boston Marathon Bombing was meant to be just one episode in a broader plot.[2] It is not a stretch to suggest that the Boston Marathon Bombing, as it was widely reported in the press, can likewise be retold as the biography of an idea.

As noted in Chapter 2, Michael Hanchett Hanson has suggested that the emerging participatory synthesis brings together aspects of individual agency with more systems-based perspectives of creativity, but it also suggests the further consideration of the practices of creativity being used for base and malevolent purposes, or, as Hanchett Hanson has put it, "the recent interests in questions of the dark side of creativity and the ethics of creativity, which require taking both individual and sociocultural factors into consideration."[3]

Participatory creativity places an emphasis on the roles that individuals play in change. And while the popular rhetoric on creativity almost exclusively frames participation in invention and innovation with positive notes, it cannot be ignored that people can—and do—participate in creativity in wicked ways as well. Of course, not all wicked instantiations of creativity exist on the level of domestic terrorism. As Carrie James has noted in her book, *Disconnected: Youth, New Media, and the Ethics Gap*, young people can likewise compromise their collective ethics through their participation in online roleplaying games by intentionally cheating other players.[4] Whether building bombs in the physical world or scamming others in a virtual world, poor ethical decisions have the potential to send the work of creativity awry, and harm others as a result.

Those of us interested in empowering young people to participate in invention and innovation within the creative classroom therefore bear the responsibility of addressing the ethics of creative participation. To empower young people in any way suggests a process of giving them power. In the creative classroom, this power is creativity itself. Conversations must therefore be had concerning how the power of creativity can be used as a force of good— without ignoring the fact that the power of creativity can just as easily be employed as a force of evil. Conversations around good and evil are difficult to have, perhaps especially with young people. Nonetheless, educators in the creative classroom cannot assume that their students are having these conversations elsewhere.

At the same time, educators in the creative classroom should certainly not assume that the students in their midst are particularly inclined towards the malevolent use of creative power. Instead, educators should assume the good intentions of all young people, and strive to provide their students with cognitive tools they can use to better think through moral and ethical issues when they arise in the creative classroom, or throughout their creative participation in life and work.

It is important to bring to light issues of ethics in the creative classroom, and I make this point here with great intention. That being said, one must not lose sight of all of the good in the world that can come from creative participation. Not all ideas developed by young people in the creative classroom will come to fruition—but whether an idea developed by young people causes a positive shift in our lived experience or not is mostly besides the point. The "good" of creative participation lies in the increased sense of agency that each young person in the creative classroom develops; the sense that he or she can effect change in the world on his or her own terms, based on his or her own strengths, from the perspective of his or her own worldview, through the interaction and engagement of others.

As educators, administrators, researchers, parents, and policymakers with a stake and an interest in the success of the creative classroom, perhaps our most important responsibility is to provide the opportunity for individual students to be themselves and build themselves through the process of creative participation. With our advocacy and support, participatory creative learning experiences can provide young people with the thrill of developing new ideas in the company of others, the pride of understanding how one's individual agency can contribute to a greater goal, and the joy involved in participating in the process of change.

Notes

1. See Mara Krechevsky, Ben Mardell, Melissa Rivard, & Daniel Wilson, *Visible Learners: Promoting Reggio-Inspired Approaches in All Schools* (San Francisco, CA: Jossey-Bass, 2013) p. xiii.
2. It has been widely reported in the press that the two brothers intended to carry out a similar attack in New York City's Times Square following the Boston Marathon bombing.
3. See Michael Hanchett Hanson, *Worldmaking: Psychology and the Ideology of Creativity.* (New York: Palgrave Macmillan, 2015), p. 180.
4. See Carrie James, *Disconnected: Youth, New Media, and the Ethics Gap* (Cambridge, MA: Massachusetts Institute of Technology Press, 2014).

References

Amabile, T. M. (1983). The social psychology of creativity: A componential conceptualization. *Journal of Personality and Social Psychology, 45*(2), 357–376.

Amabile, T. M. (1996). *Creativity in context.* Boulder, CO: Westview Press.

Aragon, C. R. & Williams, A. (2011). Collaborative creativity: A complex systems model with distributed affect. Paper presented at CHI 2011, Vancouver, BC, May 7–11.

ArtScience Labs (2011). *ArtScience Prize program replication manual.* Boston, MA: ArtScience Labs.

Baer, J. (1994). Why you should trust creativity tests. *Educational Leadership, 51*(4), 81–83.

Baer, J. (1998). The case for domain specific creativity. *Creativity Research Journal, 11*(2), 173–177.

Baer, J. (2010). Is creativity domain specific? In J. C. Kaufman & R. J. Sternberg (Eds.), *The Cambridge handbook of creativity* (pp. 321–341). New York: Cambridge University Press.

Bandura, A. (2000). Exercise of human agency through collective efficacy. *Current Directions in Psychological Science, 9*(3), 75–78.

Becker, H. S. (1982). *Art worlds.* Berkeley, CA: University of California Press.

Bernays, E. L. (1965). *Biography of an idea: Memoirs of public relations counsel Edward L. Bernays.* New York: Simon and Schuster.

Blake, A. (2012, July 18). Obama's "you didn't build that" problem. *Washington Post.* Retrieved from https://www.washingtonpost.com/blogs/the-fix/post/obamas-you-didnt-build-that-problem/2012/07/18/gJQAJxyotW_blog.html

Bourdieu, P. & Passeron, J. (1977). *Reproduction in education, society, and culture.* Beverly Hills, CA: Sage.

Brown, A. L., Ash, D., Rutherford, M., Nakagawa, K., Gordon, A., & Campione, J. C. (1993). Distributed expertise in the classroom. In G. Salomon (Ed.), *Distributed cognitions: Psychological and educational considerations* (pp. 188–228). New York: Cambridge University Press.

Brown, T. (2008, June). Design thinking. *Harvard Business Review,* 84–92.

Chang, J. (2005). *Can't stop won't stop: A history of the hip hop generation.* New York: St. Martin's Press.

Chang, J. (2009, May 4). A new deal for culture. *The Nation.* Retrieved from http://cantstopwontstop.com/reader/the-creativity-stimulus/

Clapp, E. P. (2014). *Reframing creativity as the biography of an idea: Developing learning narratives that describe creativity as a participatory and distributed process*. Student dissertation, Harvard Graduate School of Education, Cambridge, MA.

Cole, M. & Engeström, Y. (1993). A cultural historical approach to distributed cognition. In G. Salomon (Ed.), *Distributed cognitions: psychological and educational considerations* (pp. 1–46). New York: Cambridge University Press.

Crockenberg, S. B. (1972). Creativity tests: A boon or boondoggle for education? *Review of Educational Research, 42*(1), 27–45.

Cropley, A. J. (2000). Defining and measuring creativity: Are creativity tests worth using? *Roeper Review, 23*(2), 72–79.

Cross, C. R. (2014). *Here we are now: The lasting impact of Kurt Cobain*. New York: HarperCollins.

Csikszentmihalyi, M. (1988). Society, culture, person: A systems view of creativity. In R. J. Sternberg (Ed.), *The nature of creativity* (pp. 325–339). New York: Cambridge University Press.

Csikszentmihalyi, M. (1990). *Flow: The psychology of optimal experience*. New York: HarperCollins.

Csikszentmihalyi, M. (1996). *Creativity: Flow and the psychology of discovery and invention*. New York: HarperCollins.

Csikszentmihalyi, M. (1999). Implications of a systems perspective for the study of creativity. In R. J. Sternberg (Ed.), *Handbook of creativity* (pp. 313–338). New York: Cambridge University Press.

Csikszentmihalyi, M., Feldman, D. H., Gardner, H., John-Steiner, V., Moran, S., Nakamura, J., Sawyer, R. K., & Sternberg, R. J. (2003). Key issues in creativity and development. In R. K. Sawyer (Ed.), *Creativity and development* (pp. 217–242). New York: Oxford University Press.

Dawkins, R. (1976). *The selfish gene*. Oxford: Oxford University Press.

Delpit, L. D. (1988). The silenced dialogue: Power and pedagogy in educating other people's children. *Harvard Educational Review, 58*(3), 280–298.

Deming, D. J. (2015). The growing importance of social skills in the labor market. Working paper 21473. Cambridge, MA: National Bureau of Economic Research. Retrieved from: http://www.nber.org/papers/w21473

Dewey, J. (1934). *Art as experience*. New York: Perigee Books.

Ditkowsky, A. (2013). Unpublished student paper. Harvard Graduate School of Education, Cambridge, MA.

Dougherty, D. (2012, July 19) DARPA mentor award to bring making to education, *Make*. Retrieved from http://makezine.com/2012/01/19/darpa-mentor-award-to-bring-making-to-education/

Driscoll, K. (n.d.). The dark side of DIY: Makerspaces and the long, weird history of DIY hobbyists and military funding. *Civic Paths*. Retrieved from http://civicpaths.uscannenberg.org/the-dark-side-of-diy-makerspaces-and-the-long-weird-history-of-diy-hobbyists-military-funding/

Duckworth, A. L., Peterson, C., Matthews, M. D., & Kelly, D. R. (2007). Grit: Perseverance and passion for long-term goals, *Journal of Personality and Social Psychology, 92*(6), 1087–1101.

Duncum, P. (2013). Creativity as conversation in the interactive audience culture of YouTube. *Visual Inquiry, 2*(2), 115–125.

Dweck, C. (2006). *Mindset: The new psychology of success*. New York: Random House.

Edwards, D. (2008). *ArtScience: Creativity in the post-Google generation*. Cambridge, MA: Harvard University Press.

Edwards, D. (2010). *The lab: Creativity and culture.* Cambridge, MA: Harvard University Press.

Engeström, Y. (1994). Teachers as collaborative thinkers: An activity-theoretical study of an innovative teacher team. In I. Calgren, G. Handal, & S. Vaage (Eds), *Teachers' minds and actions: Research on teachers' thinking and practice* (pp. 43–62). Bristol, PA: Falmer.

Feist, G. J. (1999). The influence of personality on artistic and scientific creativity. In R. J. Sternberg (Ed.), *The Handbook of creativity* (pp. 273–296). New York: Cambridge University Press.

Foucault, M. (1980). What is an author? In *Language, counter-memory, practice: Selected essays and interviews* (pp. 113–138). Ithaca, NY: Cornell Paperbacks.

Foucault, M. (1997). *Ethics, subjectivity, and truth, Essential works of Foucault 1954–1984.* P. Rabinow (Ed.). New York: The New Press.

Fricke, D. (1994, January 27). Kurt Cobain, the *Rolling Stone interview*: Success doesn't suck. *Rolling Stone.* Retrieved from http://www.rollingstone.com/music/news/kurt-cobain-the-rolling-stone-interview-19940127

Gardner, H. (1983). *Frames of mind: The theory of multiple intelligences.* New York: Basic Books.

Gardner, H. (1993a). *Creating minds: An anatomy of creativity seen through the lives of Freud, Einstein, Picasso, Stravinsky, Eliot, Graham, and Gandhi.* New York: Basic Books.

Gardner, H. (1993b). *Multiple intelligences: The theory in practice.* New York: Basic Books.

Gardner, H. (1993c). A multiplicity of intelligences. *Scientific American Presents, Exploring Intelligence, 9*(4), 19–23.

Gardner, H. (1996). The assessment of student learning in the arts. In D. Boughton, E. W. Eisner, & J. Ligtvoet (Eds), *Evaluating and assessing the visual arts in education: International perspectives* (pp. 131–155), New York: Teachers College Press.

Gardner, H. (1999a). *The disciplined mind: What all students should understand.* New York: Simon & Schuster.

Gardner, H. (1999b). *Intelligence reframed.* New York: Basic Books.

Gardner, H. (1999c). The happy meeting of multiple intelligences and the arts. *Harvard Education Letter, 15*(6), 1–6.

Gardner, H. (2006). *Five minds for the future.* Boston, MA: Harvard Business School Press.

Gerth, J. (2012, April 17). Presidential hopeful Mitt Romney to visit Louisville for fundraiser next Thursday. *Courier-Journal.*

Glăveanu, V. P. (2014a). *Distributed creativity: Thinking outside the box of the creative individual.* Springer Briefs in Psychology.

Glăveanu, V. P. (2014b). *Thinking through creativity and culture: Toward an integrated model.* New Brunswick, NJ: Transaction Publishers.

Glăveanu, V. P., Gillespie, A., & Valsiner, J. (Eds) (2015). *Rethinking creativity: Contributions from social and cultural psychology* (cultural dynamics of social representation). New York: Routledge.

Gloor, P. A. (2006). *Swarm creativity: Competitive advantage through collaborative innovation networks.* New York: Oxford University Press.

Groff, J. (2013). Expanding our "frames" of mind for education and the arts. *Harvard Educational Review, 83*(1) 15–39.

Gruber, H. E. (1981). *Darwin on man: A psychological case study of scientific creativity,* (2nd edition). Chicago: University of Chicago Press.

Gruber, H. E. (1989a). The evolving systems approach to creative work. In D. B. Wallace and H. E. Gruber (Eds.), *Creative people at work: Twelve cognitive case studies* (pp. 3–24). New York: Oxford University Press.

Gruber, H. E. (1989b). Creativity and human survival. In D. B. Wallace and H. E. Gruber (Eds.), *Creative people at work: Twelve cognitive case studies* (pp. 278–287). New York: Oxford University Press.

Gruber, H. E. & Davis, S. N. (1988). Inching our way up Mount Olympus: The evolving systems approach to creative thinking. In R. J. Sternberg (Ed.), *The nature of creativity: Contemporary psychological perspectives* (pp. 243–270). New York: Cambridge University Press.

Gruber, H. E. & Wallace, D. B. (1999). The case study method and evolving systems approach for understanding unique creative people at work. In R. J. Sternberg (Ed.), *Handbook of creativity* (pp. 93–115). New York: Cambridge University Press.

Guilford, J. P. (1950). *Creativity.* Address of the President of the American Psychological Association. September 5, 1950. Pennsylvania State College, University Park, PA.

Hanchett Hanson, M. (2013a). Author, self, monster: Using Foucault to examine functions of creativity. *Journal of Theoretical and Philosophical Psychology, 33*(1), 18–31.

Hanchett Hanson, M. (2013b). Creativity theory and educational practice: Why all the fuss? In J. B. Jones & L. J. Flint (Eds), *The creative imperative: School librarians and teachers cultivating curiosity together* (pp. 19–37). Santa Barbara, CA: ABC-CLIO, LLC.

Hanchett Hanson, M. (2015). *Worldmaking: Psychology and the ideology of creativity.* New York: Palgrave Macmillan.

Handy, B. (1994, April 18). MUSIC: Never mind. *Time.* Retrieved from http://content.time.com/time/magazine/article/0,9171,980562,00.html

Heifetz, R. A. (1994). *Leadership without easy answers.* Cambridge, MA: Belknap Press/Harvard University Press.

Herrera, L. (2012). Youth and citizenship in the digital age: A view from Egypt. *Harvard Educational Review, 82*(3), 333–354.

Hersted, L. (2015). Creativity in a relational perspective. In T. Chemi, J. B. Jensen, L. Hersted (Eds), *Behind the scenes of artistic creativity* (pp. 229–245). Frankfurt am Main, Germany: Peter Lang.

Hutchins, E. (1995). *Cognition in the wild.* Cambridge, MA: Massachusetts Institute of Technology Press.

Hutchins, E. (1996). Learning to navigate. In S. Chaiklin & J. Lave (Eds.), *Understanding practice: Perspectives on activity in context* (pp. 35–63). Cambridge, UK: Cambridge University Press.

Hutchins, E. & Klausen, T. (1996). Distributed cognition in an airplane cockpit. In Y. Engeström & D. Middleton (Eds.), *Cognition and communication at work* (pp. 15–34). New York: Cambridge University Press.

IDEO. (2011). *Design thinking for educators toolkit.* Retrieved from https://www.ideo.com/work/toolkit-for-educators

Intelligent Collaborative Knowledge Networks (2013). Collaboration in creative learning networks. Retrieved from www.ickn.org/collaboration.html

Ito, M., Gutiérrez, K., Livingstone, S., Penuel, B., Rhodes, J., Salen, K., Schor, J., Sefton-Green, J., & Watkins, S. K. (2013). *Connected learning: An agenda for research and design.* Irvine, CA: Digital Media and Learning Research Hub. Retrieved from http://dmlhub.net/wp-content/uploads/files/Connected_Learning_report.pdf

James, C. (2014). *Disconnected: Youth, new media, and the ethics gap.* Cambridge, MA: Massachusetts Institute of Technology Press.

Jencks, C. (1988). Whom must we treat equally for educational opportunity to be equal? *Ethics, 98*(3), 518–533.

Johnson, S. (2010). *Where good ideas come from: The natural history of innovation.* New York: Riverhead Books.

John-Steiner, V. & Mahn, H. (1996). Sociocultural approaches to learning and development: A Vygotskian framework. *Educational Psychologist, 31*(3–4), 191–206.

Kaufman, S. B. (2013). *Ungifted: Intelligence redefined.* New York: Basic Books.

Kornhaber, M. L., Griffith, K., & Tyler, A. (2014). It's not education by zip-code anymore—but what is it? Conceptions of equity under Common Core. *Education Policy Analysis Archives, 22*(4). Retrieved from http://dx.doi.org/10.14507/epaa.v22n4.2014

Kozbelt, A., Beghetto, R. A., & Runco, M. A. (2010). Theories of creativity. In J. C. Kaufman & R. J. Sternberg (Eds.), *Cambridge handbook of creativity* (pp. 20–47). New York: Cambridge University Press.

Krechevsky, M. & Mardell, B. (2001). Four features of learning in groups. In Project Zero and Reggio Children, *Making learning visible: Children as individual and group learners* (pp. 284–295). Reggio Emilia, Italy: Reggio Children.

Krechevsky, M., Mardell, B., Rivard, M., & Wilson, D. (2013). *Visible learners: Promoting Reggio-inspired approaches in all schools.* San Francisco, CA: Jossey-Bass.

Lang, D. (2013). *Zero to maker: Learn (just enough) to make (just about) anything.* Sebastopol, CA: Maker Media.

Latour, B. (2005). *Reassembling the social: An introduction to actor-network theory.* New York: Oxford University Press.

Lave, J. (1991). Situating learning in communities of practice. In L. B. Resnick, J. B. Levine, & S. D. Teasley (Eds.), *Perspectives on socially shared cognition* (pp. 63–82). Washington, DC: American Psychological Association.

Leach, J. (2001). A hundred possibilities: Creativity, community, and ICT. In A. Craft, B. Jeffrey, & M. Leibling (Eds.), *Creativity in education* (pp. 175–194). New York: Continuum.

Luther, K. & Diakopoulos, N. (2007, June 13). Distributed creativity. Paper presented at Creativity & Cognition: Supporting Creative Acts Beyond Dissemination, Washington, D.C.

Mehta, J. (2014, June 20). Deeper learning has a race problem. *Education Week's Blogs—Learning Deeply.* Retrieved from http://blogs.edweek.org/edweek/learning_deeply/2014/06/deeper_learning_has_a_race_problem.html

Meinel, C & Lefier, L. (2011). Design thinking research. In H. Plattner, C. Meinel, & L. Leifer (Eds.), *Design thinking: Understand—improve—apply* (pp. xiii–xxi). New York: Springer.

Miettinen, R. (2006). The sources of novelty: A cultural and systemic view of distributed creativity. *Creativity and Innovation Management, 15*(2), 173–181.

Montanaro, D. (2012, July 23). Romney to Olympians: "You didn't get here solely on your own." *First Read on NBC News.com.* Retrieved from http://firstread.nbcnews.com/_news/2012/07/23/12904508-romney-to-olympians-you-didnt-get-here-solely-on-your-own?lite

Moran, S. (2010). The roles of creativity in society. In J. C. Kaufman & R. J. Sternberg (Eds.), *The Cambridge handbook of creativity* (pp. 74–92). New York: Cambridge University Press.

Moran, S. & John-Steiner, V. (2003). Creativity in the making: Vygotsky's contemporary contribution to the dialectic of development and creativity. In R. K. Sawyer (Ed.), *Creativity and development* (pp. 61–90). New York: Oxford University Press.

On the Media. (2015, November 20). Breaking news consumer's handbook: Terrorism edition. Retrieved from www.onthemedia.org/story/breaking-news-consumers-handbook-terrorism-edition/

Paulus, P. B. & Brown, V. R. (2003). Enhancing ideational creativity in groups: Lessons from research on brainstorming. In P. B. Paulus & B. A. Nijstad (Eds.), *Group creativity: Innovation through collaboration* (pp. 110–136). New York: Oxford University Press.

Perkins, D. N. (1993). Person-plus: A distributed view of thinking and learning. In G. Salomon (Ed.), *Distributed cognitions: Psychological and educational considerations* (pp. 88–110). New York: Press Syndicate/University of Cambridge.

Perkins, D. N. (2009). *Making learning whole: How seven principles of teaching can transform education.* San Francisco, CA: Jossey-Bass.

Perkins, D. N. (2014). *Future wise: Educating our children for a changing world.* San Francisco, CA: Jossey-Bass.

Reynolds, S. (2006). *Rip it up and start again: Postpunk 1978–1984.* New York: Penguin.

Rhodes, M. (1961). An analysis of creativity. *Phi Delta Kappan, 42,* 305–310.

Rolling, Jr., J. H. (2013). *Swarm intelligence: What nature teaches us about shaping creative leadership.* New York: Palgrave Macmillan.

Salomon, G. (Editor, 1993). *Distributed cognitions: Psychological and educational considerations.* New York: Press Syndicate/University of Cambridge.

Savage, J. (2001). *England's dreaming: Anarchy, Sex Pistols, punk rock, and beyond.* New York: St. Martin's Griffin.

Sawyer, R. K. (1997). Improvisational theater: An ethnography of conversational practice. In R. K. Sawyer (Ed.), *Creativity in performance* (pp. 171–193). Greenwich, CT: Ablex.

Sawyer, R. K. (2003). *Group creativity: Music, theater, collaboration.* Mahwah, NJ: Lawrence Erlbaum Associates.

Sawyer, R. K. (2005). *Social emergence: Societies as complex systems.* New York: Cambridge University Press.

Sawyer, R. K. (2006/2012). *Explaining creativity: The science of human invention.* New York: Oxford University Press.

Sawyer, R. K. (2007). *Group genius: The creative power of collaboration.* New York: Basic Books.

Sawyer, R. K. (2010). Individual and group creativity. In J. C. Kaufman & R. J. Sternberg (Eds.), *The Cambridge handbook of creativity* (pp. 366–380). New York: Cambridge University Press.

Sawyer, R. K. (Ed.). (2011). *Structures and improvisation in creative teaching.* New York: Cambridge University Press.

Sawyer, R. K. & DeZutter, S. (2009). Distributed creativity: How collective creations emerge from collaboration. *Psychology of Aesthetics, Creativity, and the Arts, 3*(2), 81–92.

Schoenfeld, A. H. (1987). What's all the fuss about metacognition? In A. H. Schoenfeld (Ed.), *Cognitive science and mathematics education* (pp. 189–215). Hillsdale, NJ: Lawrence Erlbaum Associates.

Scholastic Testing Services, Inc. (n.d.). Torrance tests of creative thinking. Bensenville, IL/Earth City, MO: Author. Retrieved from www.ststesting.com/ngifted.html

Seidel, S., Tishman, S., Winner, E., Hetland, L., & Palmer P. (2009). *The qualities of quality: Understanding excellence in arts education.* Cambridge, MA: Project Zero.

Shafer, J. (2015, November 16). The myth of the terrorist mastermind: Why do we need to keep telling ourselves that the plotters are special? *Politico Magazine.* Retrieved from www.politico.com/magazine/story/2015/11/the-myth-of-the-terrorist-mastermind-213367

Shenk, J. W. (2014). *Powers of two: Finding the essence of innovation in creative pairs.* Boston, MA: Eamon Dolan/Houghton Mifflin Harcourt.

Simonton, D. K. (2005). Creativity. In C. R. Snyder & S. J. Lopez (Eds.), *Handbook of positive psychology* (pp. 189–201). New York: Oxford University Press.

Snyder, A., Mitchell, J., Bossomaier, T., & Pallier, G. (2004). The creativity quotient: An objective scoring of ideational fluency, *Creativity Research Journal, 16*(4), 415–420.

Stevens, S. S. (1946). On the theory of scales of measurement. *Science, 7*(2684), 677–680.

Strauss, V. (2013, October 16). Howard Gardner: "Multiple Intelligences" are not "learning styles." *Washington Post.* Retrieved from https://www.washingtonpost.com/news/answer-sheet/wp/2013/10/16/howard-gardner-multiple-intelligences-are-not-learning-styles/

Tamm, J. W. & Luyet, R. J. (2005). *Radical collaboration: Five essential skills to overcome defensiveness and build successful relationships.* New York: Harper Collins.

Tomm, K., Hoyt, M. F., & Madigan, S. B. (1998). Honoring our internalized others and the ethics of caring: A conversation with Karl Tomm. In M. Hoyt (Ed.), *Handbook of constructive therapies: Innovative approaches from leading practitioners* (pp. 198–218). San Francisco, CA: Jossey-Bass.

Torrance, E. P. (1974). *Torrance tests of creative thinking: Norms technical manual.* Princeton, NJ: Personnel Press.

Torres, N. (2015, August 26). Technology is only making social skills more important. *Harvard Business Review.* Retrieved from: https://hbr.org/2015/08/research-technology-is-only-making-social-skills-more-important

True, E. (2007). *Nirvana: The biography.* Cambridge, MA: Da Cappo Press.

Vega, T. (2014, August, 12). Shooting spurs hashtag effort on stereotypes. *New York Times.* Retrieved from www.nytimes.com/2014/08/13/us/if-they-gunned-me-down-protest-on-twitter.html

Vygotsky, L. S. (1971). *The psychology of art.* Cambridge, MA: MIT Press.

Vygotsky, L. S. (1978). *Mind in society: The development of higher psychological processes.* Cambridge, MA: Harvard University Press.

Wallace, D. B. (1989). Studying the individual: The case study method and other genres. In D. B. Wallace & H. E. Gruber, (Eds.), *Creative people at work: Twelve cognitive case studies* (pp. 25–43). New York: Oxford University Press.

Wallace, D. B. & Gruber, H. E. (Eds.) (1989). *Creative people at work: Twelve cognitive case studies.* New York: Oxford University Press.

Weisberg, R. W. (2006). *Creativity: Understanding innovation in problem solving, science, invention, and the arts.* Hoboken, NJ: John Wiley & Sons.

Weisberg, R. W. & Hanchett Hanson, M. (2013). Inside-the-box: An expertise-based approach to creativity in education. In J. B. Jones & L. J. Flint (Eds.), *The creative imperative: School librarians and teachers cultivating curiosity together* (pp. 71–84). Santa Barbara, CA: ABC-CLIO, LLC.

Index

Notes: italics denote figures; bold denotes tables.